IMAGES
of America

AROUND BROCKPORT

Betty-
For the memories,
Love,
Judy
2002

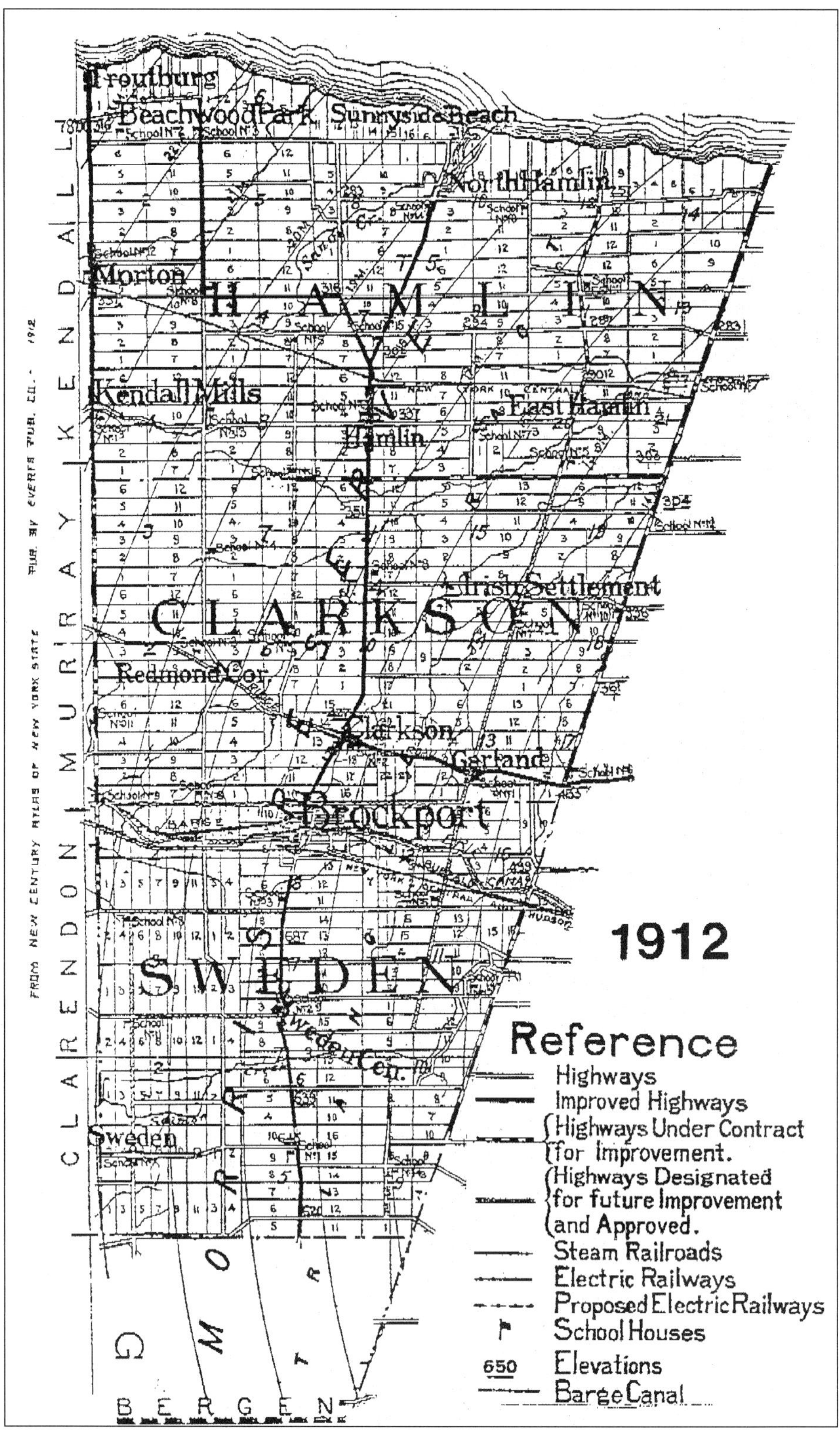
1912
Reference
Highways
Improved Highways
Highways Under Contract for Improvement.
Highways Designated for future Improvement and Approved.
Steam Railroads
Electric Railways
Proposed Electric Railways
School Houses
650 Elevations
Barge Canal
HAMLIN
CLARKSON
SWEDEN
KENDALL
MURRAY
CLARENDON
BERGEN
Troutburg
Beachwood Park
Sunnyside Beach
North Hamlin
Morton
Kendall Mills
East Hamlin
Hamlin
Irish Settlement
Redmond Cor.
Clarkson
Garland
Brockport
Sweden Cen.
Sweden
FROM NEW CENTURY ATLAS OF NEW YORK STATE PUB. BY EVERTS PUB. CO. 1912

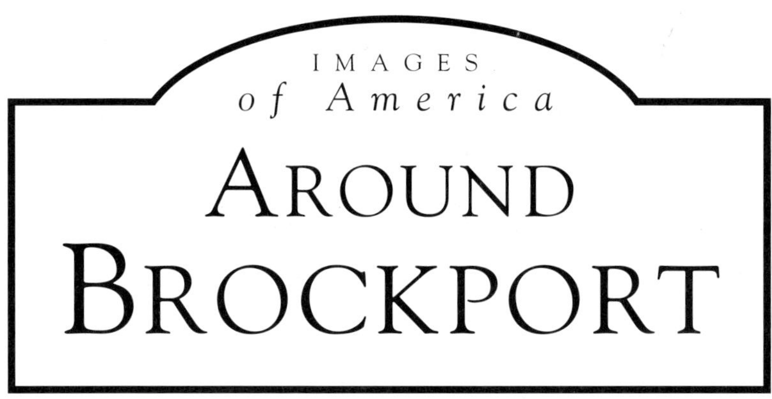

IMAGES of America

AROUND BROCKPORT

William G. Andrews

with

Eunice Chesnut, Mary Jo Gigliotti, Kathy Goetz,
Hazel Kleinbach, and Jennifer Quigley

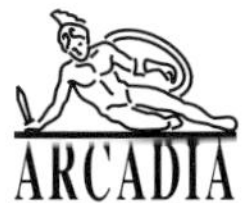

ISBN 0-7385-0990-6

First printed in 2002.

Published by Arcadia Publishing,
an imprint of Tempus Publishing, Inc.
2A Cumberland Street
Charleston, SC 29401

Printed in Great Britain.

Library of Congress Catalog Card Number: 2002100868

For all general information contact Arcadia Publishing at:
Telephone 843-853-2070
Fax 843-853-0044
E-Mail sales@arcadiapublishing.com

For customer service and orders:
Toll-Free 1-888-313-2665

Visit us on the internet at http://www.arcadiapublishing.com

To the memory of Fletcher Morgan Garlock, Squire of Brockport, gracious friend, ardent preservationist, loyal Brockporter, entrepreneur, architect, historian, philanthropist.

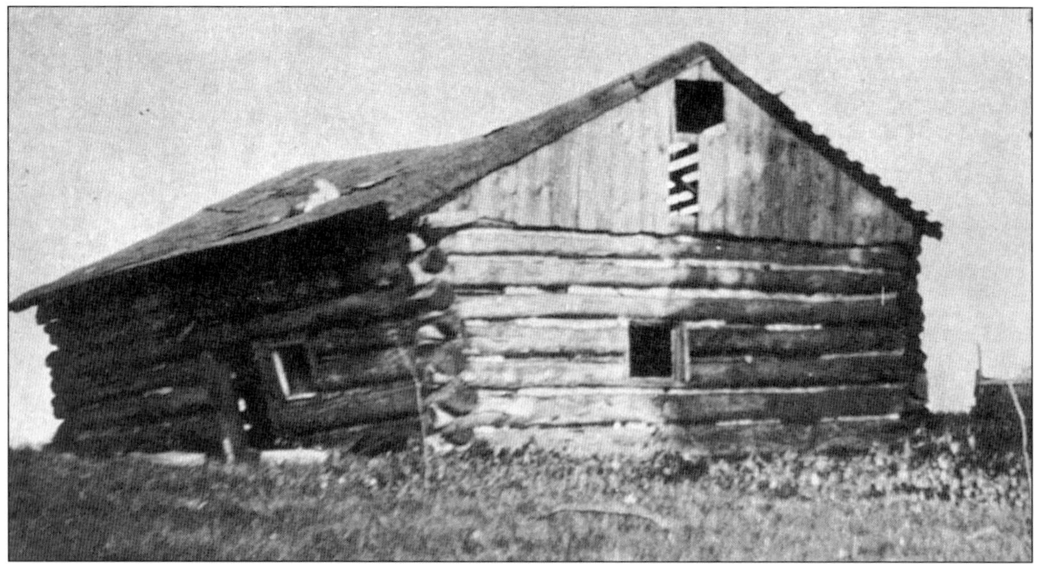

WILLIAM PETERS. Peters, a Connecticut Tory who had been persecuted by his patriot neighbors, came to the Triangle Tract around 1804 and built this cabin just south of the Sweden-Bergen town line. His great-great-grandson, Gifford Morgan (pages 27, 35, and 55), restored it in the 1930s, moved it to his property in Clarkson, and furnished it with authentic period items. Alice Garlock, widow of Morgan's grandson, Fletcher M. Garlock, now owns it.

Contents

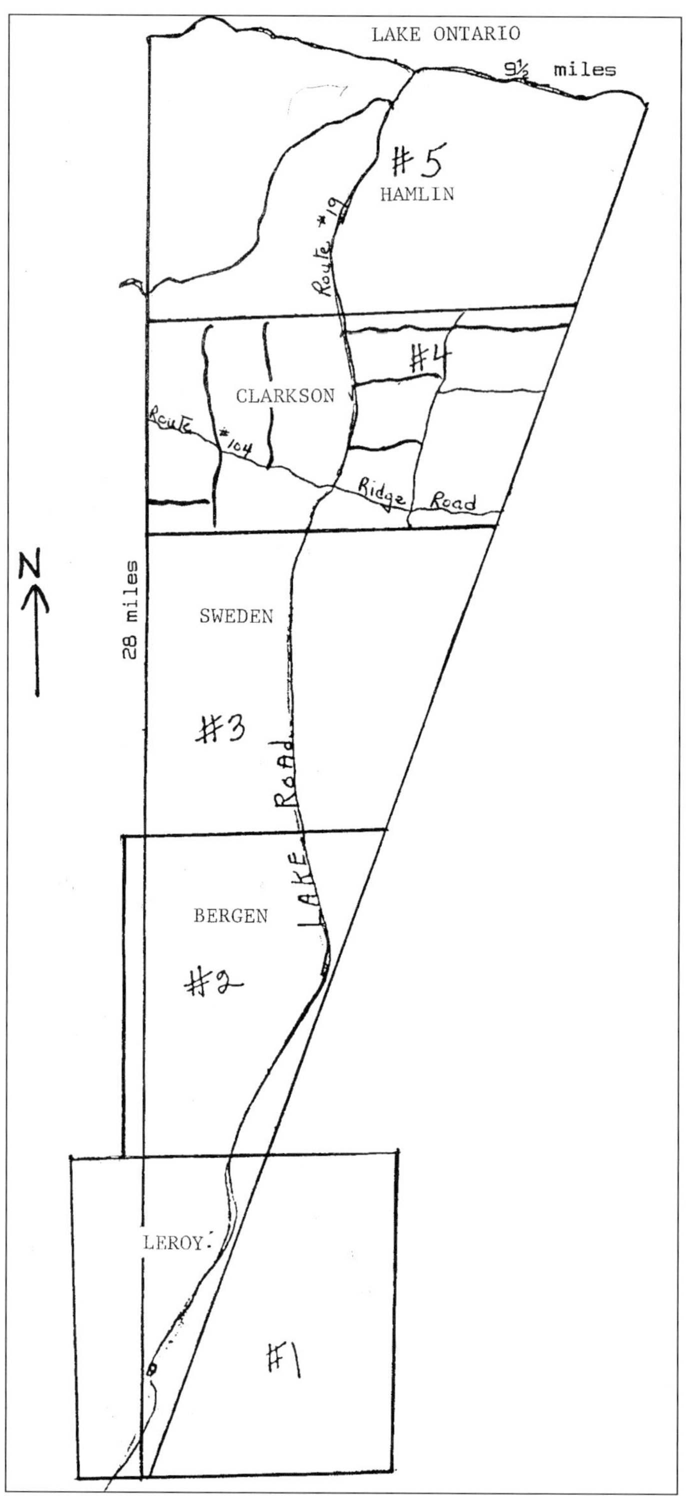

The Triangle Tract. This map shows the Triangle Tract, the towns that were carved from it, and Lake and Ridge Roads, which opened it to settlement.

INTRODUCTION

This pictorial history covers four communities on the western edge of New York's Monroe County. The town of Sweden includes the village of Brockport and the State University of New York at Brockport. The town of Clarkson abuts Sweden and Brockport on the north. Sweden (1814) and Clarkson (1819) were created from the Triangle Tract, pictured on the opposite page. Brockport was laid out in 1822 and incorporated in 1829. The antecedents of the college date to 1830.

The 87,000-acre Triangle Tract was 28 miles long and 9.5 miles wide along Lake Ontario. It lay in the town of Northhampton, in Ontario County, with a county seat at Canandaigua. It resulted from an apparent fraud attempted by the Phelps and Gorham land speculators. They had bought from the Seneca Indians an enormous expanse of central New York, including a 12-mile-wide strip along the west bank of the Genesee River. However, the surveyor ran its western boundary due north from the present site of the village of Leroy rather than parallel to the river as had been agreed. The Senecas discovered the error, reclaimed the land, and sold it to Robert Morris and associates. In 1793, they resold it to Herman Leroy, William Bayard, James McEvers, and Matthew Clarkson, who opened it to settlement in 1801. Leroy, Bayard, and Clarkson were sons-in-law of a wealthy New Yorker, Samuel Cornel. McEvers was a cousin of Bayard.

In 1807, the Triangle Tract and the land west of it separated from Northhampton to become the town of Murray. In 1814, the towns of Leroy, Bergen, and Sweden were formed in the southern part of Murray. Sweden then included what became the town of Clarendon to its west in 1821, and Murray covered what are now the towns of Clarkson, Hamlin, and, in Orleans County, Murray.

In 1802, the proprietors opened Lake Road by widening to 64 feet a Native American trail that ran north from Leroy to Lake Ontario. Ridge Road was built *c.* 1810 across Clarkson from east to west, again following a Native American trail. Both towns were originally farming communities. However, the 1823–1825 construction of the Erie Canal across the northern edge of Sweden added industrial, commercial, and transportive dimensions to Brockport's character. The founding of an institution of higher education in Brockport in 1835 made it a learning center as well.

We devote a chapter to each community, in chronological sequence by founding date: Sweden (1814), Clarkson (1819), Brockport (1822), and the college (1835). As far as practicable, the images on each pair of facing pages form a topical group; for example, Hiel

Brockway, the Gordon family, industries, churches, and so forth. As Brockport has had the largest population, been the principal focus of communal activity for all but the first 18 years, and is more diverse economically and socially, it gets more attention than its neighbors. Also, in the late 19th and early 20th centuries, the economy of the area was the most thriving and diverse and produced a rich store of relevant and interesting images. Thus, a disproportionate share of images concern that period. Therefore, this survey is neither comprehensive nor balanced, but it does, we hope, present an interesting and revealing selection of glimpses into our communities' pasts.

Many generous friends have assisted on this project. Foremost are my collaborators. Eunice Chesnut, historian of the Western Monroe Historical Society, helped select the Brockport images and drafted half of their captions. Kathy Goetz, town of Sweden historian, selected the images for that community and drafted their captions. Hazel Kleinbach, town of Clarkson historian, helped select the Clarkson images and drafted some of their captions. Jennifer Quigley and Mary Jo Gigliotti, State University of New York Brockport librarians, selected the college images and drafted their captions. I rewrote all captions for uniformity in style and format. The final draft was reviewed for accuracy by Louie D. Smith Jr., former Brockport village clerk; Jacqueline Morris, village of Brockport historian; Mary Smith, town of Hamlin historian; Dr. David G. Hale, Brockport Sesquicentennial Celebration Committee member; and my collaborators. Pam O'Neil was our patient and supportive editor.

The images came from many collections: the village of Brockport and towns of Clarkson and Hamlin historians' offices; the Emily L. Knapp Local History Museum and Library (Mary Lynne Turner); the Seymour Library (Mark Jacarino); the State University of New York's Drake Memorial Library; the Western Monroe Historical Society; Brockport Volunteer Fire Department (Scott Warthman); Rochester Public Library (Shirley Iversen); Rochester Historical Society (Ann Salter); Brockport Post (Sally Beer); Louie D. Smith Jr.; Margaret Johnson; Estel Lewis; Helen Massar; the Nativity of the Blessed Virgin Mary Church (Noel Myers, Karen Holzschuh); college photographer Jim Dusen; and my personal collection. Also, we have drawn both information and images from a number of published sources, including *Rochester and Monroe County New York* (1908); William F. Peck, *History of Rochester and Monroe County New York* (1908); *History of Monroe County New York* (1877); William F. Peck et al., *Landmarks of Monroe County New York* (1895); W. Wayne Dedman, *Cherishing This Heritage* (1969); Charlotte Elizabeth Martin, *The Story of Brockport* (1930?); Hazel Kleinbach, *Highlights of Clarkson History* (1988?) and *Chronicles of Clarkson* (1992); David G. Hale, *Village of Brockport* (1979); *Brockport Fire Department: Our History* (2001); Wilbur W. Hiler et al., *History of the Town of Sweden* (1964); Eunice Chesnut, *And Papa Cried Hoorah!* (1987), *Hoe Cakes to Hamburgers* (1993), *A Path Through the Years* (1995), *That Reminds Me . . .* (1998), *Sewing for the Heathen* (2000), and *The Canal and the Castle* (2001).

One

Town of Sweden

The town of Sweden is six miles north to south and five-and-three-quarter miles east to west, covering about 22,000 acres. The first settlers arrived in 1807. Many early residents came from New England, especially Connecticut, traveling several weeks by wagon over generally poor roads. They paid $2.00 to $2.50 an acre for their farmland. Nathaniel Poole and Walter Palmer arrived first, homesteading on Lake Road between Sweden Center and Brockport. Later that year, four other families arrived. In 1808, nine new families settled in the town, including four Stickney brothers. By 1813, Sweden in its present limits had 140 households, one single person, and a total population of 819. The average family size was 5.8 persons, and the average number of children under 18 per household was 3.4.

The uncertainty and dangers created by the War of 1812 and the difficulties of shipping products to market inhibited settlement, but after the Erie Canal was built to Brockport in 1823, land in the town was quickly occupied. During the early decades, Sweden Center on Lake Road and West Sweden near the town line had a few commercial businesses, but they faded after Brockport was founded. The town outside Brockport has never had a substantial manufacturing enterprise and was almost entirely agricultural for over a century. The development of Sweden Village, a housing tract southeast of the village, and several nearby apartment complexes in the 1960s stimulated the growth of a shopping-mall economy in the town. Meanwhile, improvements in transportation led to the sprinkling of a commuter population along its rural roads.

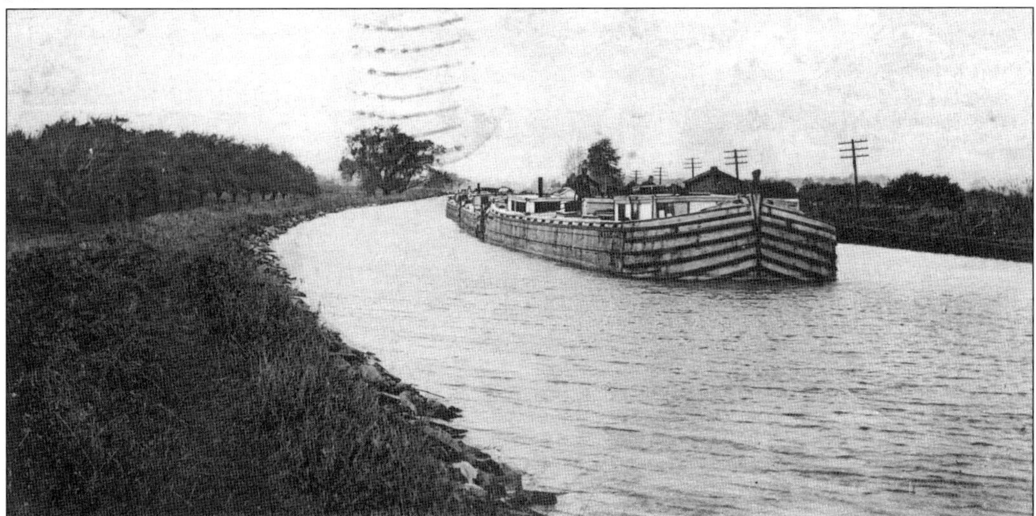

The Erie Canal. The canal was vital to Sweden's prosperity. It provided farmers the most economical and efficient means to transport their bulky commodities to market for many decades. Eventually, railroads superceded it in that role. This barge is traveling the recently reconstructed waterway through Sweden c. 1914, when the canal had already passed its heyday.

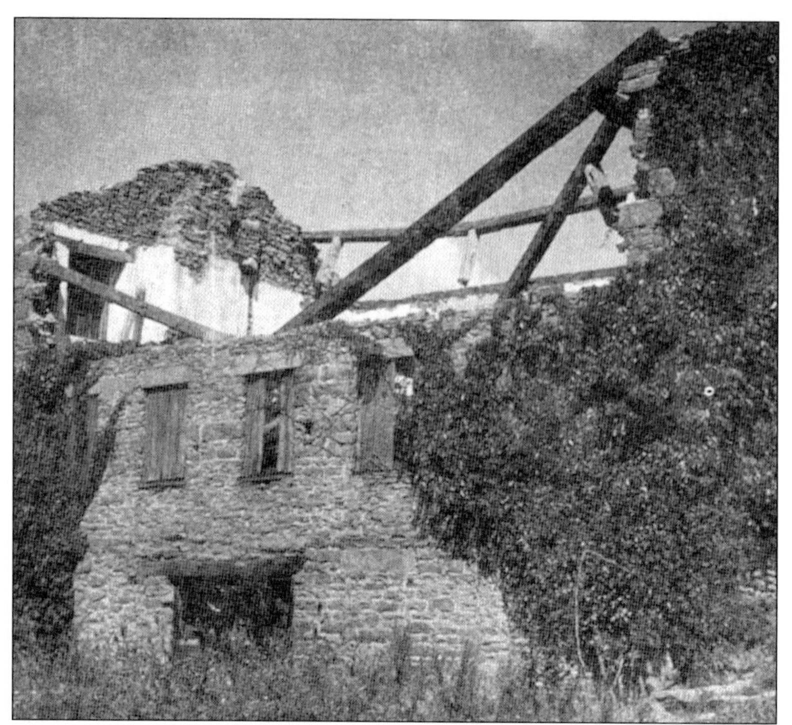

BEEDLE TAVERN. Johnson Beedle arrived in Sweden in about 1808 and built a tavern and store on Lake Road just south of Sweden Center near Swamp Road. Even the ruins in this 1964 photograph had disappeared by 2002. Beedle was part of a large clan of Beadles (spelled various ways), several of whom were early settlers. His father, Capt. John Beedle, had seen land in this area while serving in Sullivan's army during the Revolution.

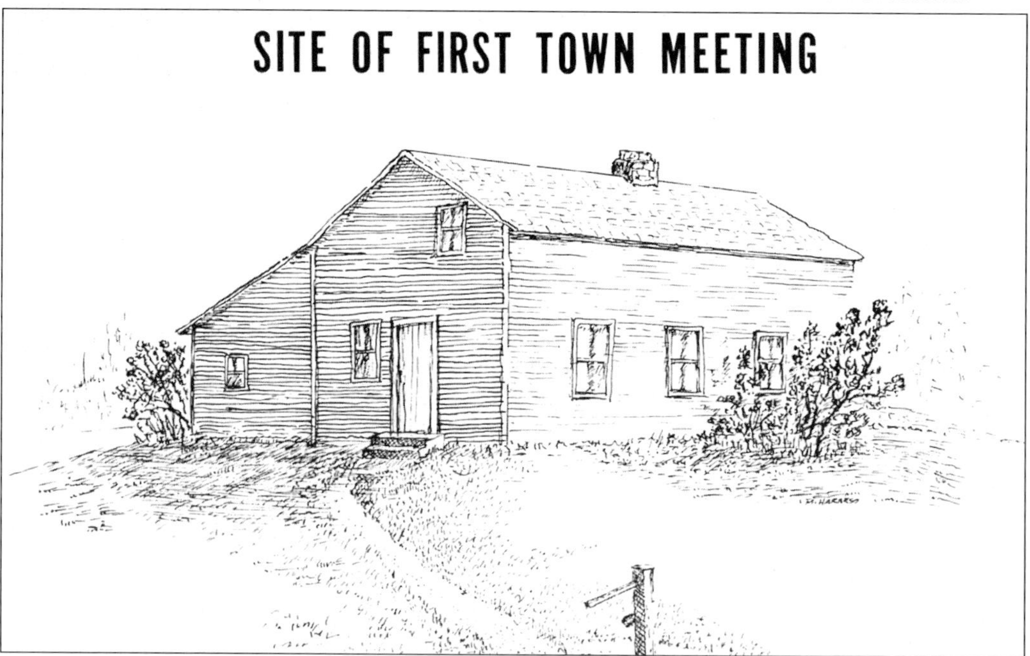

THE FIRST TOWN MEETING SITE. In 1809, Maj. Reuben Stickney's home, at Lake and Swamp Roads, was the first frame structure in the town of Sweden. On April 5, 1814, the first town meeting convened in his barn. Virtually all of the town's estimated 147 men were eligible to attend and vote. Many brought their wives, and the occasion became a two-day celebration with much drinking. Nevertheless, they elected 40 town officers, including Supervisor John Reed who claimed, at one time, to own 1,400 acres, though not all in Sweden.

THE CAPEN FAMILY. Benjamin F. Capen came to Sweden in 1814 and cleared and farmed a large piece of land in its southwestern corner near what is now Capen Road. His son, Franklin F. Capen (1835–1898) (right), became a leading citizen (pages 51 and 80), including service as the youngest Monroe County town supervisor in the 19th century, from 1870 to 1871, and as four-term Brockport mayor. He began his career working the family farm (below) but, in 1882, began selling implements and other farm products. In 1887, he organized a shoe factory that merged with the Moore-Shafer Shoe Manufacturing Company, of which he became president. In 1892, he formed the Brockport Piano Company as its president. He was prominent in farm organizations as first master of the Brockport Grange and chair of the executive committee of the state Grange for 20 years.

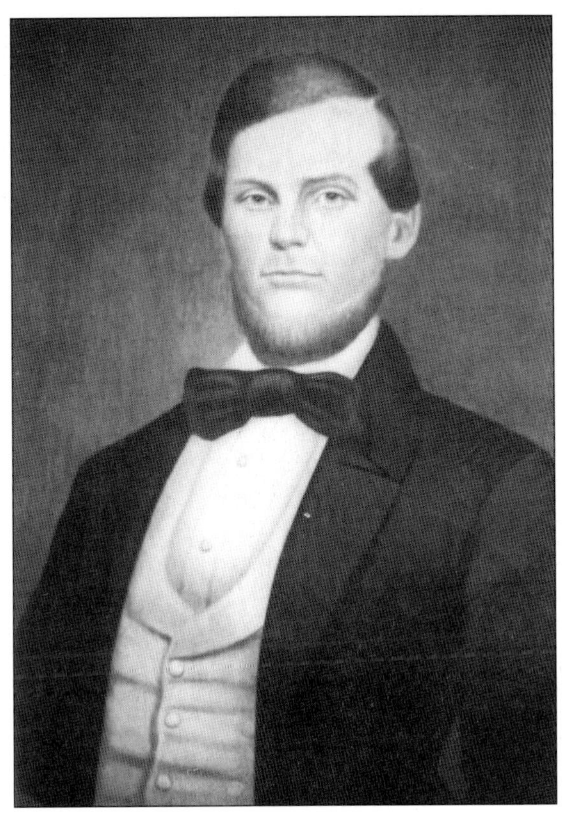

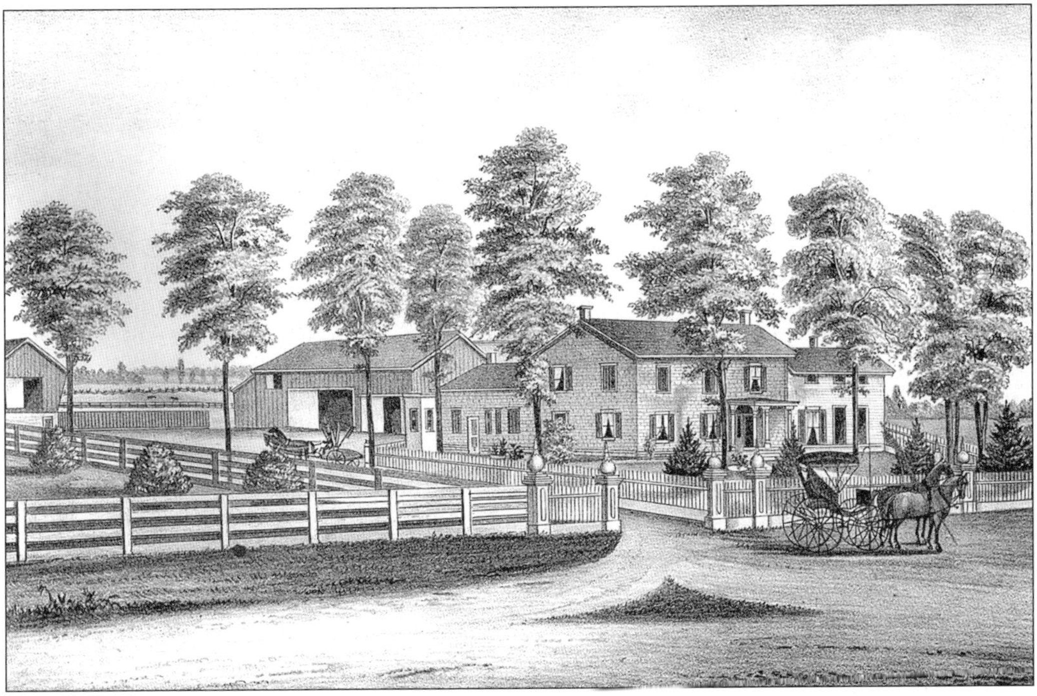

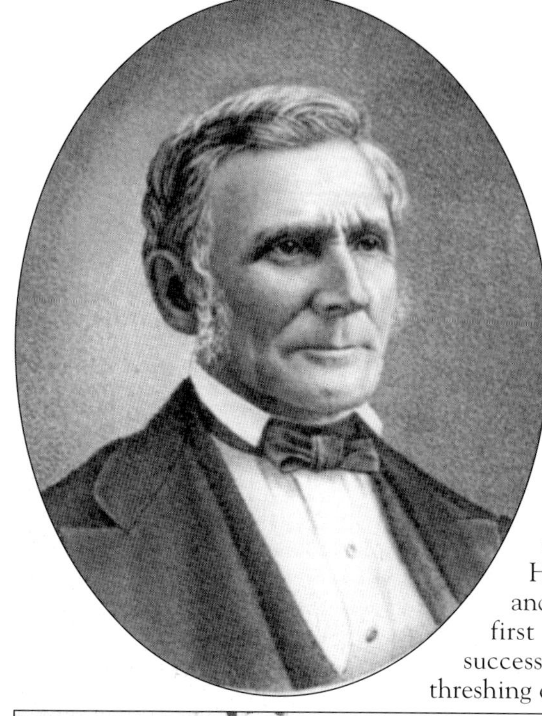

FREDERICK P. ROOT. Root (1814–1904) was Sweden's leading rural citizen and its largest landowner at one time, with 700 acres. His father and two uncles settled in Sweden in 1818. He was the first president of the New York State Farmers Alliance, an organizer of the state Grange, and longtime county leader of the Agricultural Society, the Farmers' Cooperative Insurance Company, and the Patrons Fire Relief Association. He served in the New York State Assembly, was town supervisor for five years, and was a justice of the peace. He was an agricultural journalist, a lecturer, and a local historian. His farm was the site of the first field demonstration of the world's first successful production-model reaper. Below is a threshing crew on his farm.

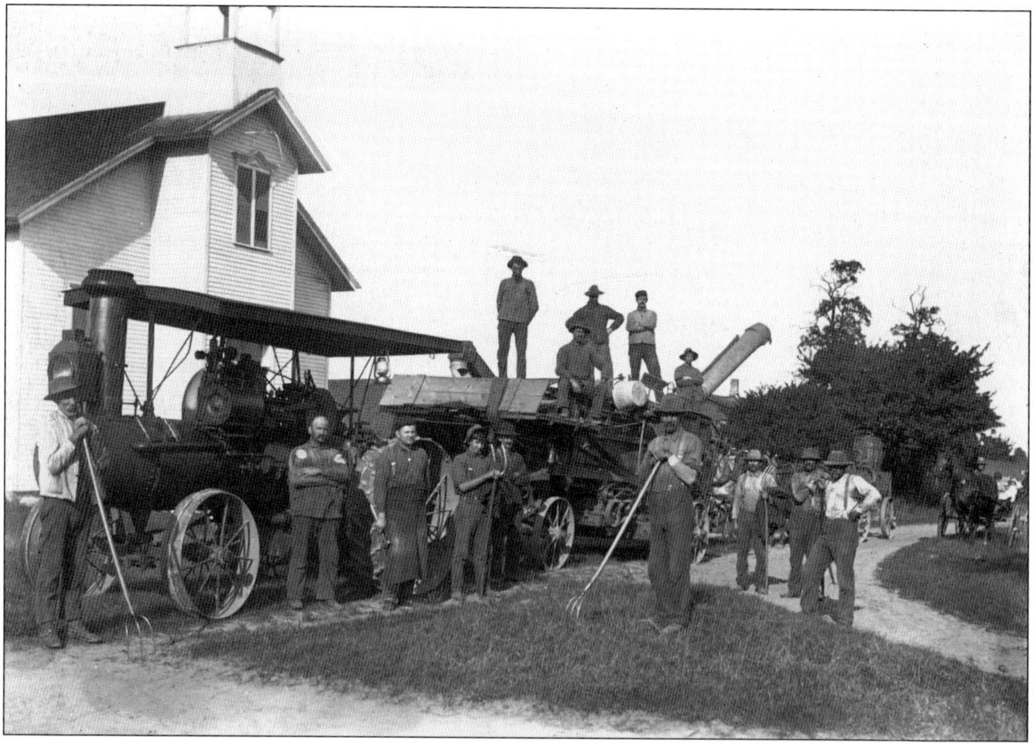

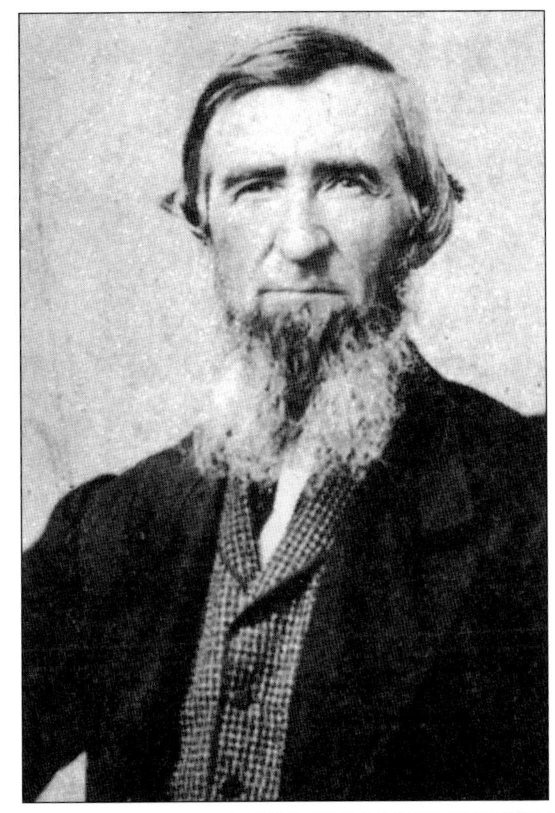

ASA ROWE. Rowe (1806–1894) became proprietor of his family's hotel and tavern on Ridge Road in Greece when orphaned at age 16. He pioneered in the American nursery business in 1826. He was town clerk, school inspector, supervisor (1835, 1836, 1838), and postmaster (1837–1842). In 1828, he married Ruby Mann Reed, daughter of John Reed (page 10), and they moved to Sweden and entered farming in 1842. He served as Sweden town supervisor in 1850. The Reeds' home (below), which survives, stood on their 350-acre farm on Reed Road on the south edge of the town. Their sons, Albert Oscar and Edwin Andrew, and later, grandson Burton, succeeded to the property.

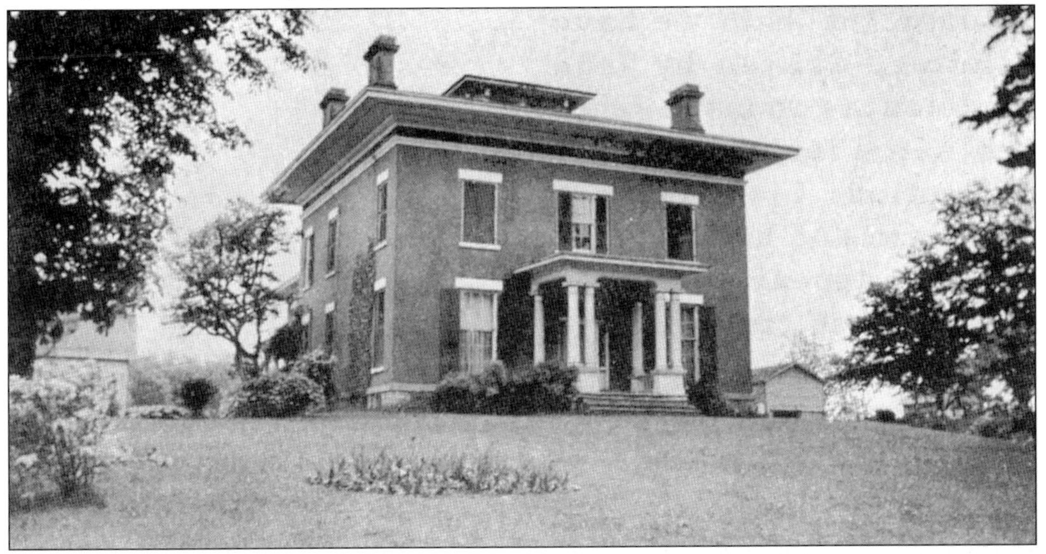

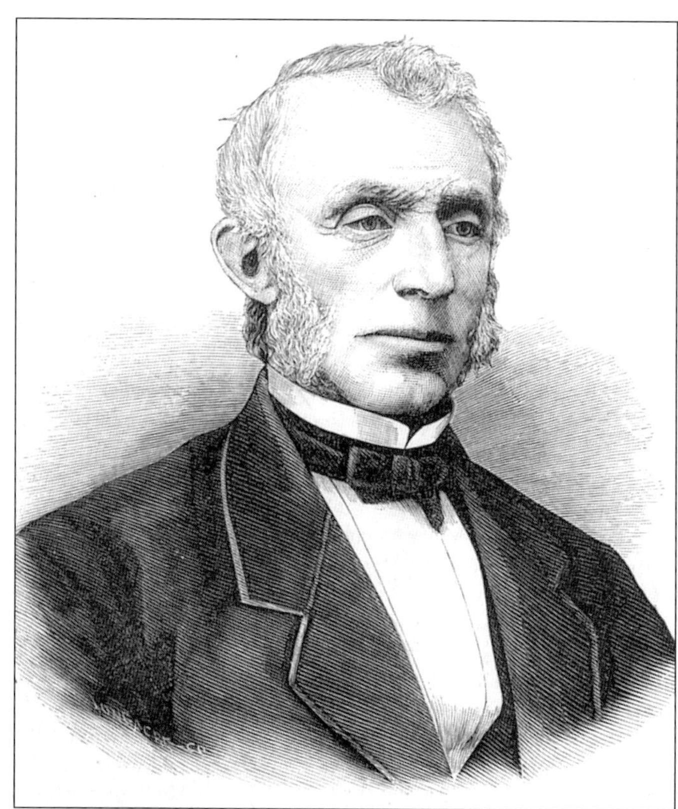

CHAUNCEY WHITE. John White and his family came from Madison County to West Sweden and White Roads in 1821. His son, Chauncey S. White (1814–1880) (left), succeeded his father in 1865. In 1866, Arthur M. White joined his uncle, who was childless, and, in 1880, succeeded him. Arthur's son, John H. White, had a nearby farm on West Sweden Road. The White Homestead is a bed and breakfast today, operated by Christine Hunt, a great-granddaughter of Reuben C. Stickney, who farmed across the road. The boys with the goat cart on the White farm (below) are, from left to right, William Farnsworth, Roland Farnsworth, Herbert White, and Earl Farnsworth.

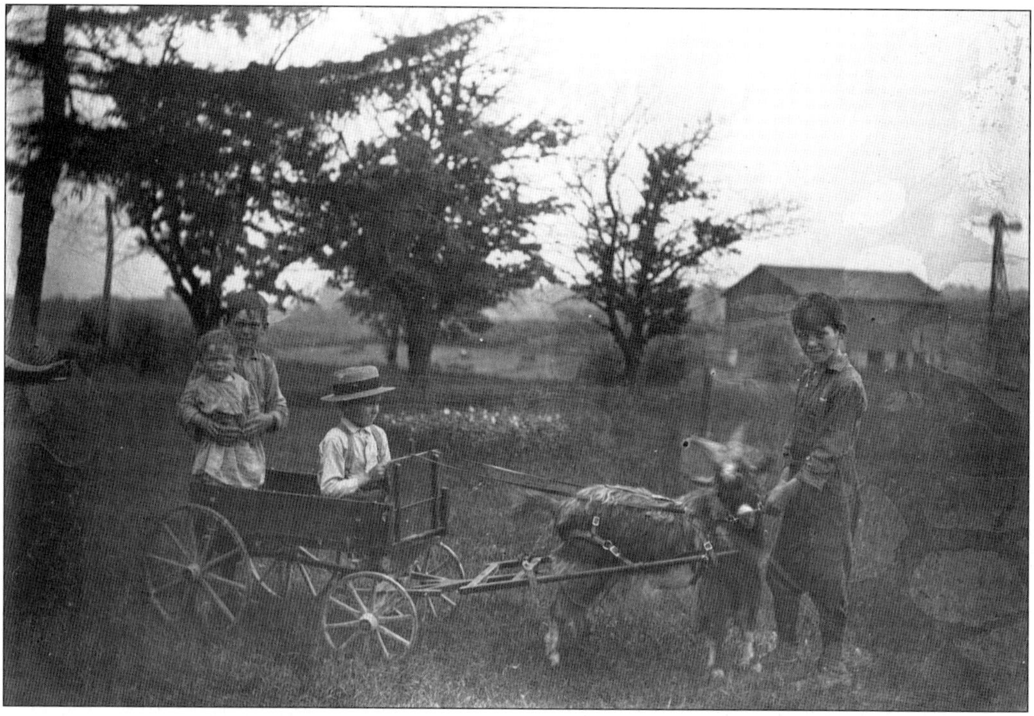

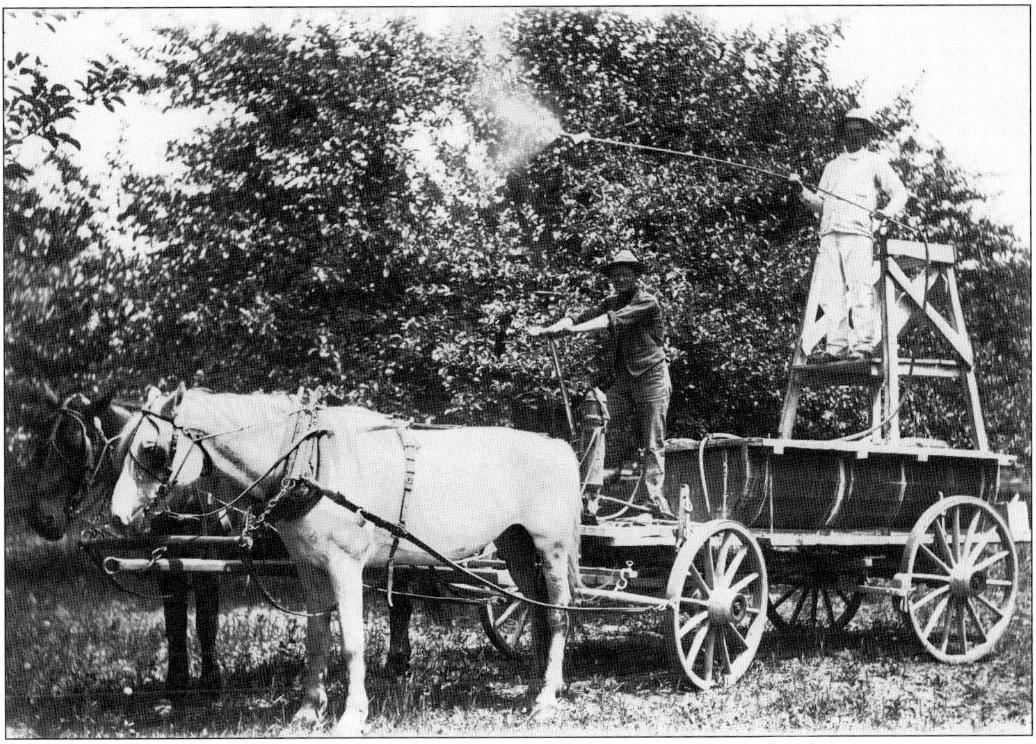

FARM WORK. These two 1907 photographs from the White Homestead collection show apple spraying (above) and corn harvesting (below).

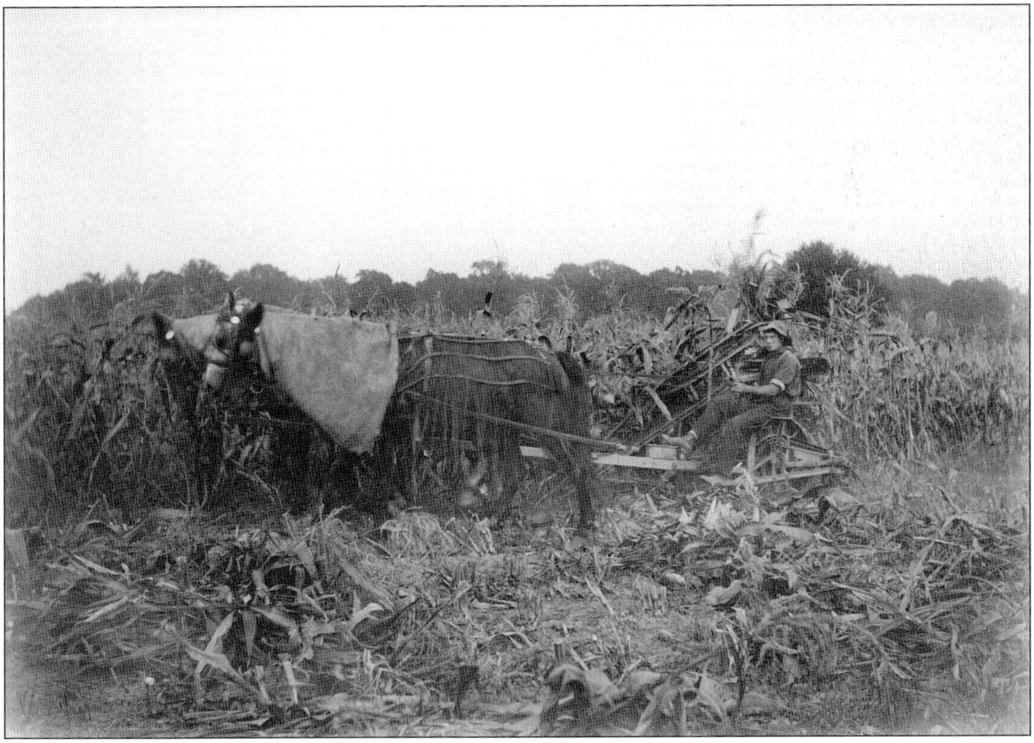

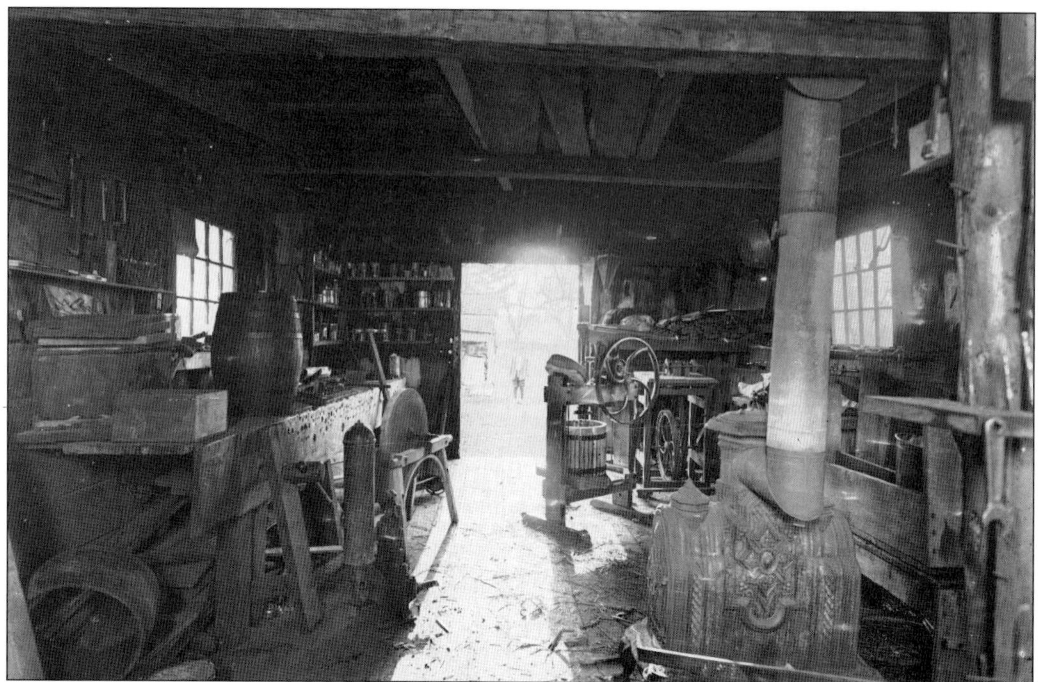

FARM SHOPS. During the 19th century, farm-to-town roads were primitive and farmers did more repair and maintenance work than is usual now. This required an adequate shop, such as the one in the 1907 photograph (above). Similarly, a blacksmith shop (below) was a common feature of larger farms, necessary when horses were shod or iron implements made or repaired.

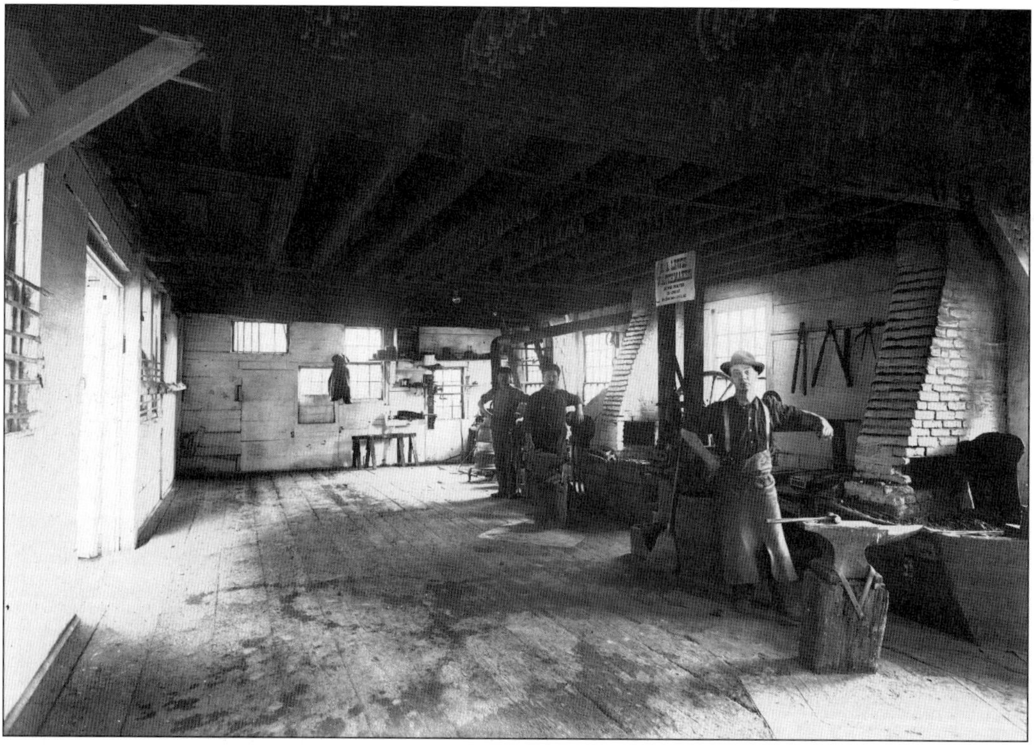

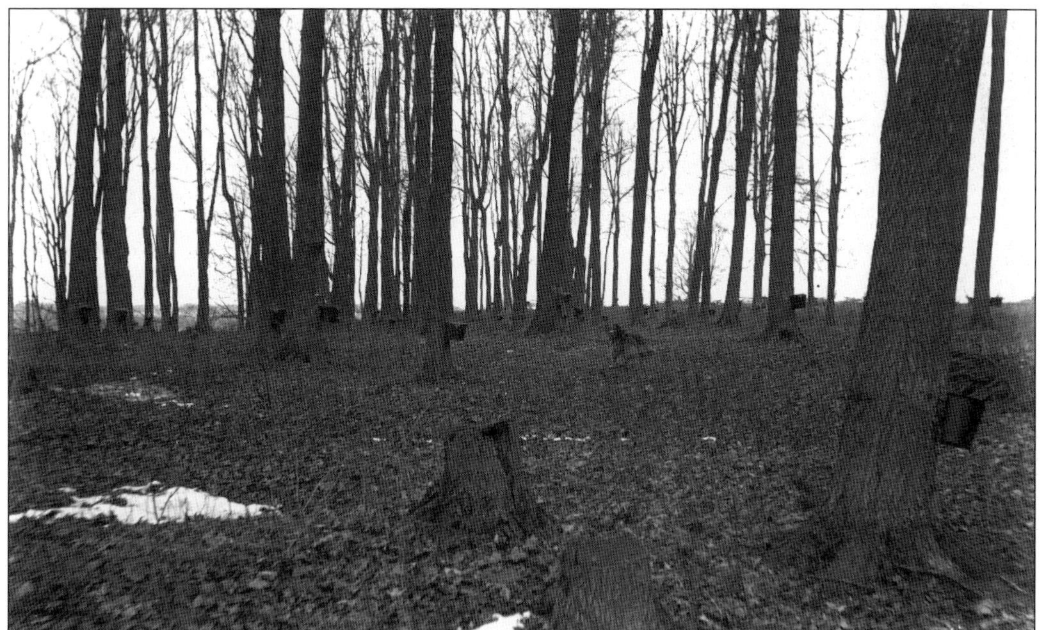

WOOD LOTS. Early Sweden was densely forested, and the first dwellings were log cabins. Much pioneer effort was spent clearing land for agriculture. Nevertheless, many farms kept a wood lot for maple sugar and syrup, as on the William H. Elwell farm, on Fourth Section and West Sweden Roads (above), and for firewood and lumber (below). The Elwell farm, which tapped 500 trees, and that of Albert Davies, which tapped 1,000, were among the largest producers of maple sugar and syrup in the town.

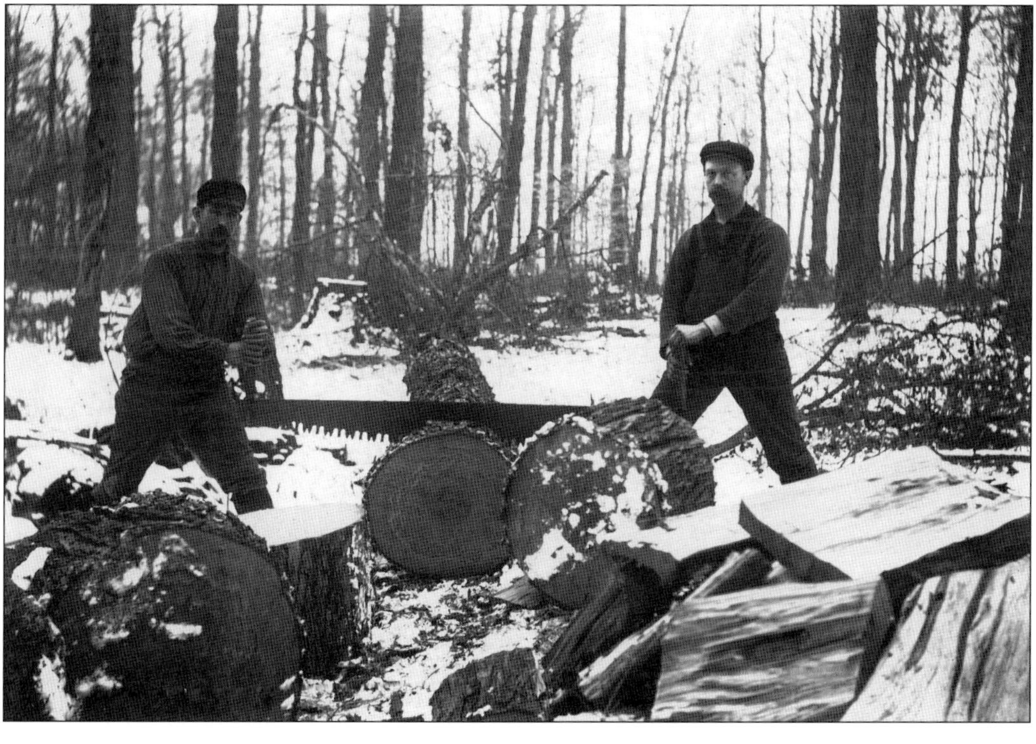

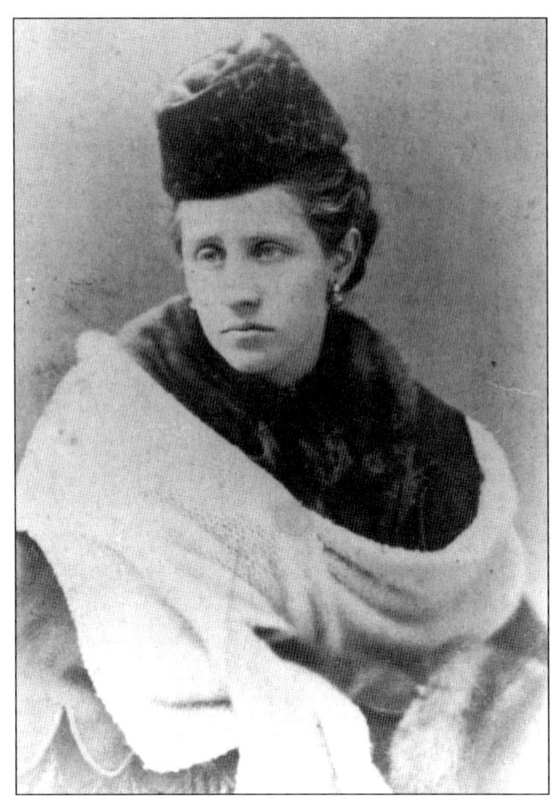

CALICO JACK. Emma Tripp Hunt was Sweden's great eccentric. Known as "Calico Jack," she earned her nickname by carrying a sealskin sack as she rode into Brockport on a cream-colored horse with a white mane and tail. Her horse pulled a buggy in which a small boy sat, holding the horse's tail over the dashboard. She smoked cigars lit with $10 bills. Her mother began building Hunt's Castle, their $20,000, 12-room mansion on Colby Street, in 1860, and Calico Jack continued the work, which was never finished. She went bankrupt, lost the property, and ended her days as a charwoman in Rochester. Nothing remains of the castle.

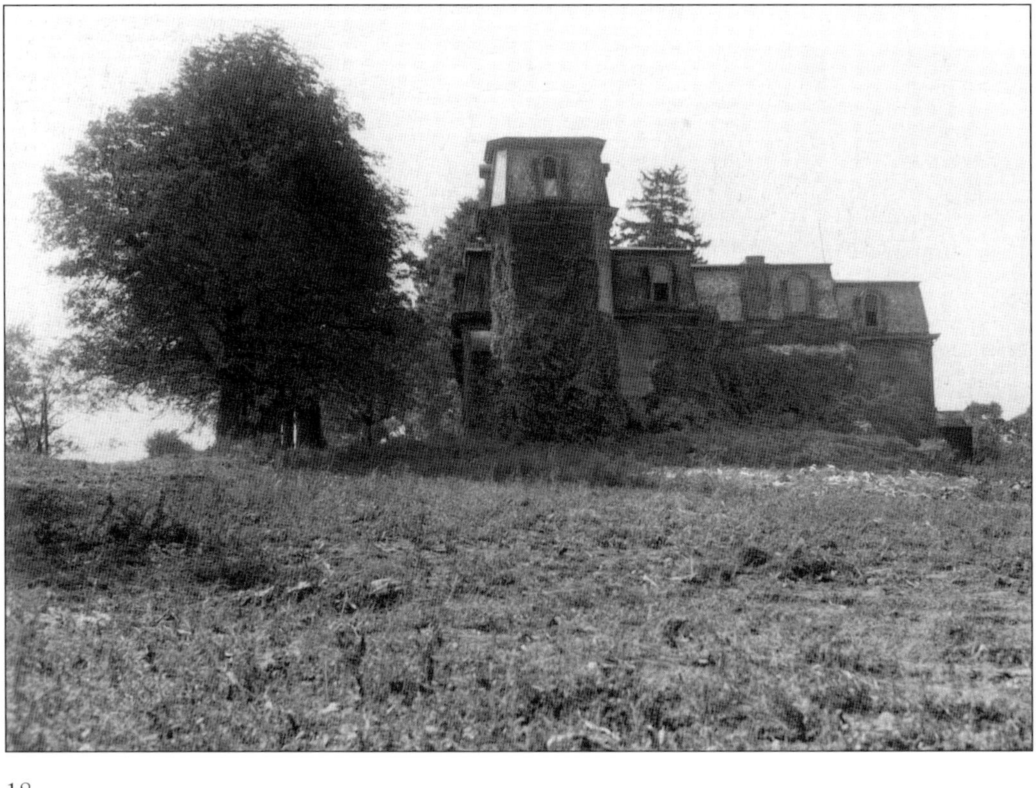

SCHOOLS. The first schools in the town were located on Lake Road. District No. 1 was at LaDue Road, and District No. 2 (right) is now a private home in Sweden Center. District No. 7 (below), was in West Sweden. In 1877, the town outside Brockport had 11 grade schools. With improvements in transportation after 1900, enrollment in the rural schools dwindled. The decline accelerated after the consolidated Brockport Central School system was formed in 1927. In 1939, four remained. By the early 1960s, all had closed.

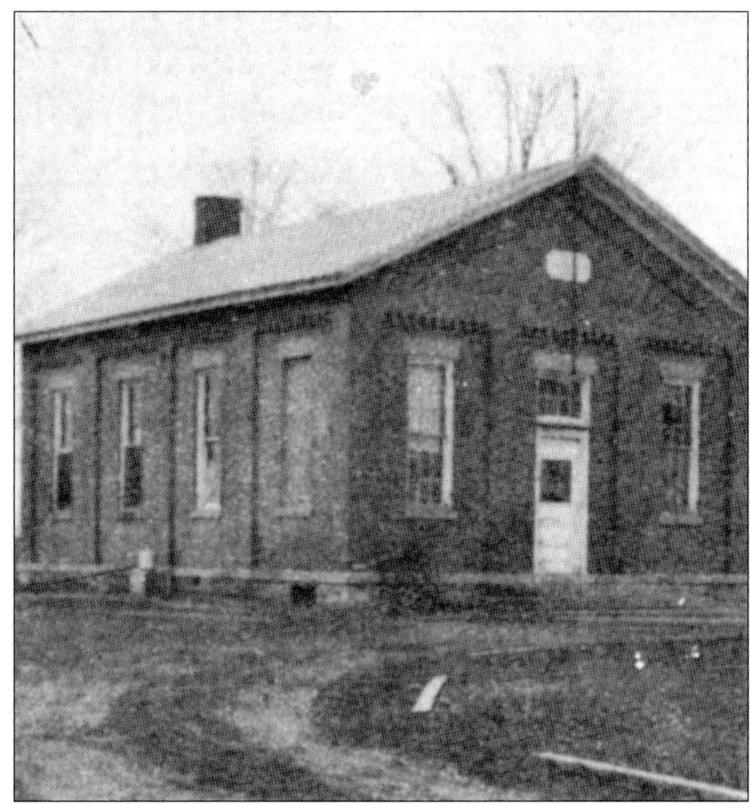

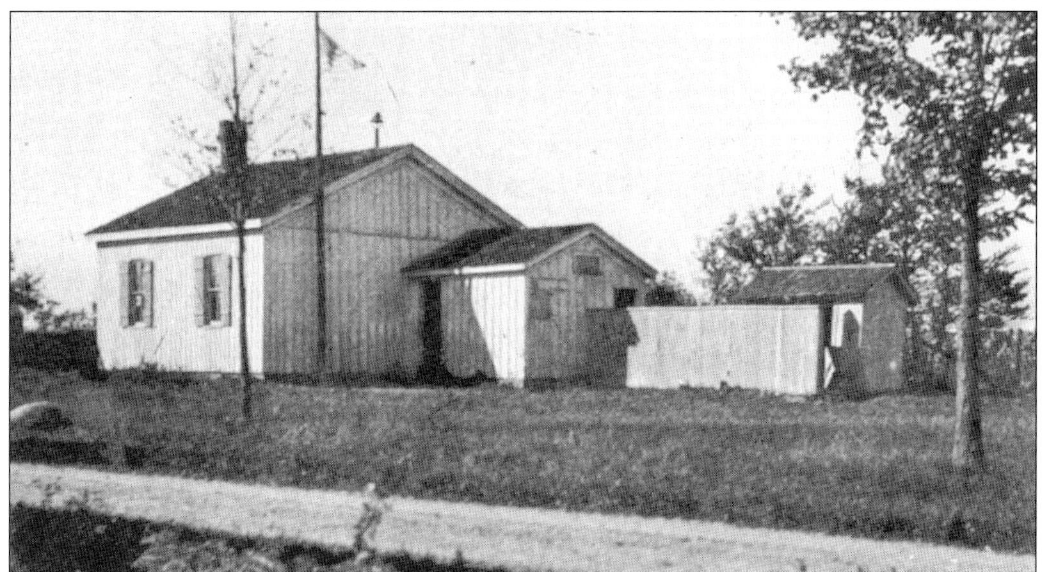

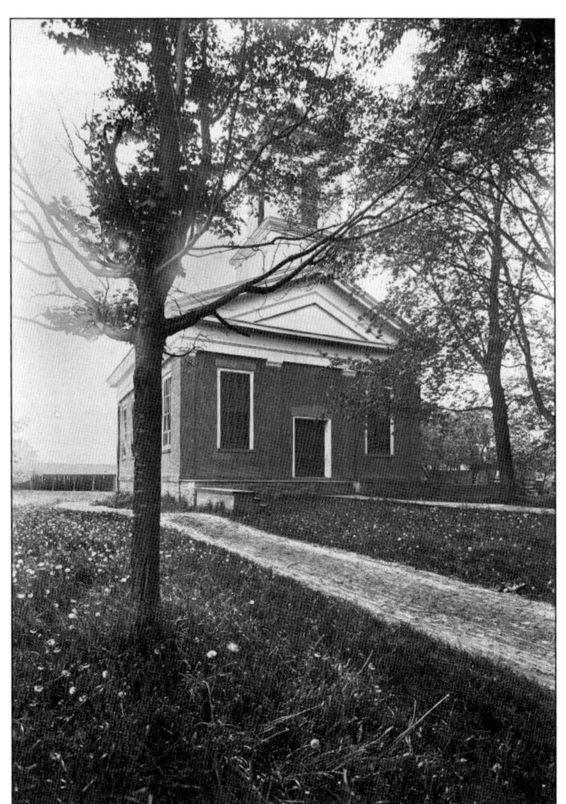

PRESBYTERIANS AND METHODISTS. The first religious organization in Sweden was Congregational, formed in Sweden Center in 1817 by 16 members. The members built a wooden church in 1821, changed denominations to Presbyterian in 1833, and replaced their original structure with a brick edifice (left) in 1836. They merged with the First Presbyterian Church in Brockport in the 1930s, and the building was razed. A Methodist Episcopal congregation formed in West Sweden in 1835 and erected a building (below) in 1836. Because of internal dissension, the group dissolved in 1855 and was succeeded in the same structure in 1860 by a Free Methodist congregation, which dissolved in the third quarter of the century. Another Methodist Episcopal church existed in Sweden Center for about 40 years after 1855.

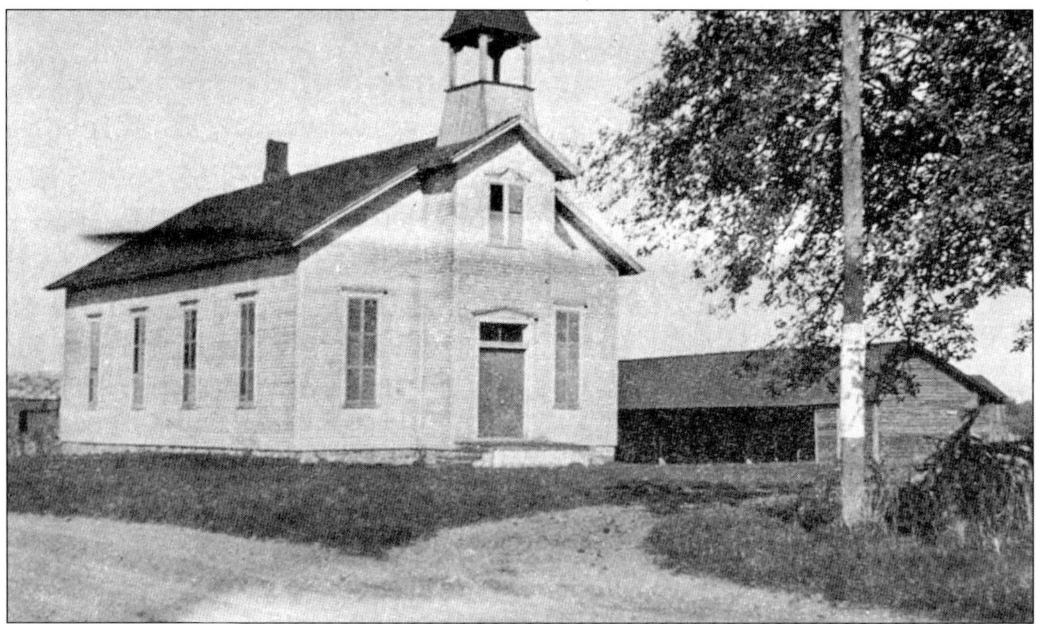

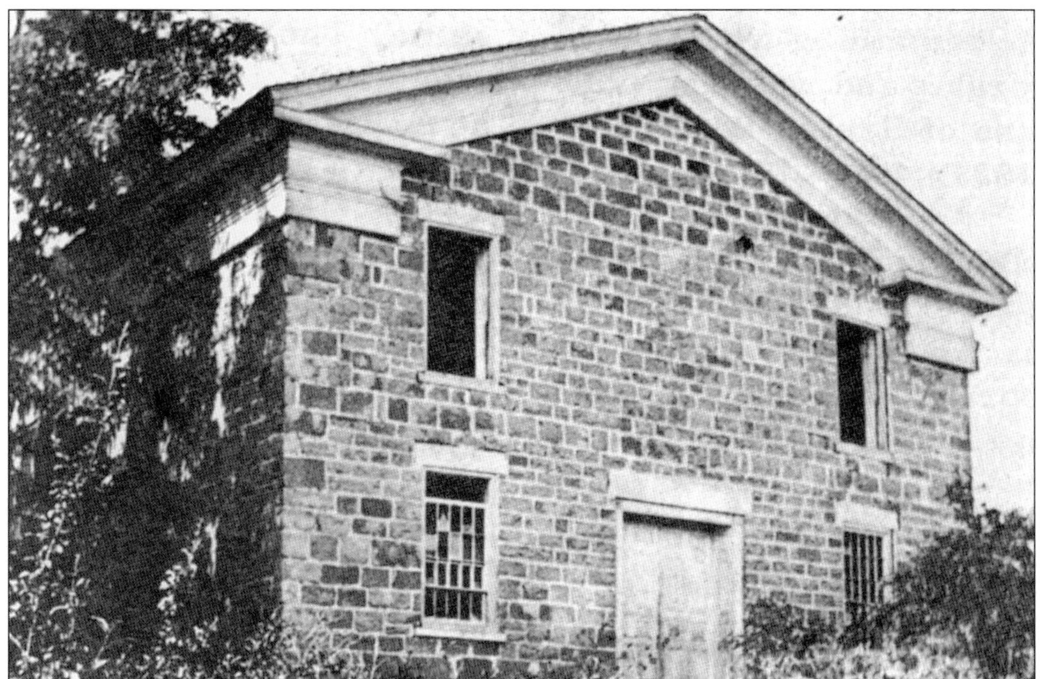

BAPTISTS. A Baptist congregation was formed by 29 members in East Sweden in 1819. The church was built 1836, and it led a fitful existence until the late 1850s. Another Baptist congregation was organized by 33 members in 1835. The church was built the same year, and it survived until 1864. In 2002, Sweden outside Brockport had three churches: Concordia Lutheran, Free Methodist (both on Fourth Section Road), and Grace Baptist on South Lake Road.

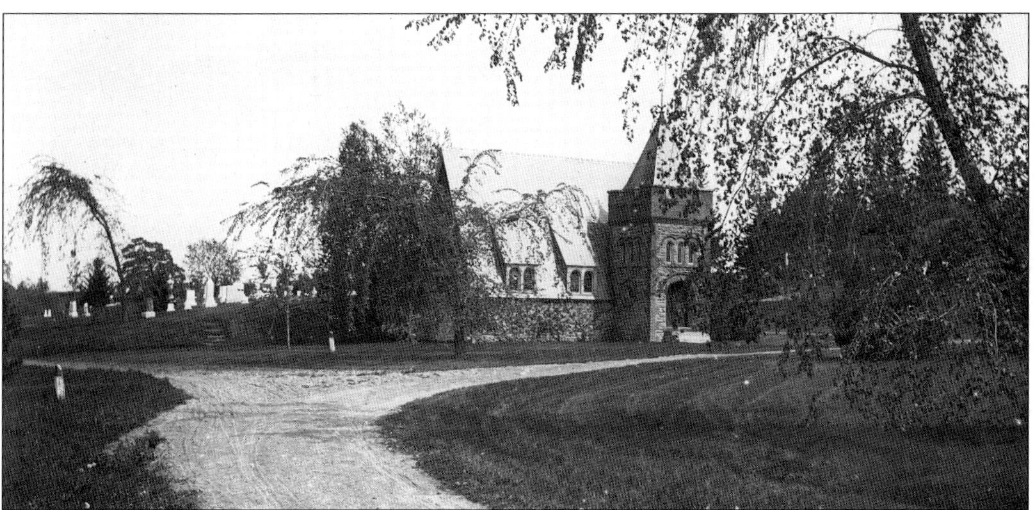

THE CEMETERY. The main cemetery in the town of Sweden is the combined Lakeview-Beach Ridge Cemetery, on Lake Road one mile south of Brockport. The first interments in Beach Ridge date to 1812. Lakeview, immediately adjacent to it, was founded in 1891, when a cemetery association bought 30 acres of the Burrows farm and engaged W.W. Parce of Rochester as landscape architect. A receiving vault (now gone) and Medina sandstone chapel (above) were built. The cemeteries merged in 1973.

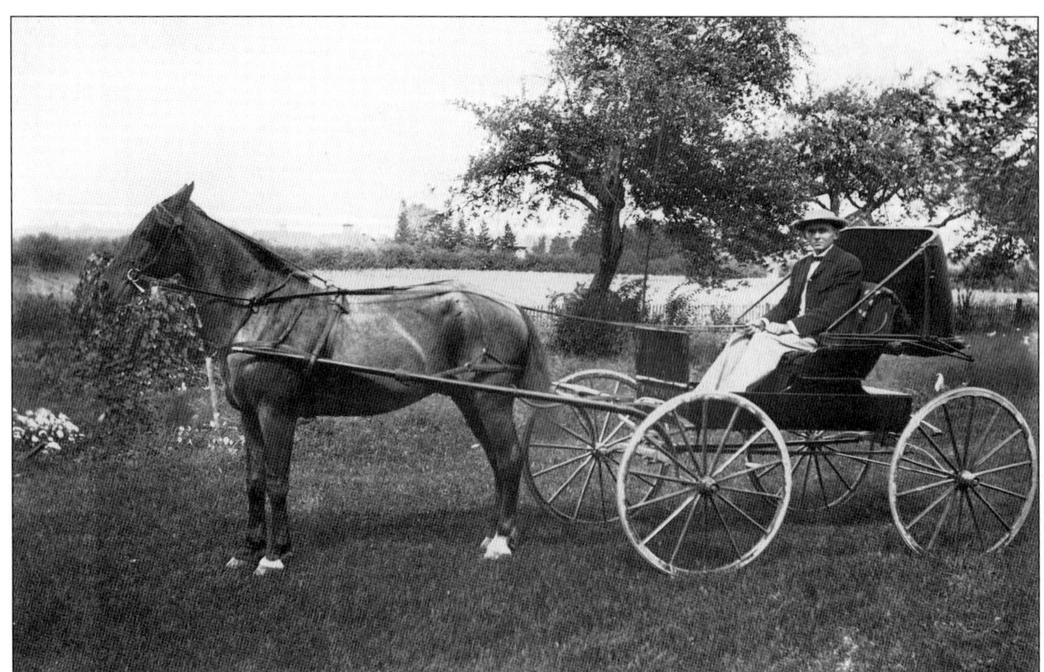

VEHICLES. Early pioneers reached Sweden on foot, by wagon, or horseback. Only after roads were built and the country became more settled did the horse and buggy become the main means of vehicular transport in rural Sweden. Early in the 20th century, the purchase of an automobile was a major event in the life of a farm family. The Sweden group below seems to be celebrating such an occasion.

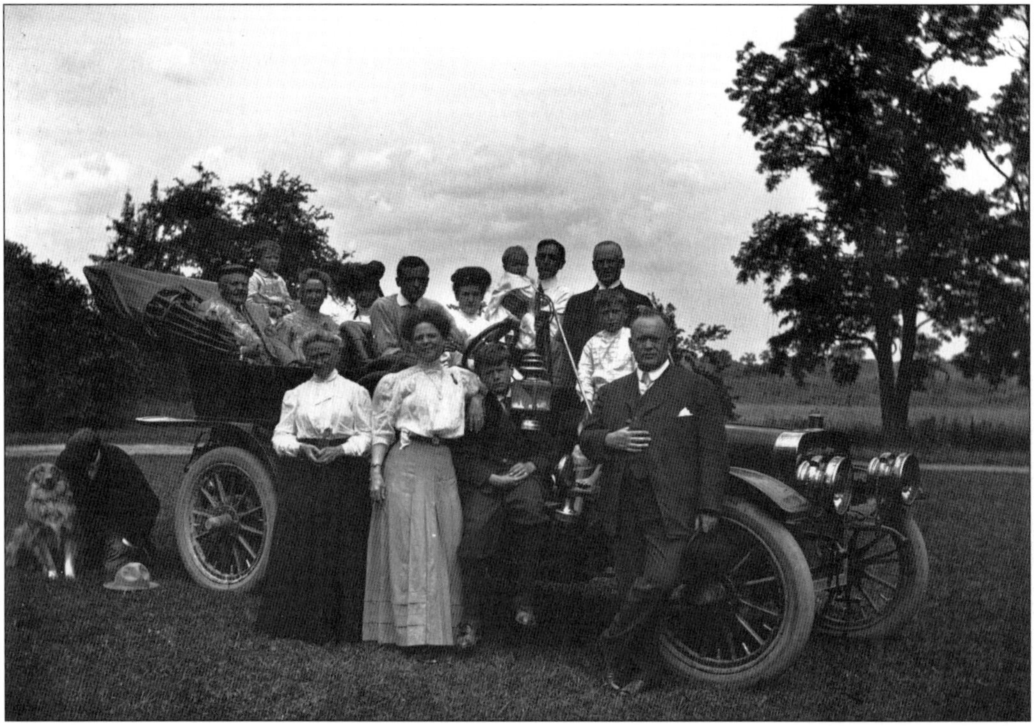

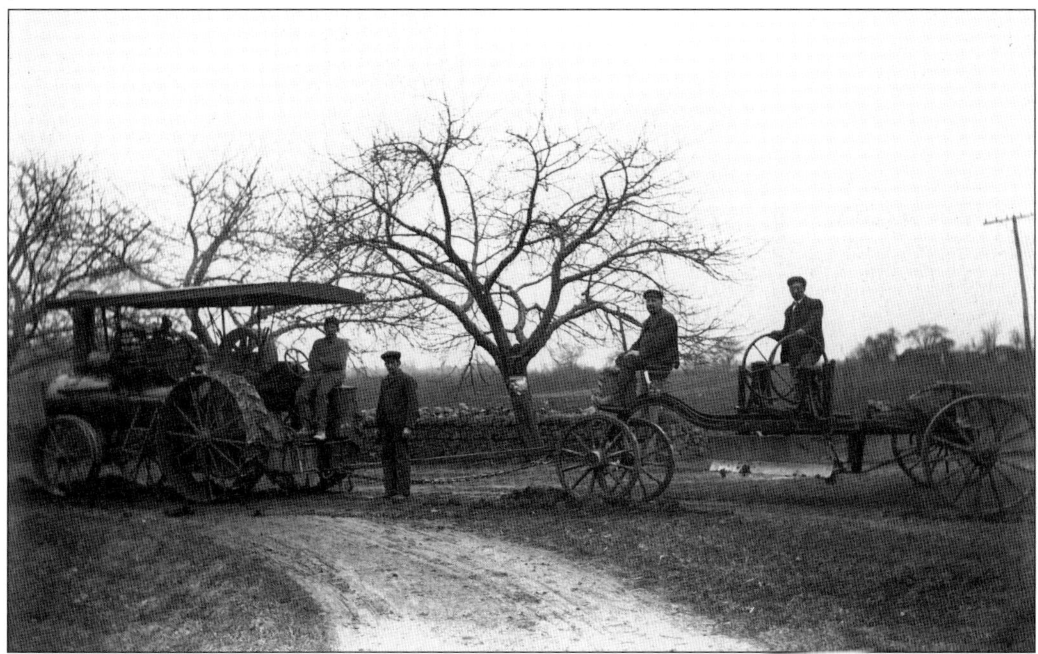

ROADS. The swath that opened the Triangle Tract for settlement gradually became a passable road as the pioneers arrived and used it. Years passed, however, before decent roads were cut through the disappearing wilderness to the increasing number of remote farmsteads. In the early 20th century, the town became one of the first in the area to build surfaced roads. The steam roller is working on such a project. The crew (below) appears to be paving a road with crushed stone, which in 1891 cost $1,431 for a seven-mile stretch.

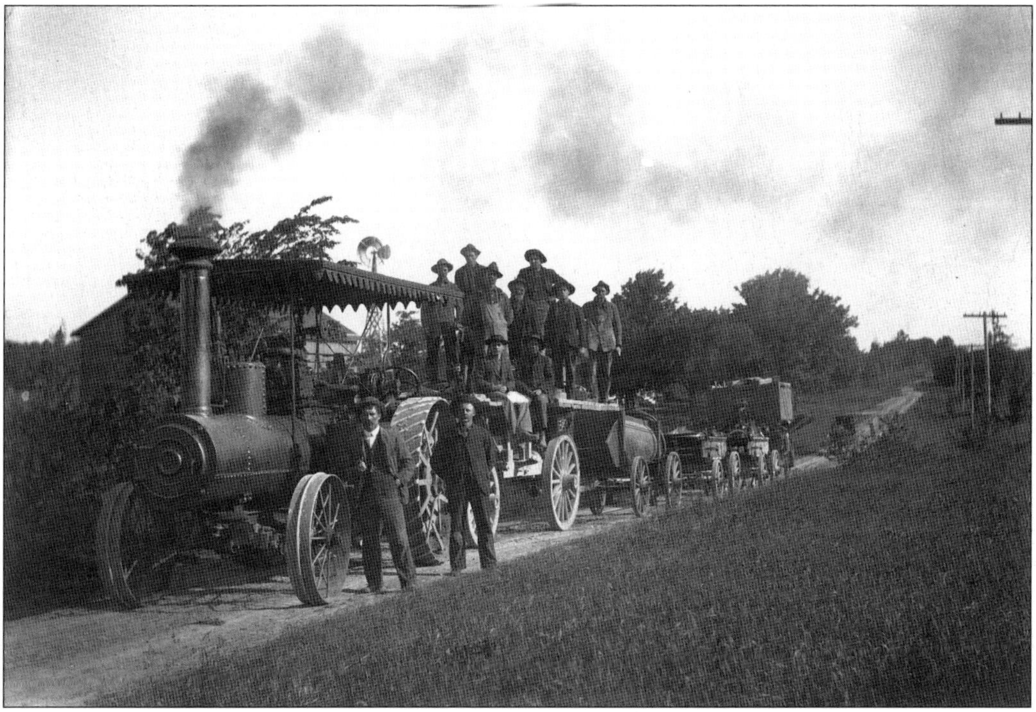

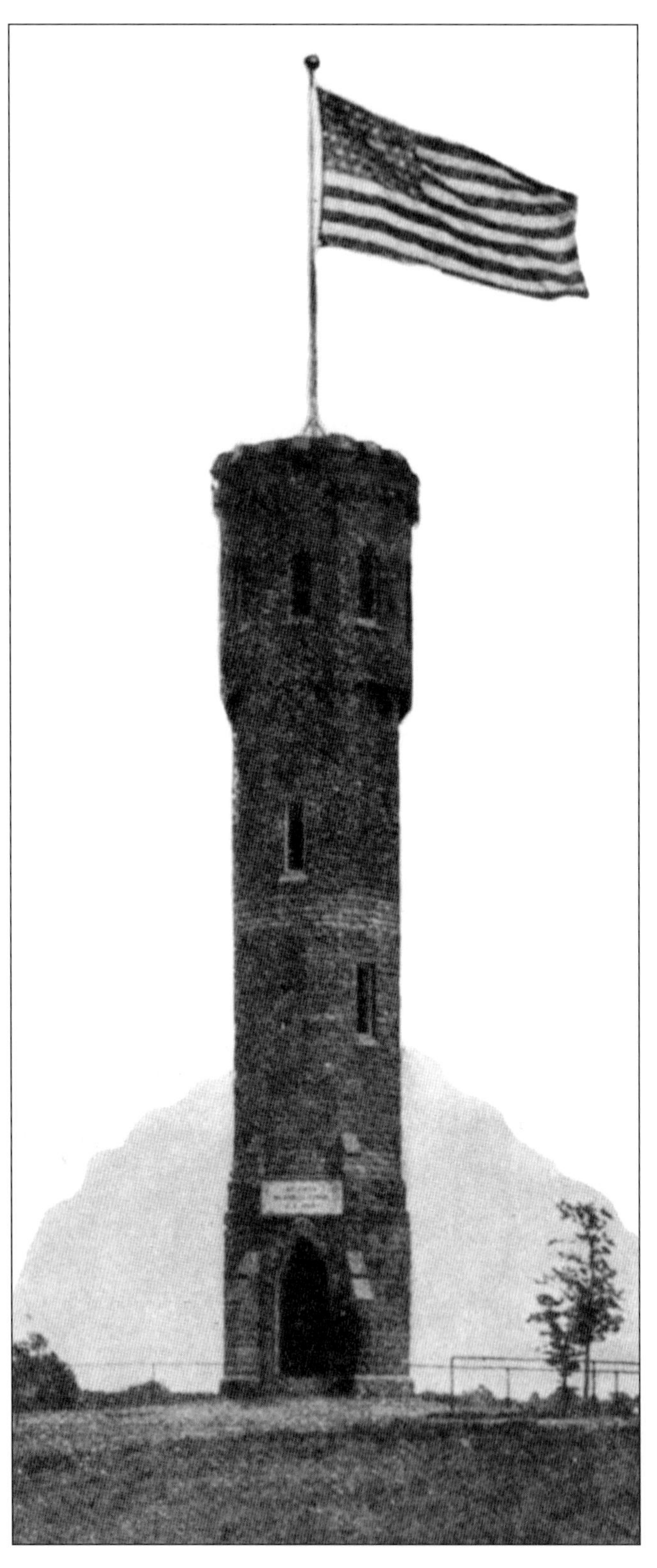

THE SOLDIERS' MONUMENT. This 52-foot Medina sandstone tower at the Brockport Rural Cemetery on Owens Road is a memorial to local Civil War veterans. The cemetery association offered "free interment of all loyal soldiers who have died or may die in Brockport or the towns of the vicinity." The dedication on September 1, 1893, was one of the grandest in the town's history, with several bands, entertainment, orations, and exhibition drills. The New York Central Railroad promoted it as an attraction along its Niagara Falls line, which ran adjacent to the property, and thousands of visitors climbed the iron staircase to the top. However, very few veterans took up the burial offer and the structure and cemetery were soon abandoned. The landmark is listed on the State and National Registers of Historic Places. A local committee is trying to restore the tower.

Two

TOWN OF CLARKSON

When the town of Clarkson was carved out of the old town of Murray in 1819, it included what later became the town of Hamlin. That town was separated from Clarkson in 1852, being first called Union and, after 1861, Hamlin. Clarkson is over 32 square miles in area, averaging about four miles north to south and eight miles east to west. The first settler, Moody Freeman, arrived in 1803, although some evidence suggests that squatters were there earlier. James Sayres, Joel Palmer, and Eli Blodgett bought property in Clarkson in 1804, but apparently settled later. Clarkson Corners emerged early as the main population center, being at the intersection of Lake Road, which had been built in 1802, and Ridge Road, which was widened from a Seneca Indian trail *c.* 1810. The first town government was organized in 1820, with Aretas Haskell as supervisor and 58 other offices. Clarkson's economy has always been heavily agricultural, though recent transportation improvements have brought some housing tracts, whose residents largely commute to other parts of the Rochester area. Clarkson has never had a major manufacturing enterprise and has had only a sprinkling of commercial ones.

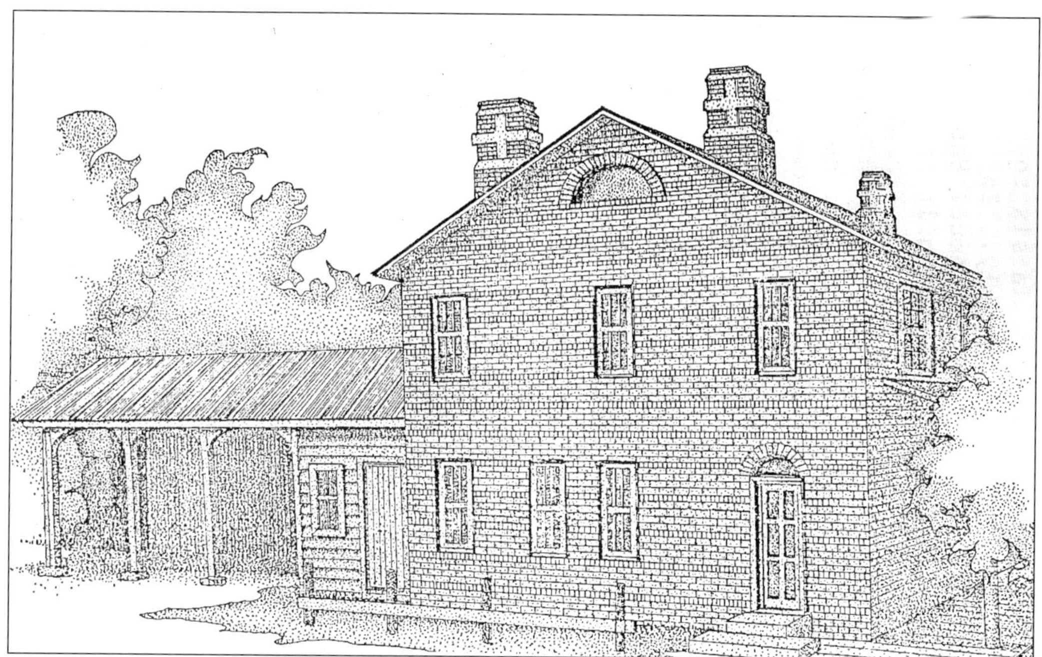

THE GENERAL STORE AND TAVERN. This is the brick building that housed Hiel Brockway's tavern in 1816 and in which James Seymour (page 26) rented space for his store from 1817 to 1818.

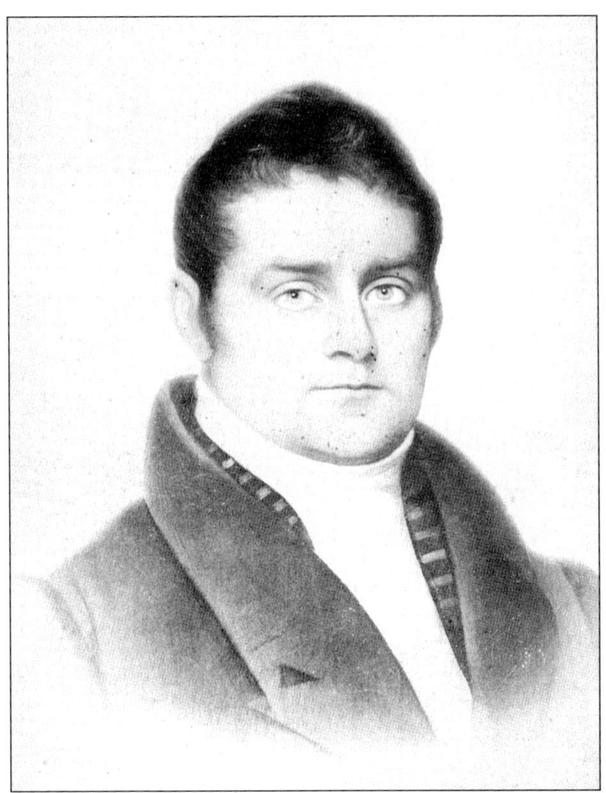

JAMES SEYMOUR. Seymour (1791–1864) came to Clarkson (then Murray) in 1817, opened a general store, and was elected Murray town supervisor. When he learned that the canal would pass south of Clarkson, Seymour bought 247 acres in Sweden and cofounded Brockport. He opened another general store there and was again elected town supervisor. Later, he helped organize Monroe County and became its first sheriff. He was president of Rochester's first bank, vice president of its first railroad, first treasurer of the Rochester Atheneum (now Rochester Institute of Technology), and a Rochester city alderman. In 1845, he moved to Michigan, became supervisor of Lansing, served in both houses of the Michigan legislature, and was an organizer of the national Republican party. Lansing, Michigan's state capital, was built partly on land Seymour owned.

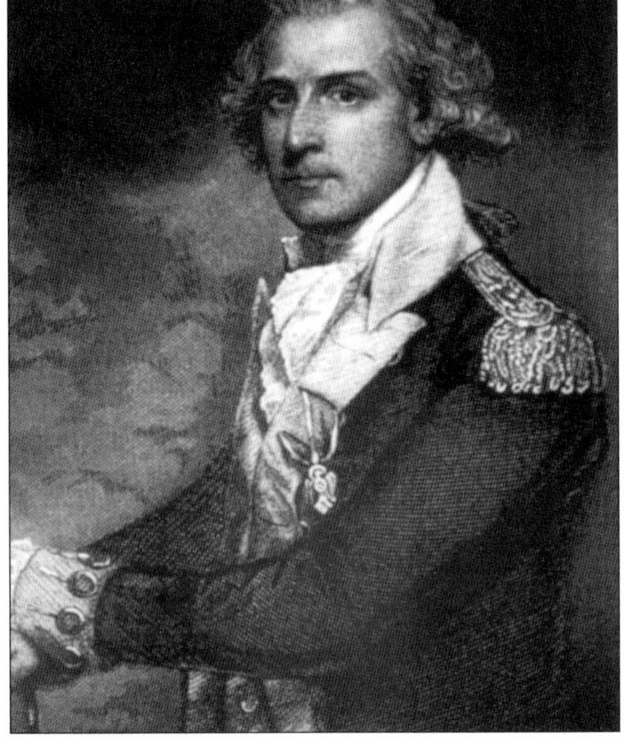

GENERAL CLARKSON. Maj. Gen. Matthew Clarkson (1758–1825) was an original proprietor of the Triangle Tract. He had been a distinguished officer in the Continental army, was a prominent New York City banker and philanthropist, and served in both houses of the state legislature. Local tradition says his son was the first white child born in Clarkson, but no evidence exists that he ever visited the town. In 1804, he placed his interest in the tract in trust for his children.

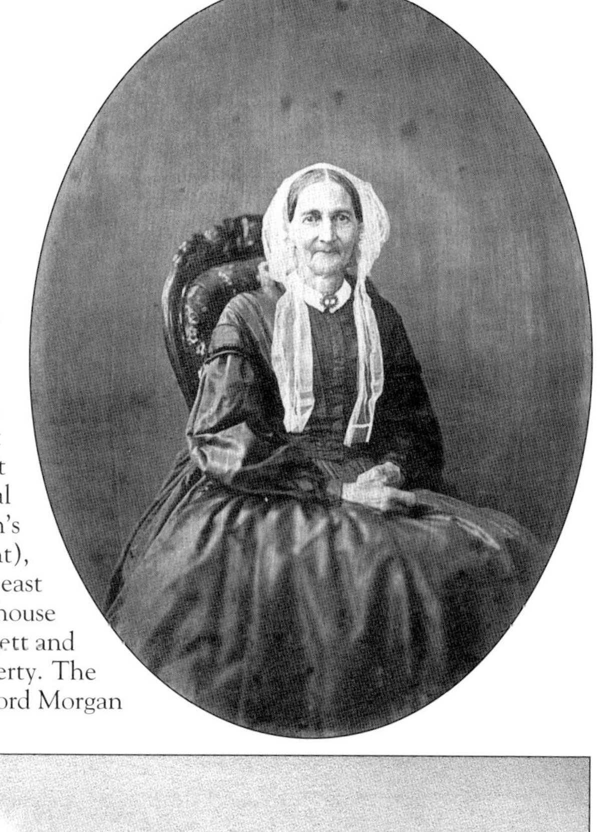

THE BLODGETT FAMILY. Early settlement of Clarkson was faster than settlement of Sweden. By 1805, twelve lots had been sold there, compared with three in Sweden. Eli Blodgett bought the second of them in 1804 but apparently did not occupy it for several years. In 1814, his son, John, and John's wife, Lucy Jane Barlow Blodgett (right), made their home on the property on the east side of Lake Road. They built their house (below) in 1825. It still stands. Eli Blodgett and Hiel Brockway built a mill on the property. The dam and millpond were restored by Gifford Morgan in the 1930s and are still there as well.

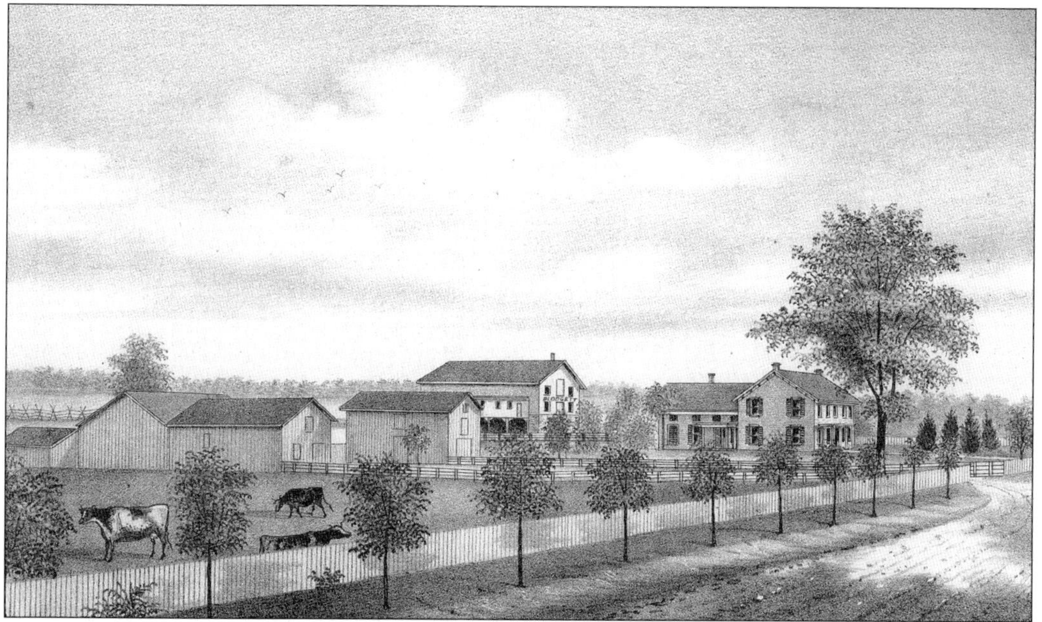

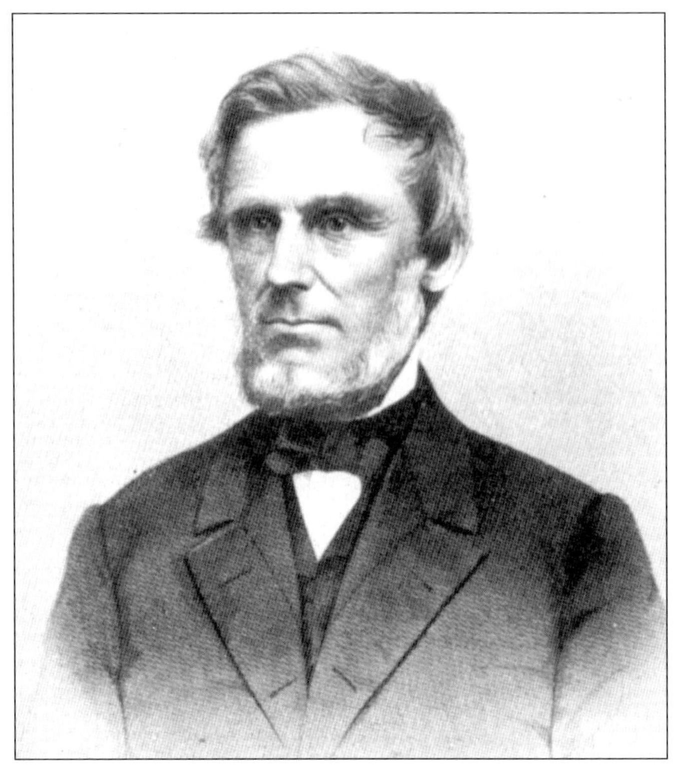

HENRY R. SELDEN. Selden (1805–1885) was one of early Clarkson's most distinguished residents. He was New York State lieutenant governor (1856–1862) and a court of appeals judge (1862–1864). Also, he was a founder of the Western Union Telegraph Company and served as suffragist Susan B. Anthony's lawyer. He is widely believed to have been the anonymous person who paid her fine when she was convicted of having voted illegally in 1872. His wife was the daughter of Abel Baldwin (page 37).

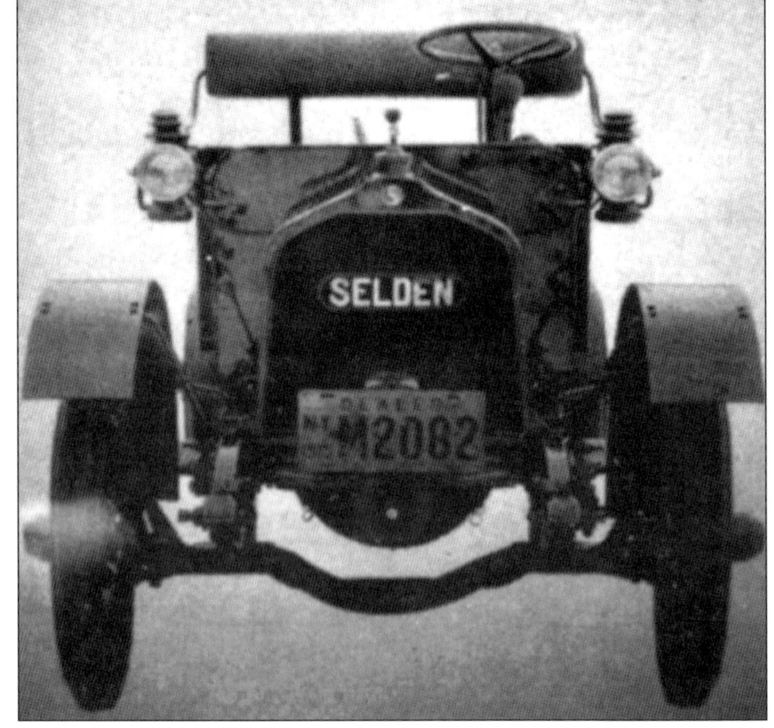

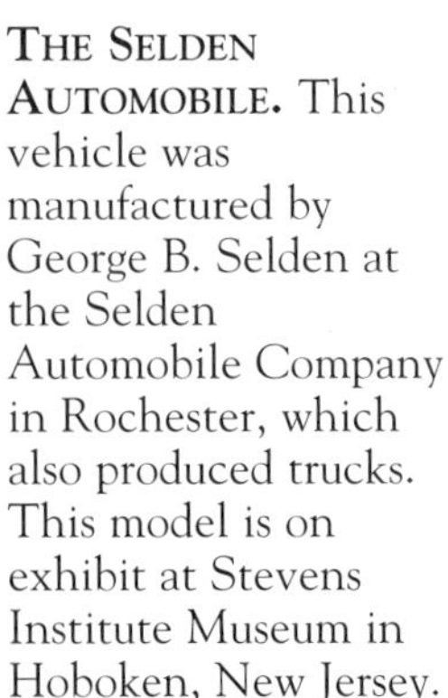

THE SELDEN AUTOMOBILE. This vehicle was manufactured by George B. Selden at the Selden Automobile Company in Rochester, which also produced trucks. This model is on exhibit at Stevens Institute Museum in Hoboken, New Jersey.

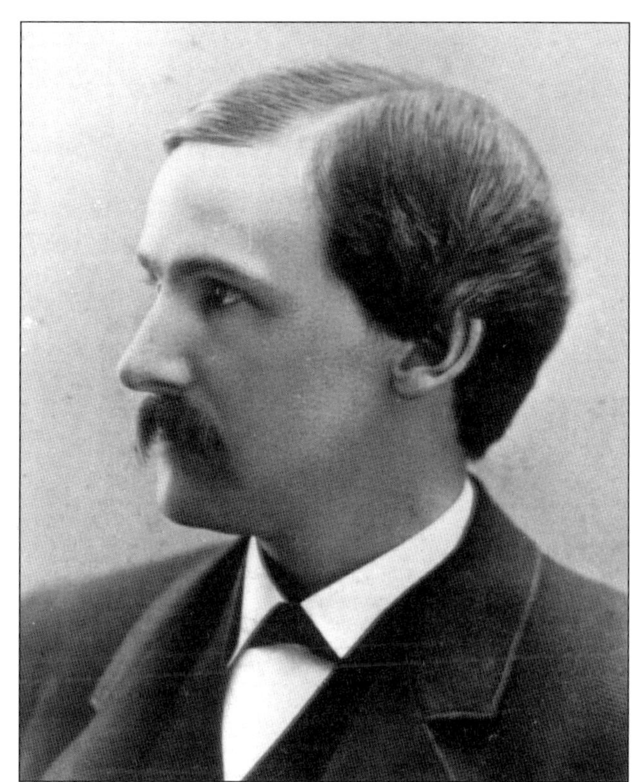

GEORGE B. SELDEN. Henry Selden's son George B. Selden (1846–1922) was a patent lawyer and inventor. From age 15, he was interested in mechanical invention. After Civil War service and law study, he worked to develop a gasoline-powered vehicle. His 1879 patent application for the device was denied but, after improvements, was approved in 1895. He collected royalties on his patents from automobile manufacturers until 1911, when Henry Ford won a lawsuit declaring his claims invalid. The illustration (below) is from his 1895 patent application. (George B. Selden Portrait Courtesy Rochester Public Library Local History Collection.)

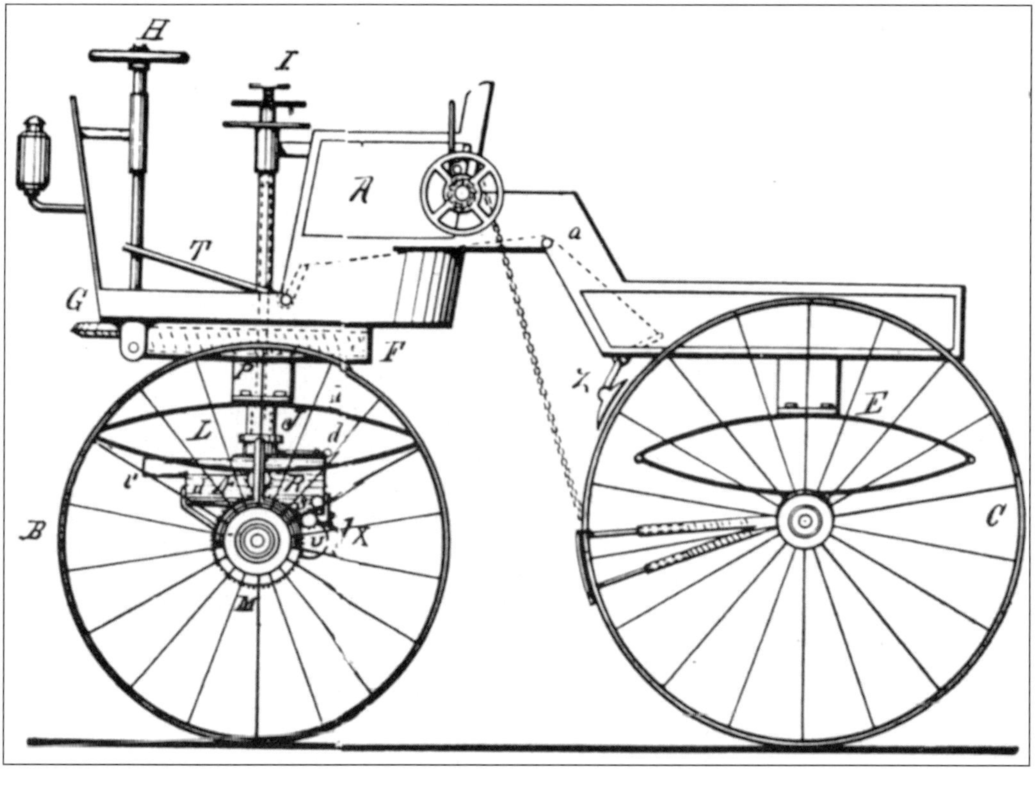

No. 184 BROCKPORT AND CLARKSON One Shares.

PLANK ROAD COMPANY.

CAPITAL STOCK $30,000—SHARES $50.

Clarkson, August 18 1863.

This is to Certify, That Shubal Harmon is entitled to one Shares in the Capital Stock of the BROCKPORT AND CLARKSON PLANK ROAD COMPANY, transferable at their office in Clarkson, by the said Shubal or his attorney.

In Witness Whereof, The Secretary has hereunto affixed his signature, this 18th day of August 1863

Secretary.

PLANK ROAD. In 1848, the Brockport and Clarkson Plank Road Company built, mostly of hemlock planks, a private toll road along Lake Road from Wilkie's Corners on the north edge of Brockport 12 miles through Clarkson and into Hamlin, with a branch running west to Redman Road. By 1868, the company was failing and the town of Clarkson bought its part of the road for $200. This certificate for one $50 share of stock was issued to Shubal Harmon on August 18, 1863.

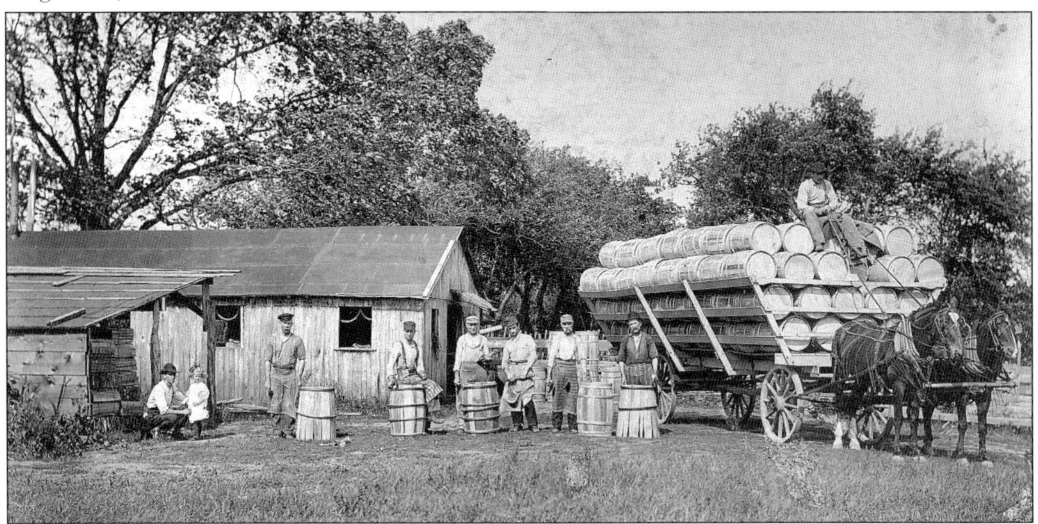

THE BARREL FACTORY. In the 19th and early 20th centuries, Clarkson was home to a number of small, artisanal family industries, but never on the scale of the manufacturing plants in Brockport. They included brickyards, potasheries, tanneries, flour mills, sawmills, distilleries, smithies, and cigar-rolling and fruit-drying shops. This is the Fowler Barrel Factory on the west side of Lake Road south of Ridge Road.

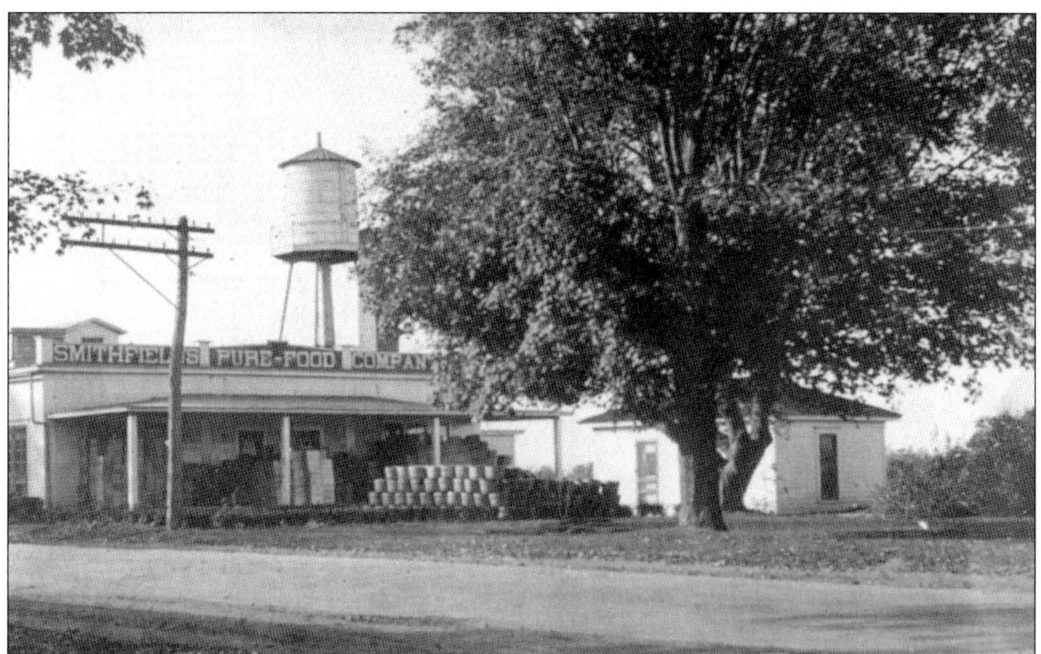

CANNING, CARRIAGES, CASKETS, AND CREAM. Perhaps Clarkson's most substantial industry was the Smithfield Canning Company's plant in Garland. From 1913 to 1930, it employed as many as 75 workers. When it closed, its machinery was moved to the company's other plant in Hilton. The cobblestone building (below), at Clarkson Corners, housed a blacksmith shop that produced carriages and caskets. Another processing plant was the Ridge Road Creamery, founded by Albert J. and W.N. Gallup c. 1890. In 1913, the creamery building housed a feed mill and later a glass business, and today it is a private residence, located immediately west of the Clarkson Community Church.

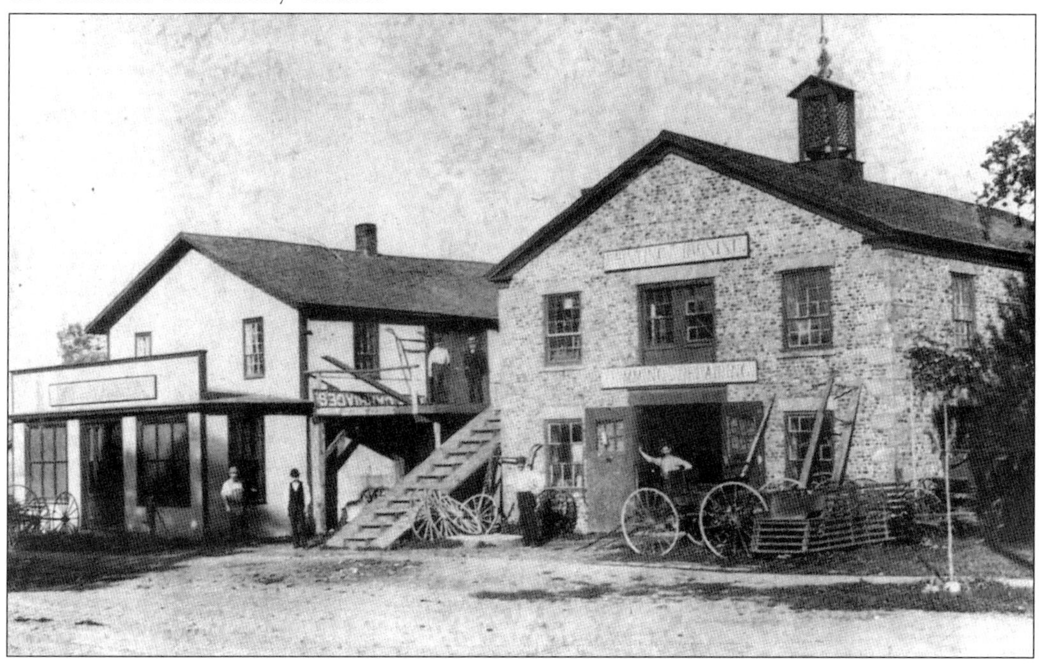

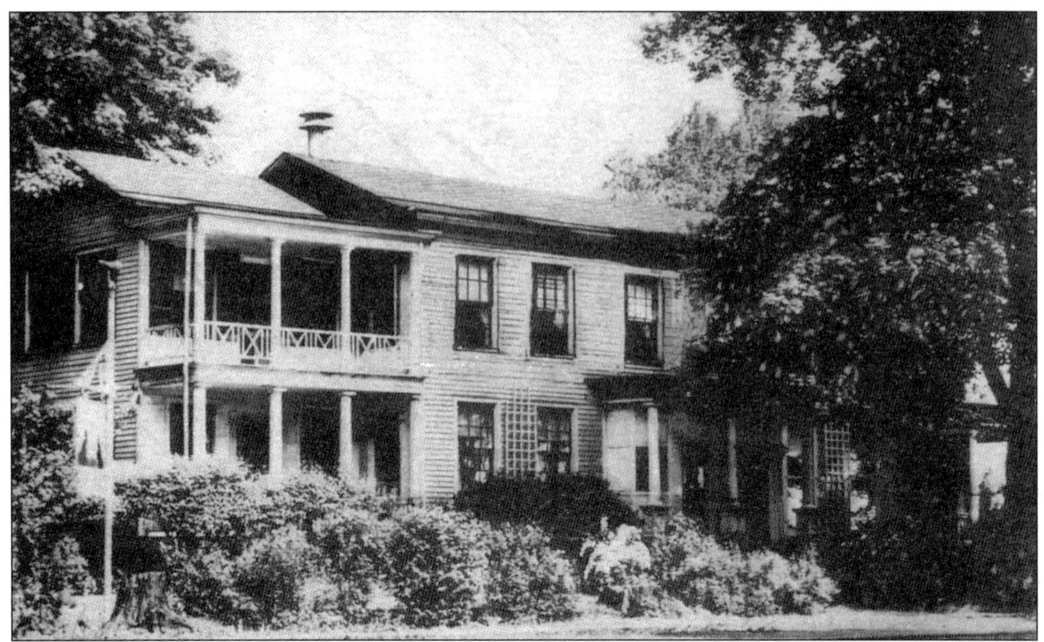

HOTELS. Hiel Brockway built Clarkson's first hotel in 1816, and the Walbridge Hotel was established c. 1817. Over the decades, other hotels, taverns, inns, and bed and breakfasts have succeeded one another. Clark Haven (above), which operated on Lake Road at the southern border of the town for several decades, was razed in 1959. Levi P. Morton, 22nd vice president of the United States and uncle of the owner, was a guest there. Its west wing was a tollhouse for the Plank Road. The Houston Tavern (below) was built by Isaac Houston in 1842 on Ridge Road in what was once called Dog's Hollow. Isaac Houston also had a tannery, cooper and cobbler shops, and a sawmill. He was town supervisor from 1845 to 1846.

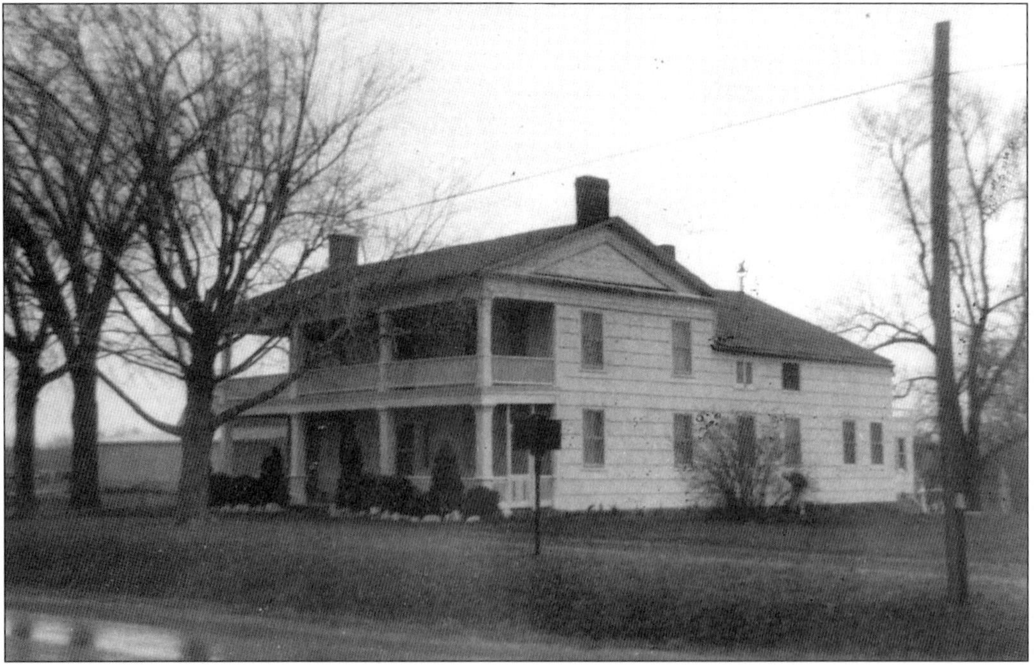

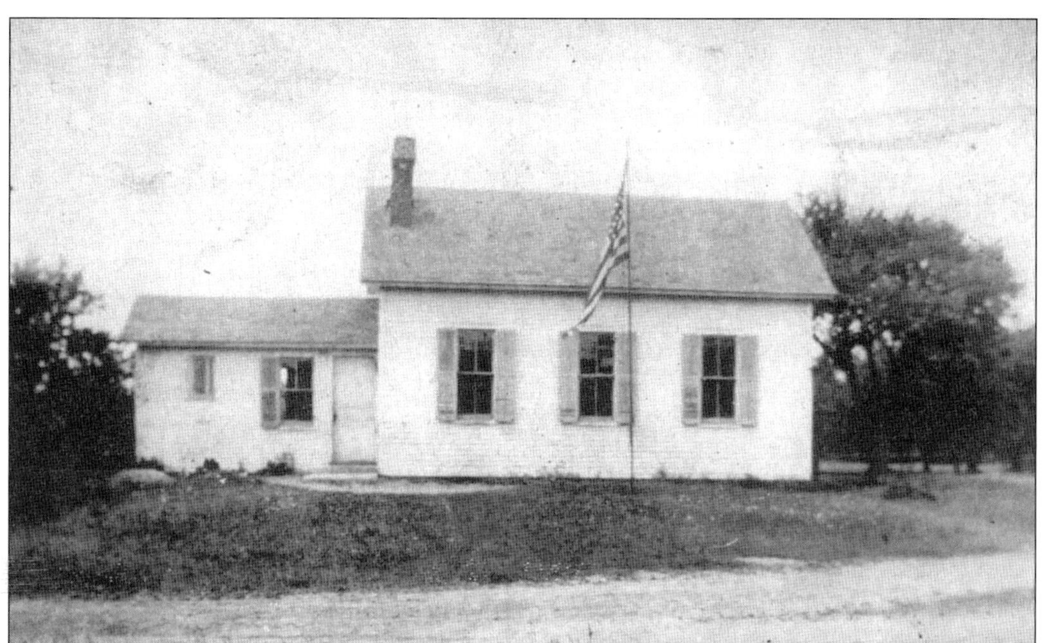

SCHOOLS. Clarkson's first school was a log cabin west of Clarkson Corners *c.* 1810. During most of the 19th century, the town had nine or ten district grade schools. Typical was District School No. 10 (above), at Ireland and Clarkson-Parma Town Line Roads. The Clarkson Academy offered private secondary schooling from the late 1820s until *c.* 1867. In 1837, it enrolled 76 boys and 51 girls. Of those, 8 girls and 38 boys lived outside Clarkson, from as far as New York City and Michigan. In 1853, the wooden structure burned and was replaced by a new building (right) that still stands. The school offered classes through eighth grade until 1934. Until 1956, two teachers offered first through sixth grade classes.

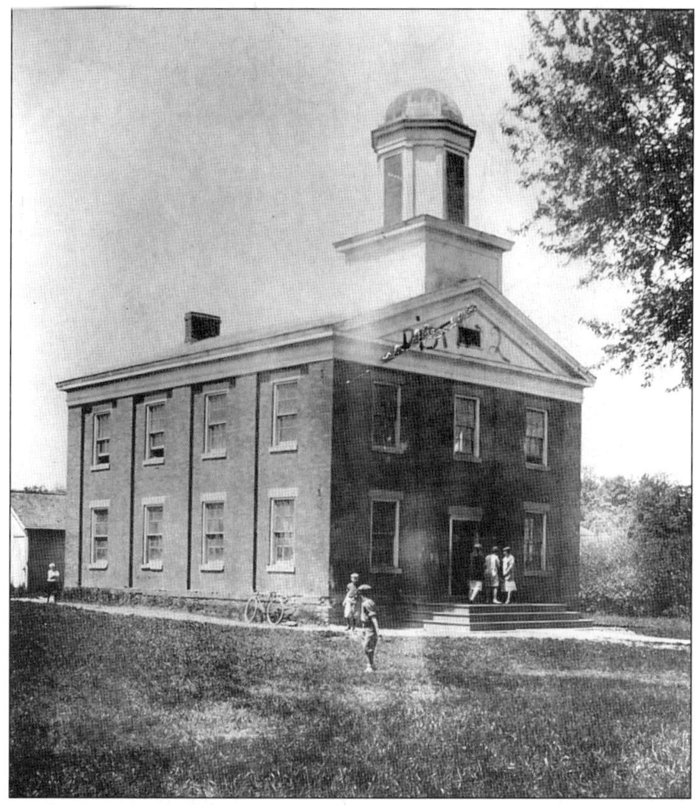

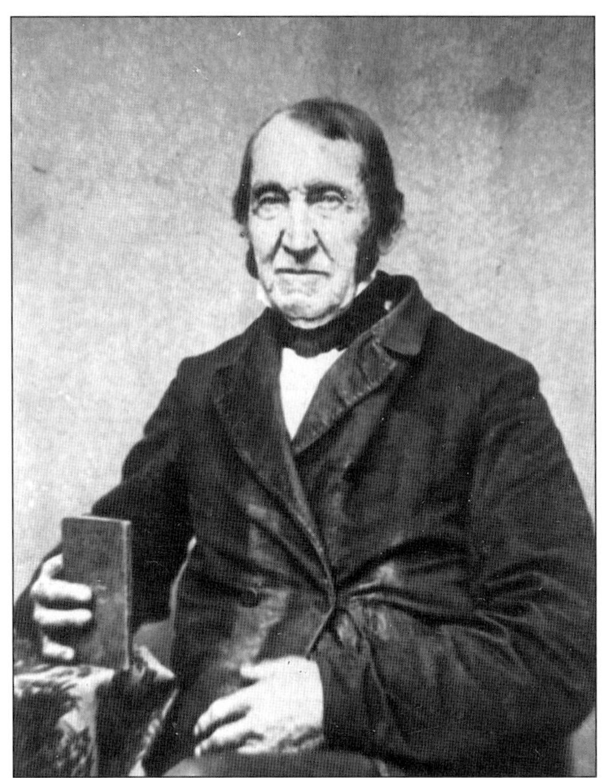

EARLY CLERGY. Eli Hannibal, an early settler, may have been Clarkson's first pastor. He was an itinerant preacher with Free Will Baptist congregations in Hamlin, Morton, Walker, Hilton, and Parma, as well as in the Garland neighborhood of Clarkson. Also, he was Clarkson's first overseer of the poor, in 1820.

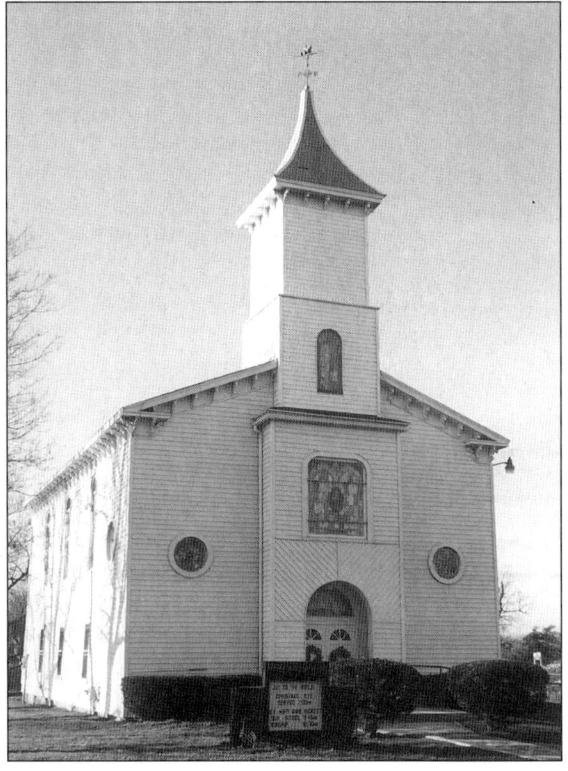

METHODISTS. In 1825, a Bethel Methodist Episcopal congregation organized in Garland and built this church. The Reverend Benajah Williams was the preacher. The building was remodeled extensively in 1869. It now serves a United Methodist congregation. Another Methodist Episcopal congregation was formed and built a church north of Garland in 1848. In 1860, some of its members organized a Free Methodist congregation and built a church across the road the following year. Both churches closed in the 1920s.

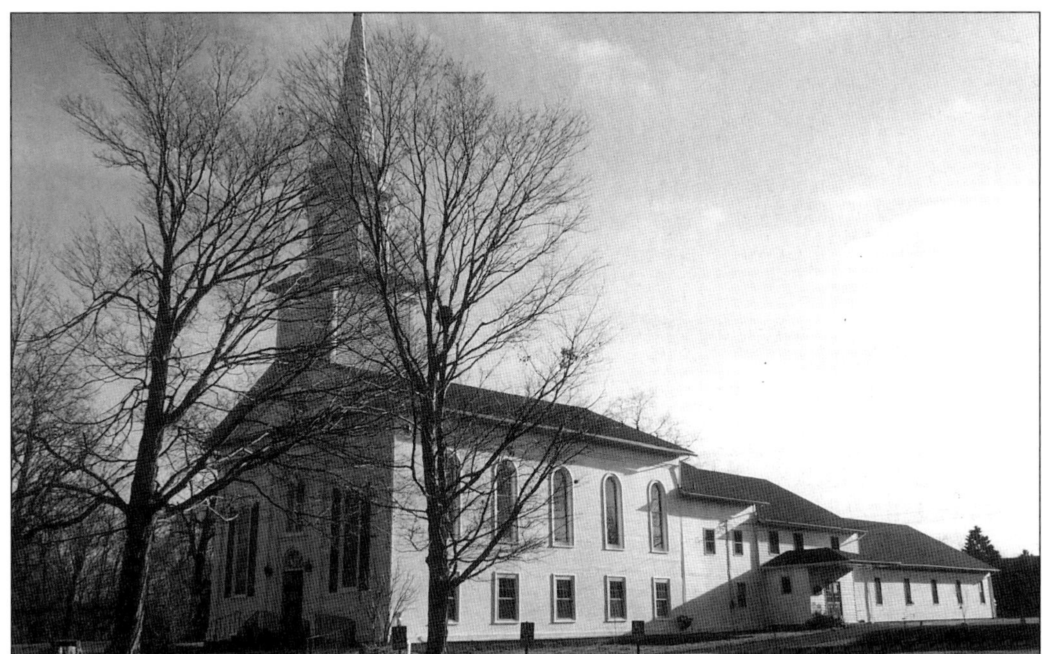

PRESBYTERIANS. A Congregational Society organized at Clarkson Corners in 1816 and built its church in 1825. It became Presbyterian in 1830, Congregational again in 1853, Presbyterian in 1869, and, finally, a Community Church in 1969. Besides the two historic churches, Clarkson today has the Open Bible Church on Redman Road, the Hamlin New Testament Church on Lake Road at the Hamlin line, the Kingdom Hall of Jehovah's Witnesses on Sweden-Walker Road, and the Church of Jesus Christ of the Latter Day Saints on Lake Road near Sweden.

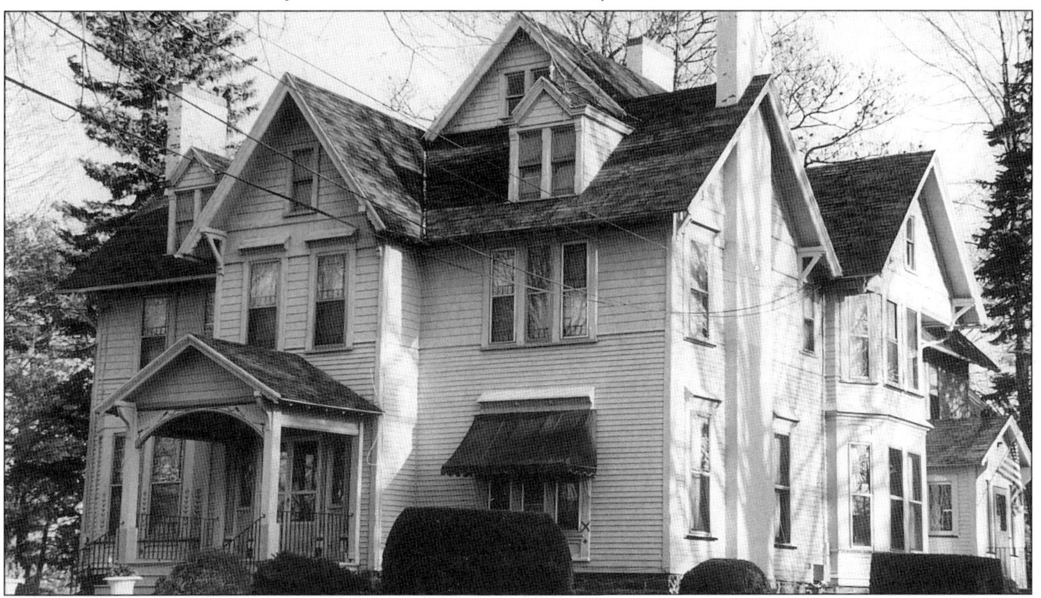

THE GIFFORD MORGAN HOUSE. This home on the east side of Lake Road just north of Sweden was built in 1884 by Brockport industrialist Gifford Morgan (pages 27 and 53). The structure was remodeled c. 1900 with poured concrete interior walls. After Gifford Morgan died in 1944, his widow resided there until she died in 1968 at age 92.

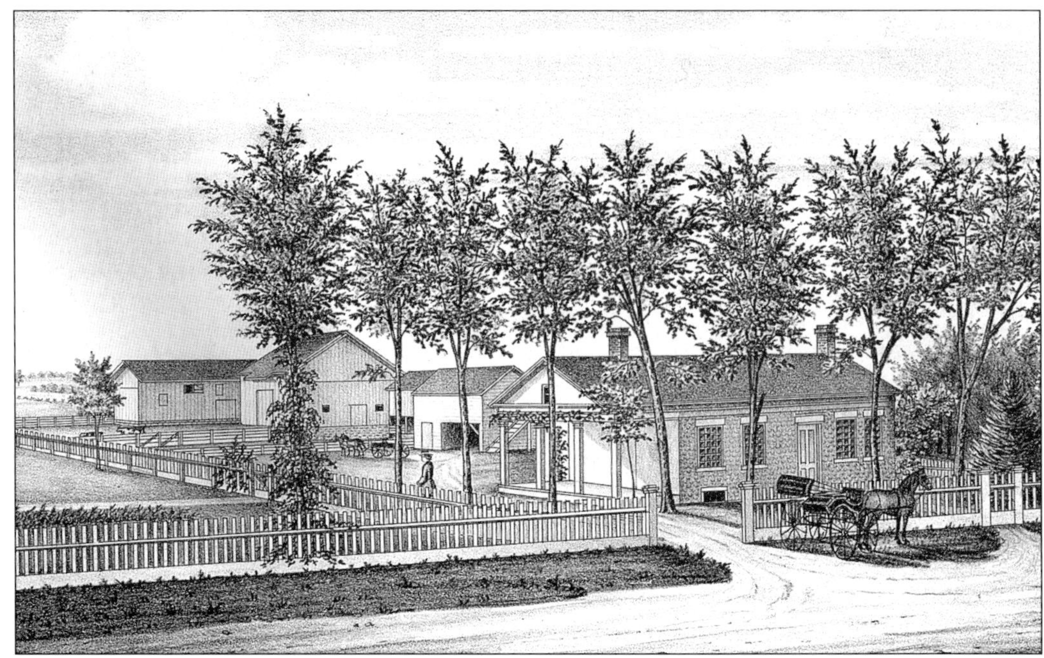

The Allen and Selden Homes. Isaac Allen Sr., a hatter, was born in Enfield, Connecticut, in 1794, and settled in Clarkson in 1816. After farming in Hamlin from 1819 to 1823, he returned to Clarkson and operated his business (above) on Ridge Road just west of Clarkson Corners. The Clarkson Corners home (below) of Henry R. Selden (pages 28 and 29) is where son George Selden was born.

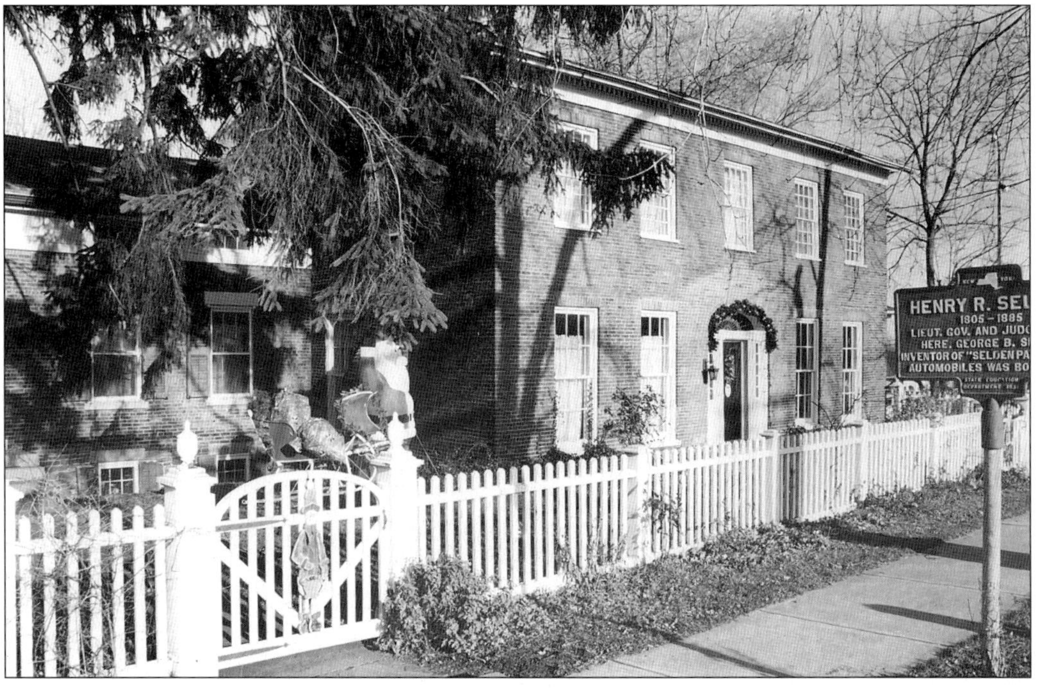

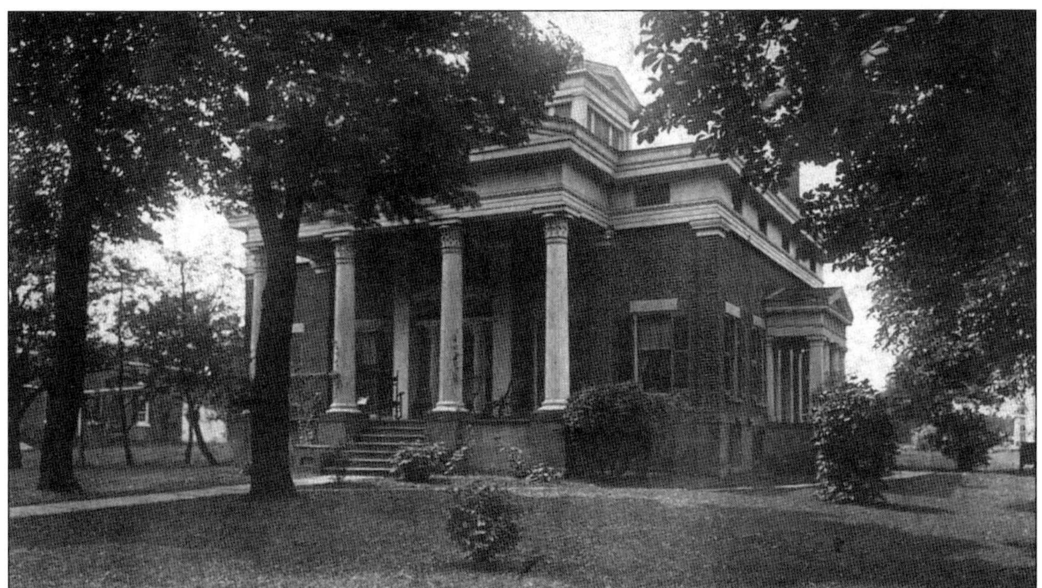

The Bowman and Baldwin Homes. John M. Bowman built a classic Greek revival home (above) *c.* 1850 for Eliza Bellinger, his betrothed. He changed his mind at the last moment and they never married—anyone. James Warren, a farmer and canal packet boat captain who had settled in Clarkson in 1810, bought the house and lived there until he died in 1888. He was town supervisor (1849–1852, 1853, 1855–1857) and Monroe County sheriff (1863). The house is now a bed and breakfast owned by Ronald E. and Anne Klein. A native of Norwich, Vermont, Dr. Abel Baldwin arrived in Clarkson in 1811 and built a frame home on the northwest corner of Ridge and Lake Roads. He ran a hotel there from *c.* 1816 to 1825, when he built another home (below) and became a successful farmer. Baldwin was town supervisor in 1826.

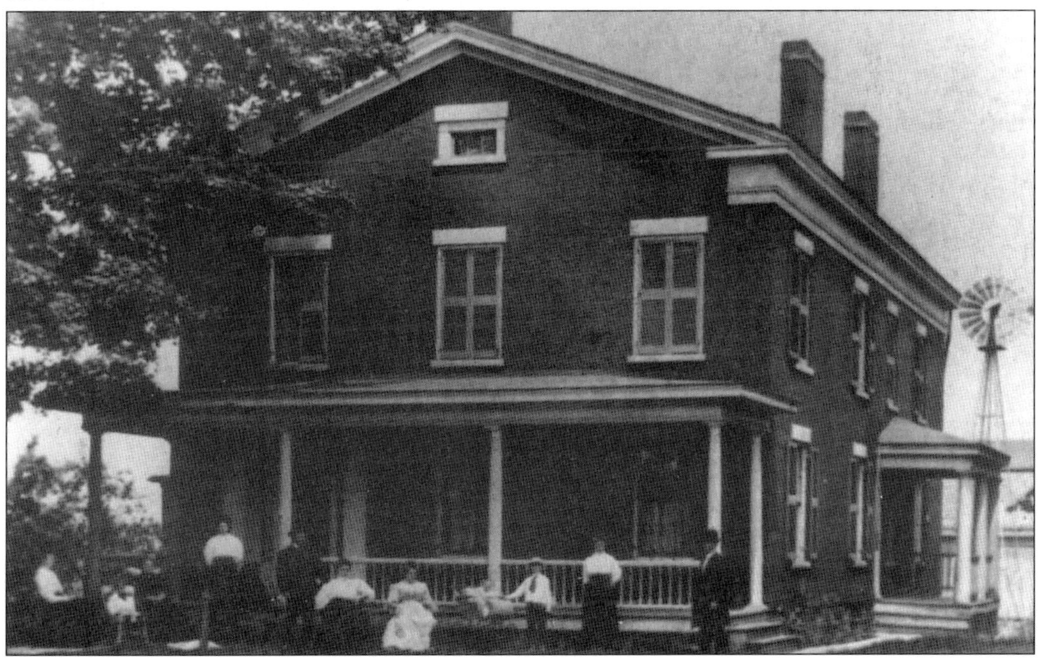

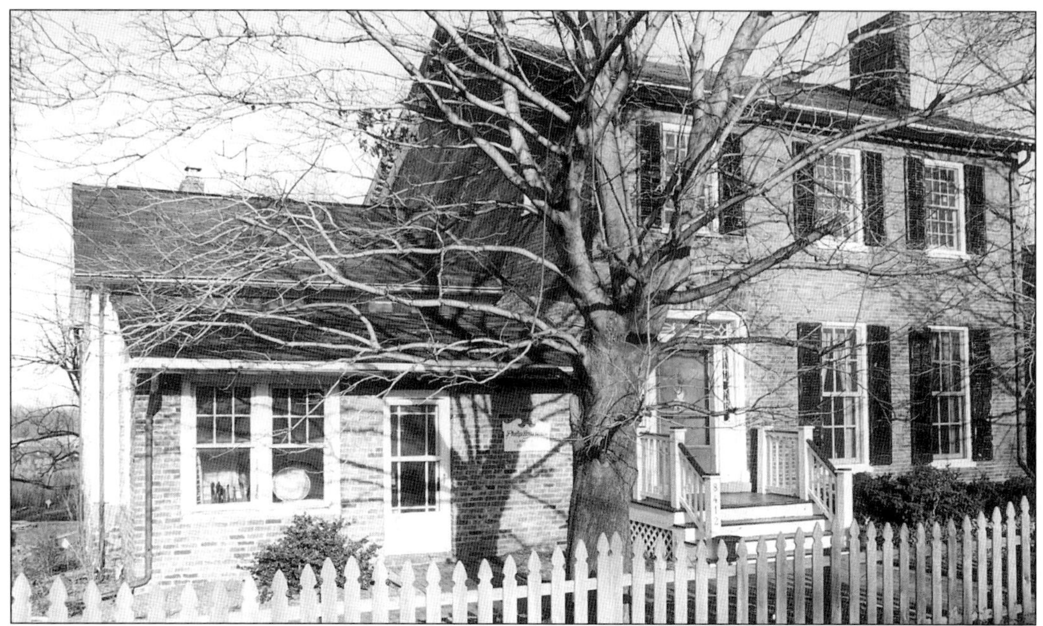

PHILIP BOSS. Philip Boss arrived in Clarkson in 1817 and built a house in 1820. He was a cabinetmaker and an amateur artist. His home and cabinetmaking shop burned in 1827, killing his young son and an apprentice. He built another home c. 1830, before moving to Rochester and becoming a popular portrait artist. Washington L. Rockwell, the next owner of the house, was town supervisor (1874–1876), a state legislator, a 20-year justice of the peace, and town tax collector. Isaac Allen Sr. (page 36) owned the property from 1867 to 1885. The portraits below of early Clarkson residents Deacon Joel Palmer, a tanner, and his wife, Phebe Palmer, are attributed to Boss.

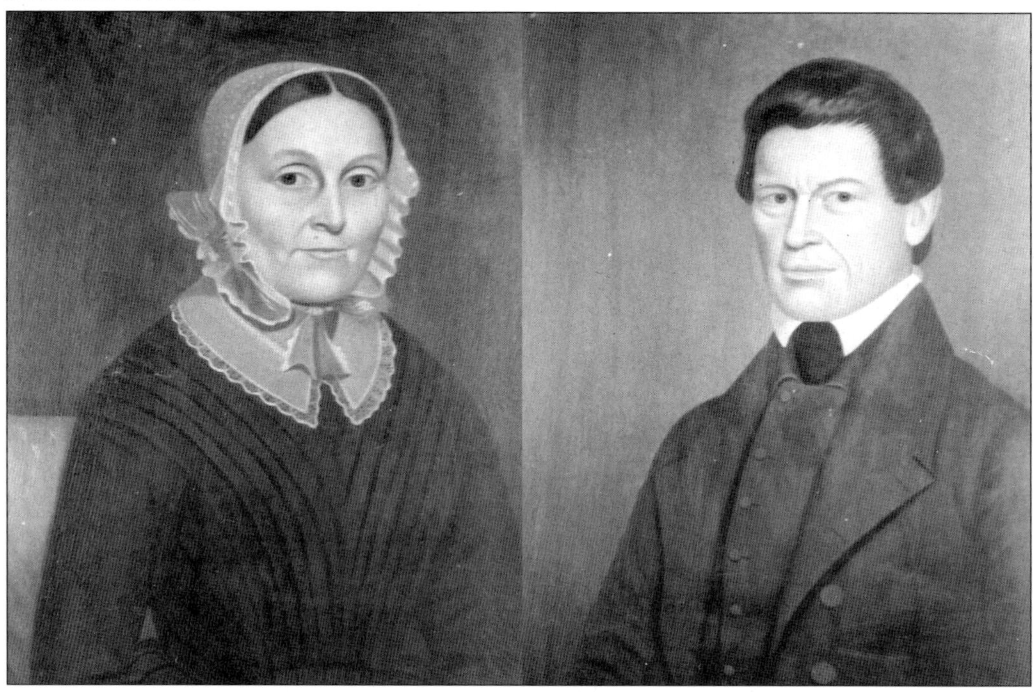

Three

VILLAGE OF BROCKPORT

Two factors determined Brockport's location: the Seneca Indian trail, coming up from present-day Leroy, which became the first north–south road in the area; and the lip of the Medina escarpment in northern Sweden, which became the most practicable route for the Erie Canal en route to Lockport. In 1822, Hiel Brockway hired Zenas Case to lay out a village where these two routes intersected. Brockway owned the land on the west side of Lake Road and had an interest in much of the land on the east side, owned mainly by James Seymour. A partner of Seymour and a first cousin were canal commissioners and got the canal extended from Rochester to Brockport in 1823. For two years Brockport was the canal's western terminus, which the community an early boost. By 1880, railroads had become superior transportation means and Brockport began a long decline, recovering only after World War II with the rise of the college and the popularity of the village as a bedroom community and commercial center.

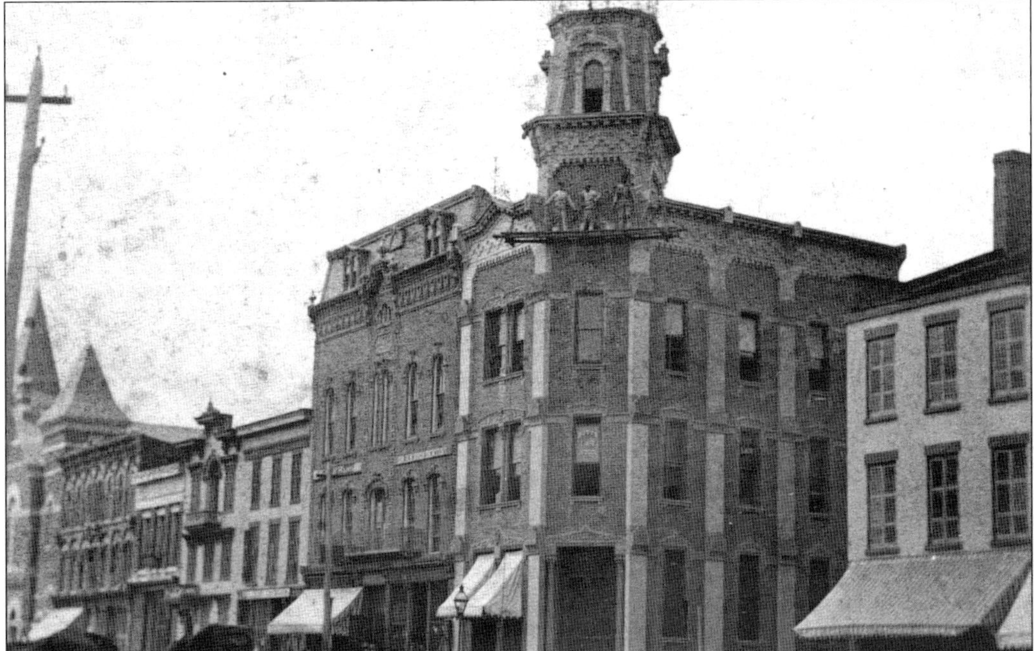

VANISHED GLORY. Brockport has the best-preserved, finest Victorian commercial structures in the area. Most buildings erected late in the 19th century have survived (pages 64 to 69). However, these gems have disappeared. The First National Bank (with the tower) was built in 1873 and demolished in 1927. The Ward Opera House (left of the bank) was built in the 1870s and was the most popular entertainment center in Brockport. In 1911, a fire badly damaged the third floors of both buildings. They were repaired and the opera house survived, without the auditorium, as a commercial structure until its demolition in the 1940s.

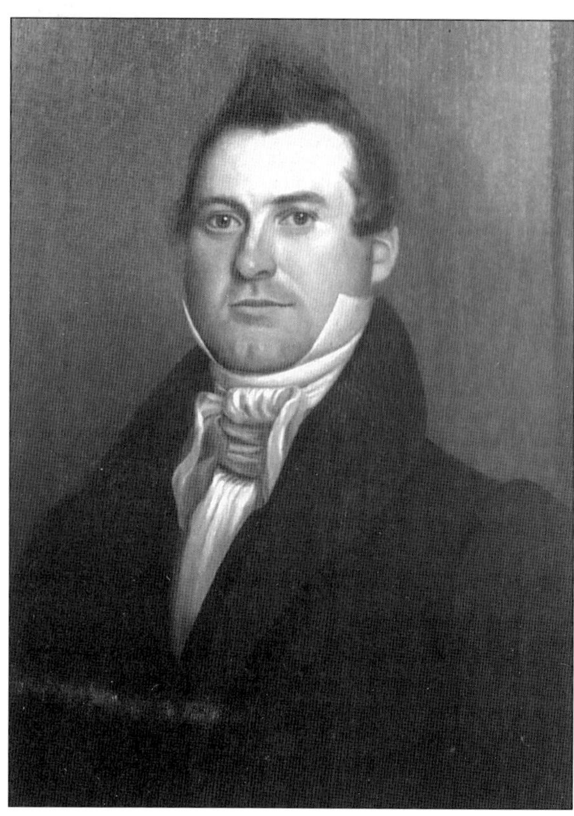

Hiel Brockway. Brockway (1775–1842) was born in Old Lyme, Connecticut, and moved to New York State *c.* 1800. For some 14 years, he and his wife, Phebe, lived near Geneva, where he practiced his trade as a builder and speculated successfully in land. In 1816, he moved to Clarkson and, in 1817, began buying land where, in 1822, he and James Seymour (pages 26, 39, 43, 78, and 91) founded Brockport. He also speculated in land elsewhere in the area and operated a brickyard. His boatyard was said to be the world's largest builder of canal packet boats at one time. His Red Bird Packet Line (below) was a major passenger line on the canal. His son-in-law Elias B. Holmes owned a competing "Opposition Line." Holmes and another of Brockway's sons-in-law, Dr. Davis Carpenter, served in Congress.

ROCHESTER
AND
ALBANY.

Red Bird Line of Packets,
In connection with Rail Road from Niagara Falls to Lockport.

1843. 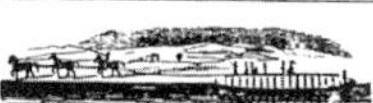 1843.

12 *hours ahead of the Lake Ontario Route!*

The Cars leave the Falls every day at 2 o'clock, P. M. for Lockport, where passengers will take one of the following new

Packet Boats 100 Feet Long.
THE EMPIRE!
Capt. D. H. Bromley,
THE ROCHESTER
Capt. J. H. Warren,

and arrive in Rochester the next morning at 6 o'clock, and can take the 8 o'clock train of Cars or Packet Boats for Syracuse and Albany, and arrive in Albany the same night.

☞ Passengers by this route will pass through a delightful country, and will have an opportunity of viewing Queenston Heights, Brock's Monument, the Tuscarora Indian Village, the combined Locks at Lockport, 3 hours at Rochester, and pass through the delightful country from Rochester to Utica by daylight.

N. B.---These two new Packets are 100 feet long, and are built on an entire new plan, with

Ladies' & Gentlemen's Saloons,

and with Ventilators in the decks, and for room and accommodations for sleeping they surpass any thing ever put on the Canal.

For Passage apply at Railroad and Packet Office, Niagara Falls.

September. 1843. T. CLARK, J. J. STATIA, Agents

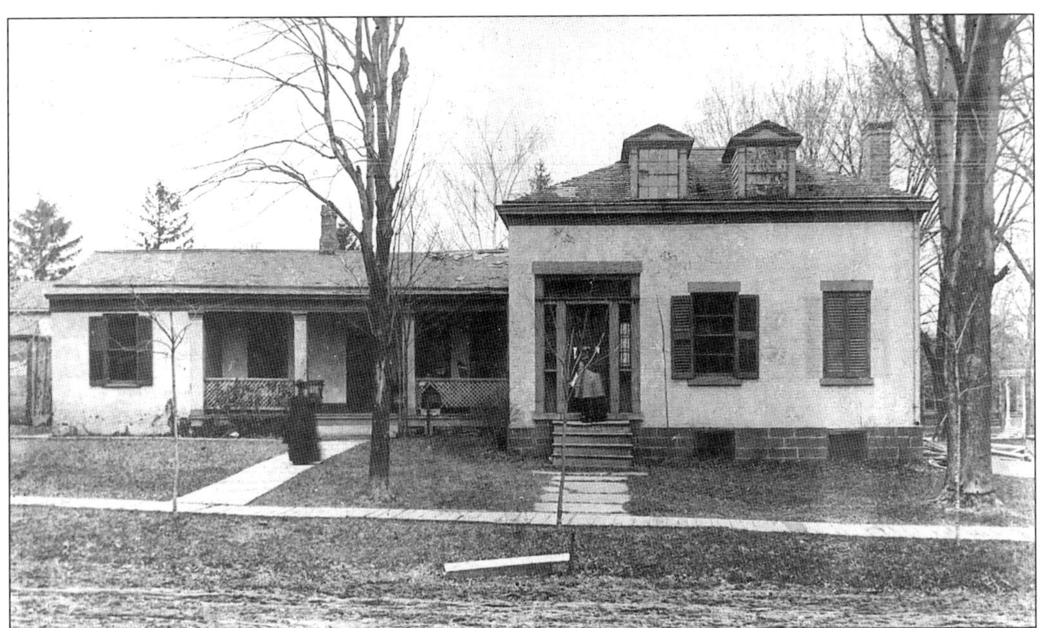

BROCKWAY HOMES. Another of Hiel Brockway's many occupations was home construction. Tradition says that he built a home for each of his 13 children. His house on Main Street (above) was built *c.* 1820 and served as the family home for many years. His house at Utica and Erie Streets (below) was built *c.* 1831 by Henry Davis. Brockway, his wife, Phebe Brockway, and a granddaughter lived there the last six months of his life. Phebe Brockway remained there until her death nine years later. The granddaughter married James Adams, later a Brockport postmaster, and the couple resided there.

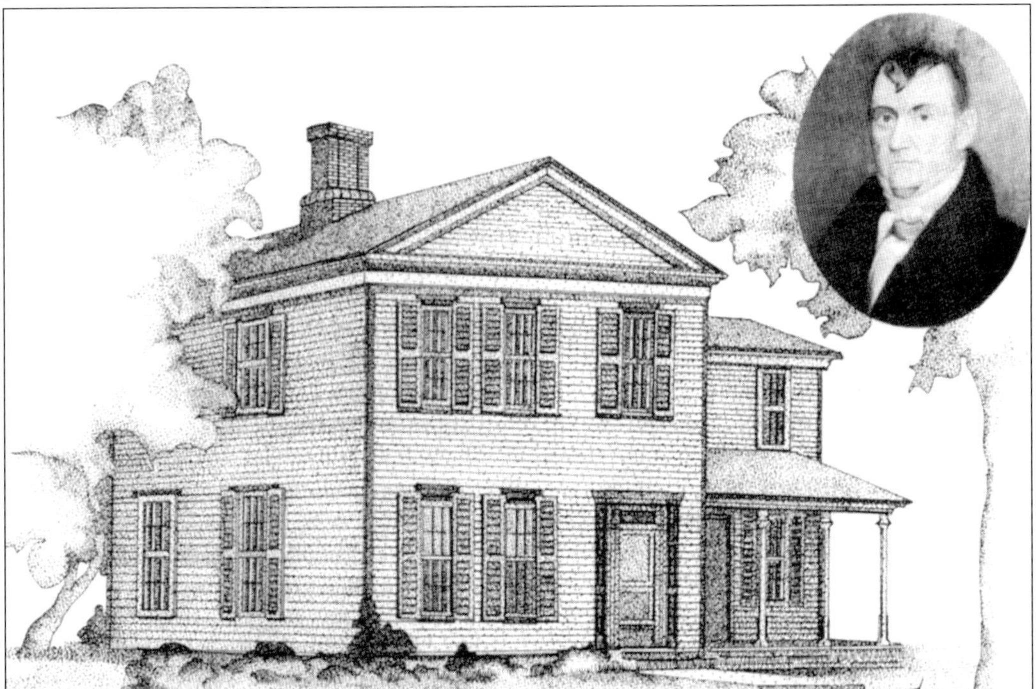

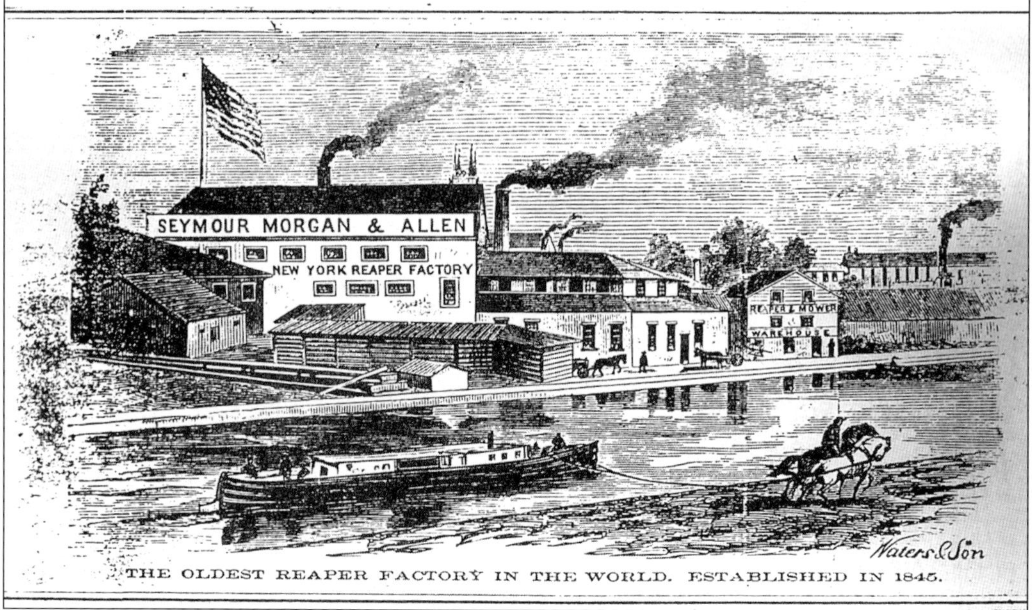

THE OLDEST REAPER FACTORY IN THE WORLD. ESTABLISHED IN 1845.

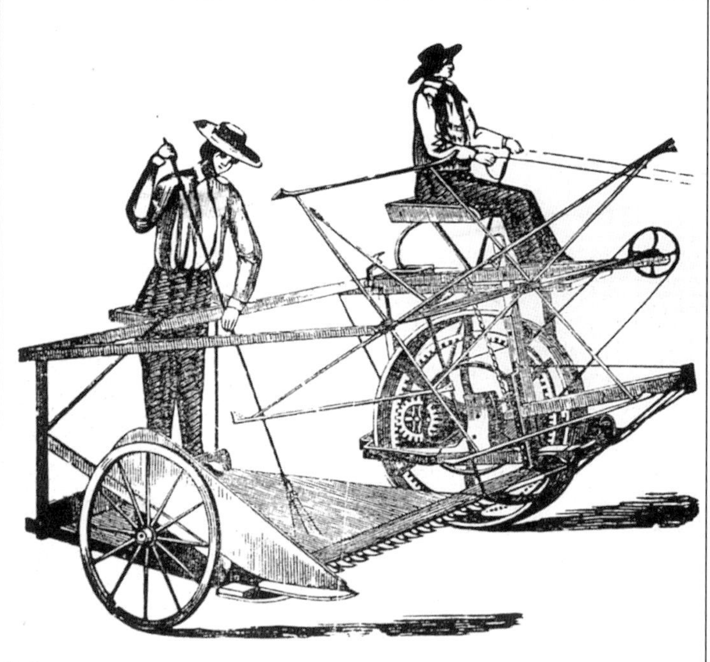

Printed from the Original Wood Engraving of the First Reaper
Seymour & Morgan, Brockport, N. Y.

Compliments of The Brockport Republic-Democrat

SEYMOUR, MORGAN & ROBY. The Industrial Revolution came to the world's agriculture at Brockport in 1846, with the manufacture of the first farm machines. Cyrus McCormick began work on a reaper in 1831, but could not solve the problem of producing his invention in quantity. He came to Brockport in 1845 and hired Backus, Fitch & Company to make 100 of his machines. None worked. He turned, then, to Seymour, Morgan & Roby, which built 100 reapers that did work. The company's Plant No. 1 (above) is pictured sometime between 1852 and 1872. The wood engraving advertises the firm's first reaper.

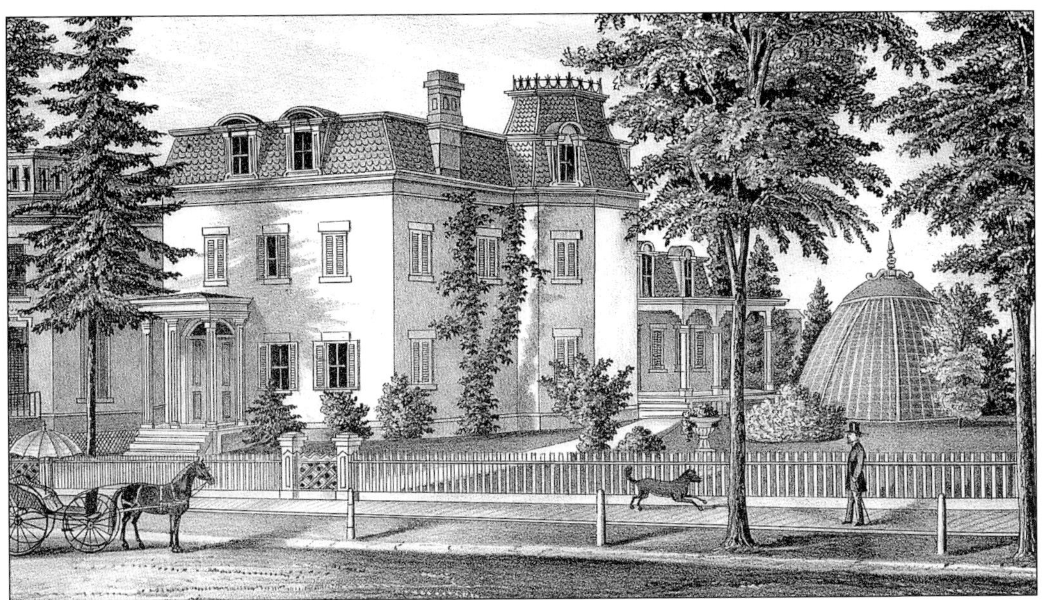

William H. Seymour. Peletiah Rogers built this home in the mid-1820s. In the early 1830s, he sold the house to William H. Seymour (1802–1903), husband of his niece, Nancy Pixley, the first school teacher in the village. Rogers moved to Hamilton, Ontario, and helped found a company that became Massey-Ferguson. Seymour resided here until his death. Seymour, younger brother of James Seymour (pages 26, 39, 78, and 91), clerked in his brother's store in 1818 and moved with him from Clarkson to Brockport in 1823. He succeeded his older brother as Brockport postmaster and acquired his business when James Seymour moved to Rochester in 1827. In 1845, William Seymour started a foundry with two partners. He retired from the reaper business in 1875 and joined his son, Henry, in the lumber business until 1882. He is shown (below) on his 100th birthday, July 15, 1902, riding with Wilson H. Moore (page 50) in Brockport's first automobile, a Steam-Locomobile.

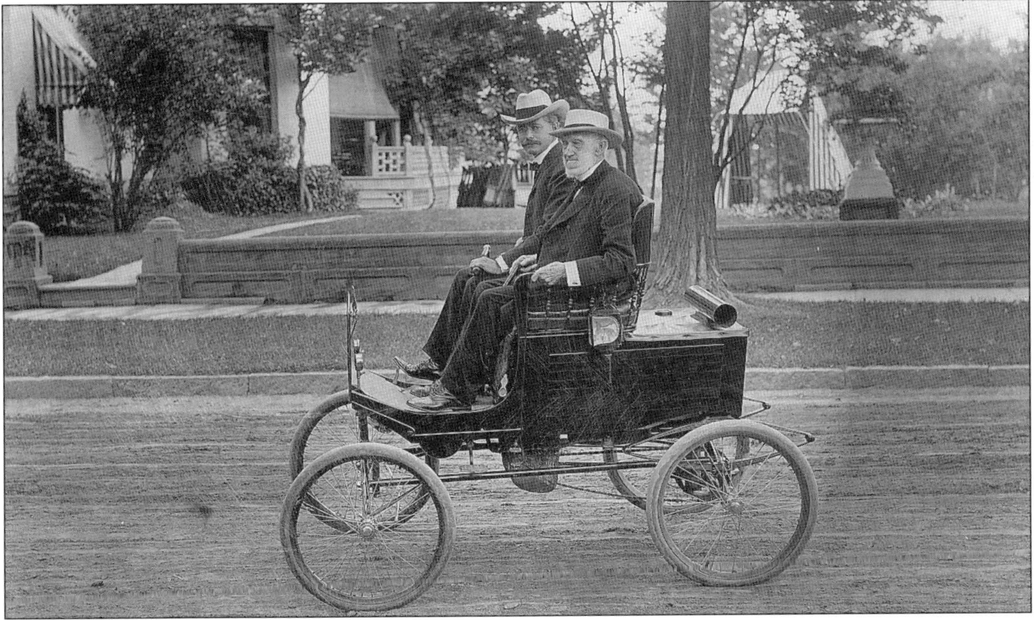

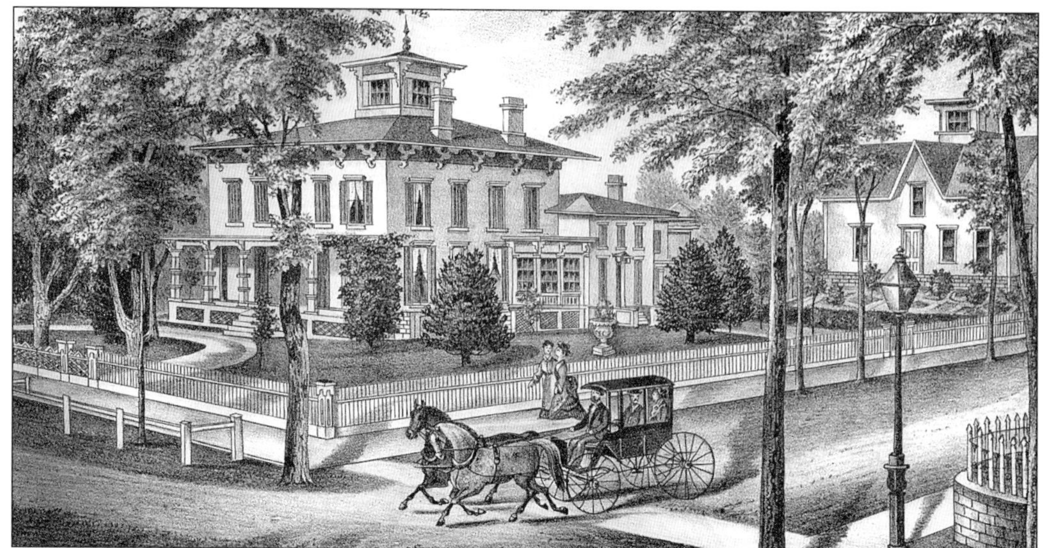

THE MORGAN HOMESTEAD. John Ostrom, a retired farmer from Medina, built the red brick Morgan-Manning House at Main and South Streets in 1854. In 1864, Dayton Samuel Morgan married Susan Joslyn and moved into the house, owned then by James Guild. Morgan bought the home in 1868. A 1964 house fire killed Sara Morgan Manning, the last surviving Morgan child, at age 97. The property was acquired and repaired by the Western Monroe Historical Society to serve as its headquarters. It is listed on the State and National Registers of Historic Places.

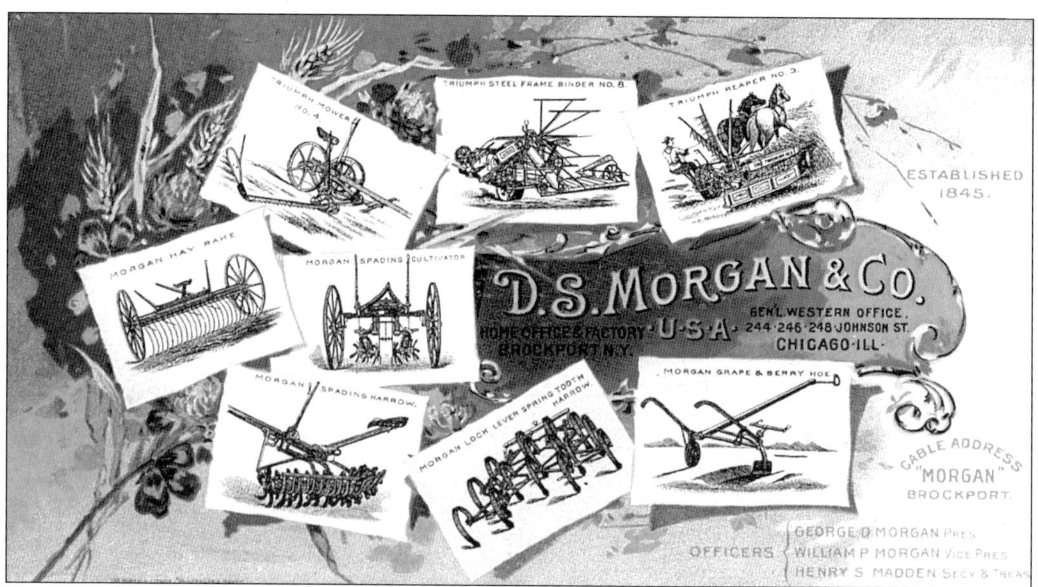

DEMISE. Seymour, Morgan & Roby lost money for five years before Dayton Morgan died. His son, George O. Morgan, strove to recover solvency by diversifying production, making reapers, binders, cultivators, rakes, harrows, and hoes. However, the Panic of 1893, the company's technological obsolescence, and its inconvenient location forced it to close in 1894. Plant No. 1 burned in 1895. The Phelps Piano Case Company occupied the site for a year before it burned in 1904. The Emily Knapp Local History Museum displays a Morgan reaper, and the Morgan-Manning House displays a salesman's model.

Dayton Samuel Morgan. Morgan (1819–1890) was born in Ogden, New York, and grew up in Brockport. He worked for a Brockport merchant for four years, before becoming a junior partner to William H. Seymour (page 43) in 1844. He bought out Seymour in 1875 and continued to manufacture farm implements until his death. Also, he developed the West Pullman suburb of Chicago, was a Union Pacific Railroad vice president, and invested in farms and timber. Proceeds from his estate built Buffalo's first steel-frame skyscraper. His maternal uncle founded Dayton, Ohio.

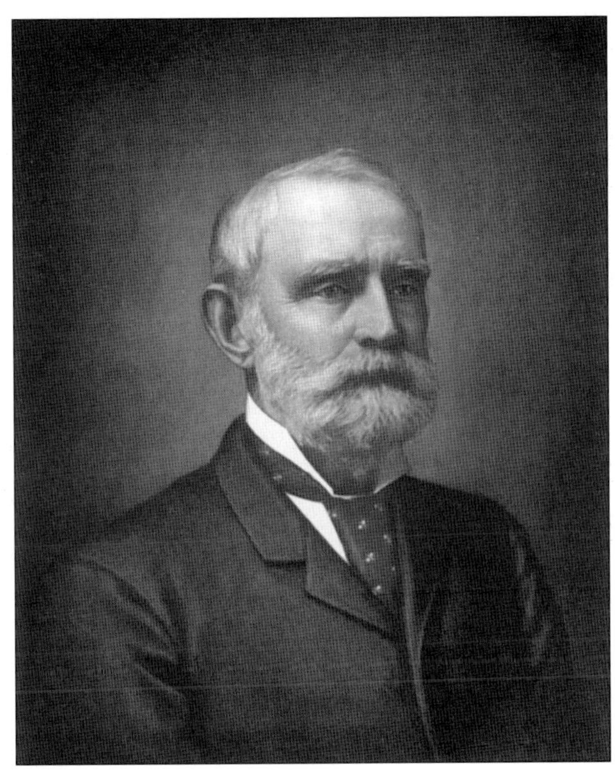

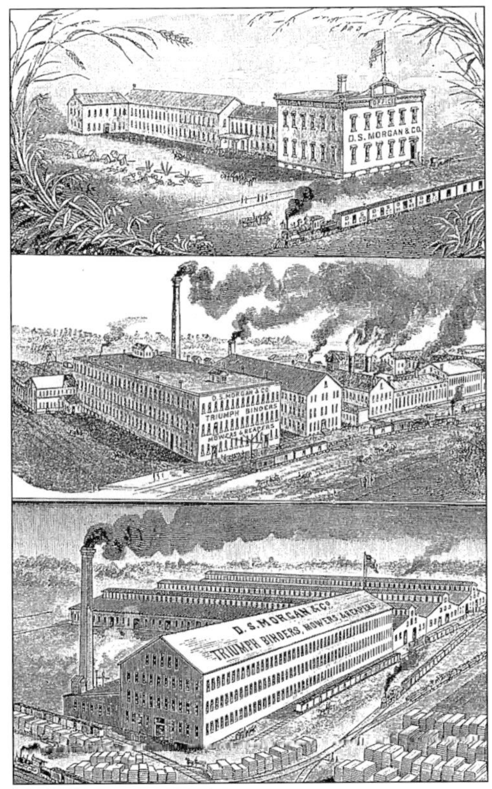

Company Buildings. This 1888 illustration is an artist's conception of Seymour, Morgan & Roby's Market Street office building, their Plant No. 1 across the street on the canal, and their Plant No. 2, which had been built in 1885 at the end of Spring Street. Much of the company's success resulted from the invention by Aaron Palmer and Stephen Williams of a quadrant platform for the reaper. The company's 1888 catalog lists reapers, mowers, and self-binding harvesters.

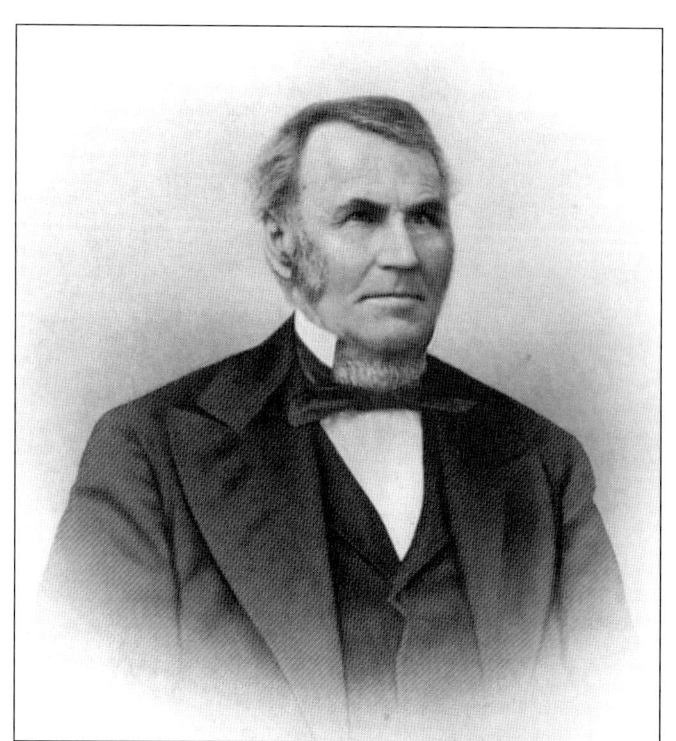

GEORGE F. BARNETT. Barnett (1804–1897) settled in Brockport in 1826. His early career was in architecture and construction. In 1840, Cyrus McCormick hired him to help develop the reaper. In 1845, he joined Seymour, Morgan & Roby in solving the problem of the quantity production of that machine and in making design improvements. In 1850, he entered the farm-implement manufacturing business with George L. Whiteside. That firm employed some 30 workers. Whiteside died in 1880 and Barnett retired in 1886.

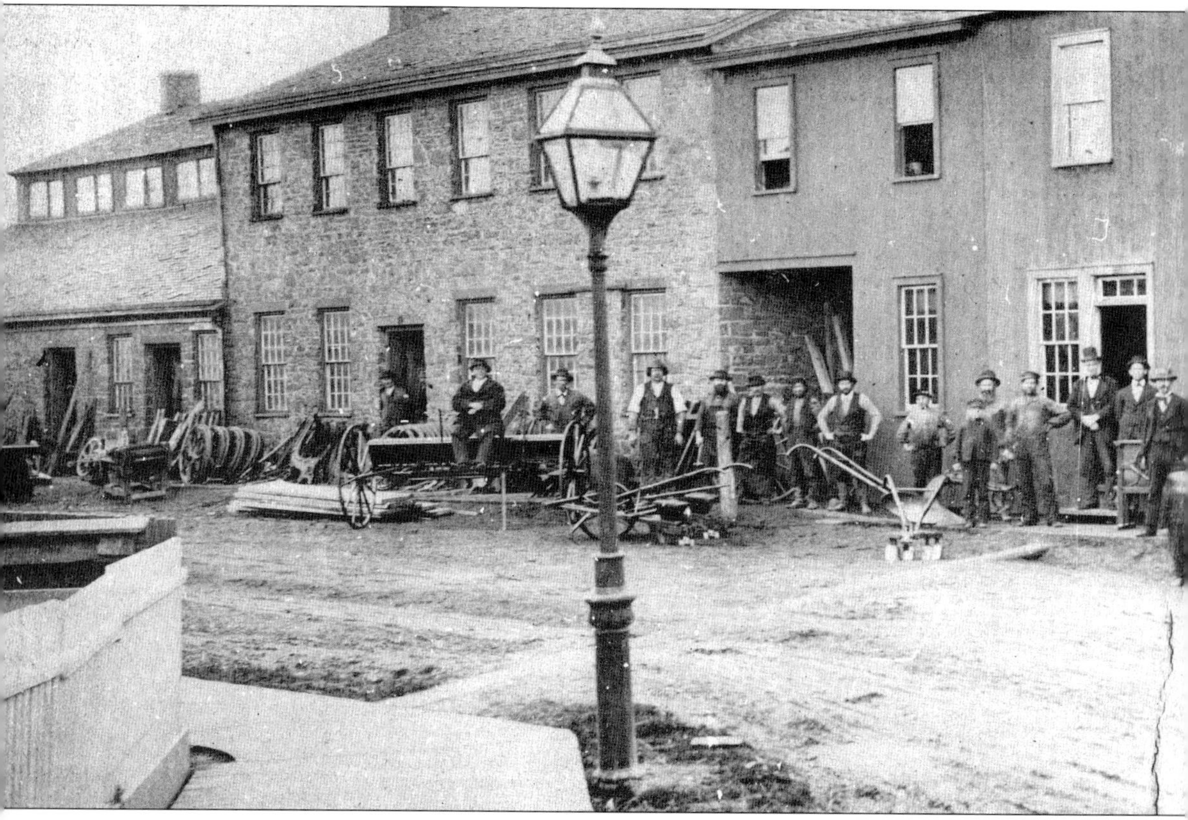

WHITESIDE, BARNETT & COMPANY. The 1880 advertisement (right) attests to the variety of farm implements the firm manufactured. Its Clinton Street plant (below) was erected in 1850 on the site of Hiel Brockway's brickyard and boatyard that had burned in 1848. After Barnett's death, the structure was occupied by a lumberyard until 1904. It then became a food processing plant of the Monroe Canning Company until 1945. Since 1948, it has housed Fay's Garage. The building is listed on the State and National Registers of Historic Places.

BROCKPORT AGRICULTURAL WORKS.
ESTABLISHED IN 1850!

WHITESIDE, BARNETT & CO.,

Manufacturers of the New

Empire Grain Drill,

With Walter Marks' new Phosphate Distributor.

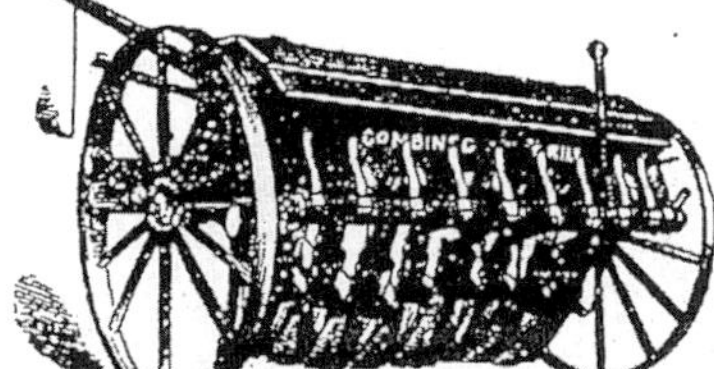

ACCURATE
AND
RELIABLE!

A positive force feed without clogging in any kind of commercial manures. Sowing the same quantity with the same combination of gear. No more guess work, but the CLIMAX OF ACCURACY.

We also Manufacture the

ITHICA WHEEL RAKE,

With or Without the Self-Dump.

Bean Planter, and Cultivators. A New Bean Screen and Separator.

Wiard, Curtis and Brockport PLOWS, both Chilled and Steel, Steel Gang Plows, and many other Farm Implements. All for sale on reasonable terms.

BROCKPORT, Jan. 29th, 1880. WHITESIDE, BARNETT & CO.

41

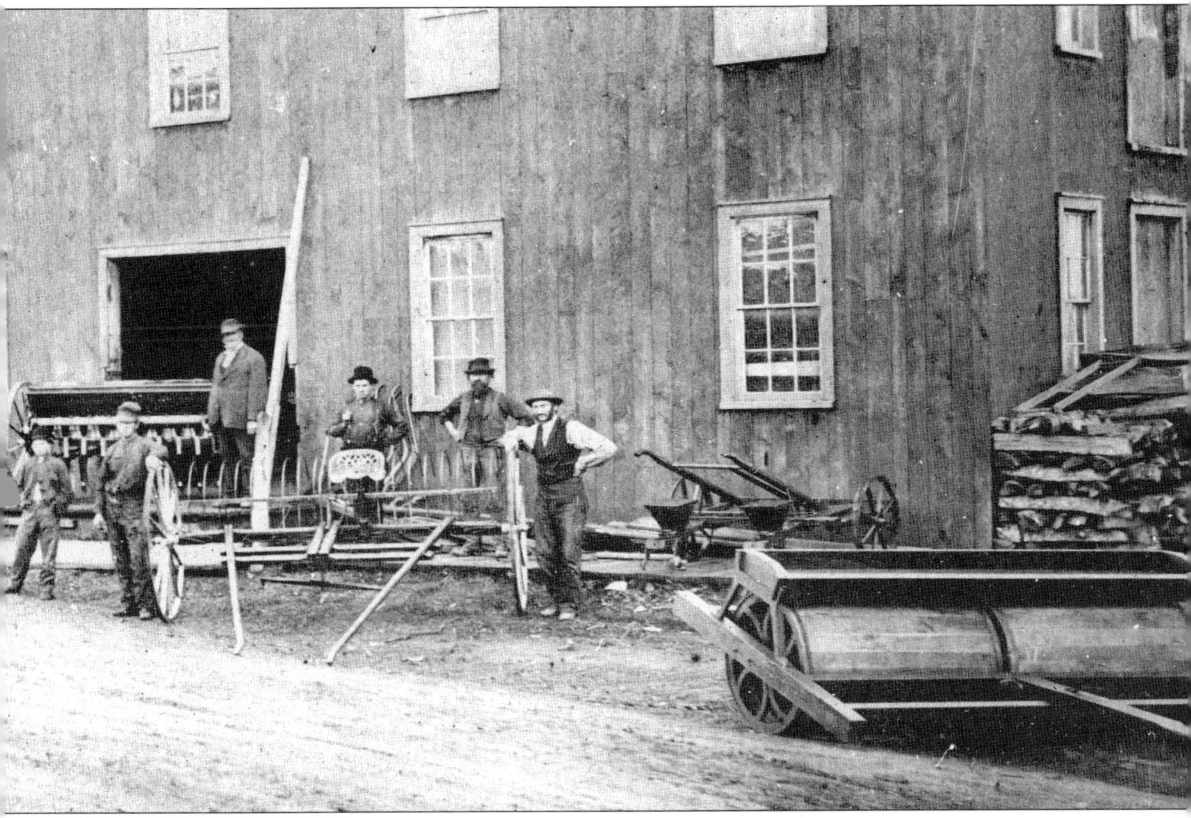

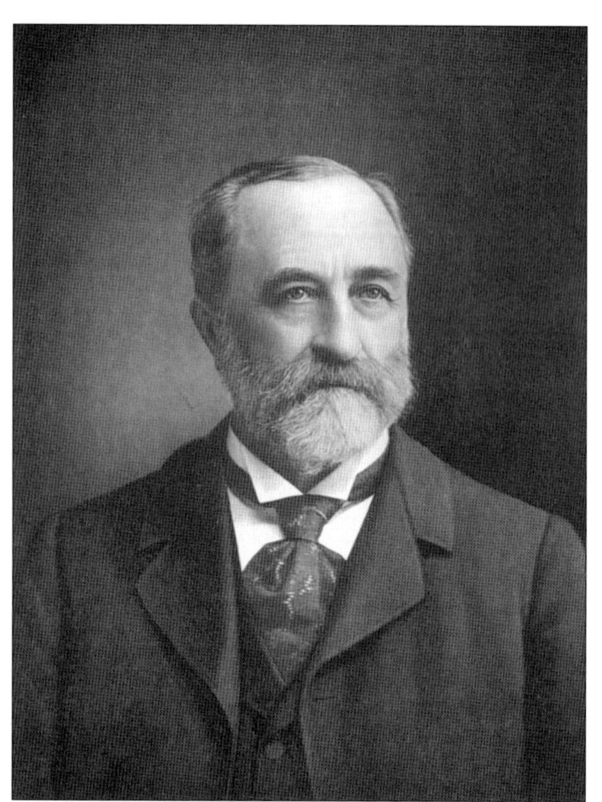

JOHNSTON HARVESTER COMPANY. Byron Huntley (1825–1906) (left), a philanthropist and industrialist, came to Brockport in 1844 as a partner in the Ganson, Huntley & Company foundry. In 1868, he and Samuel Johnston formed the Johnston Harvester Company. Johnston was the creative partner and Huntley the businessman. After 1870, Huntley made annual trips to Europe as the company's foreign general agent. The firm's plant on North Main Street (below) was destroyed by a fire of incendiary origin in 1882. The company rebuilt in Batavia, with its better shipping facilities.

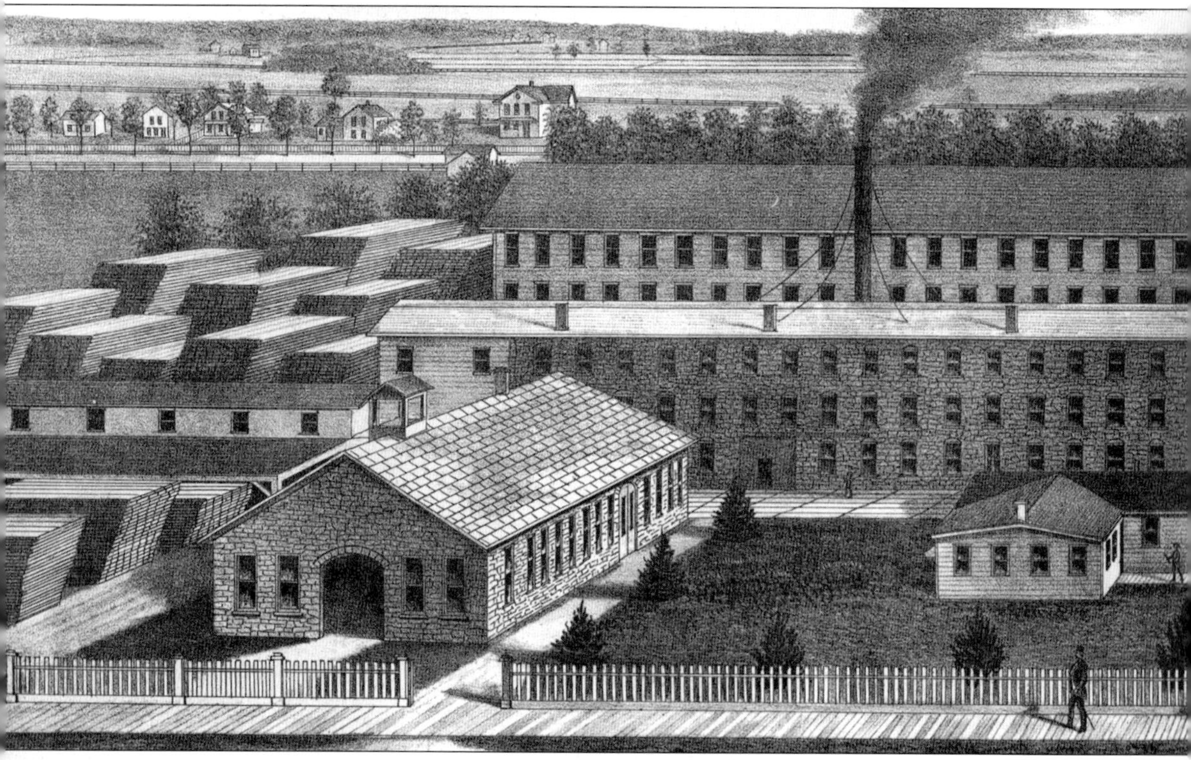

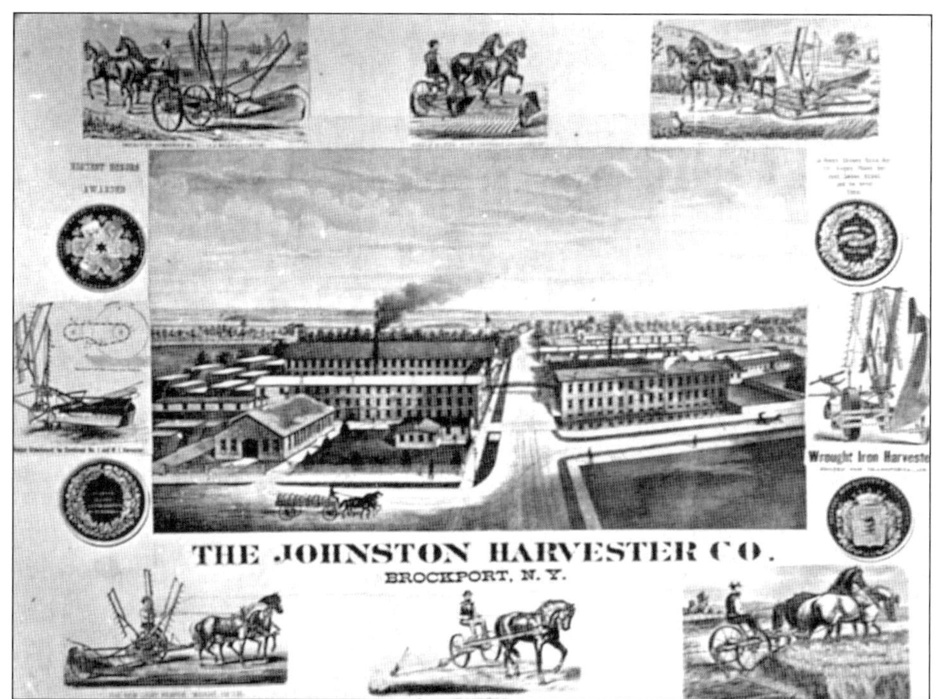

AN ADVERTISING CARD. Pictures of the plant and of several of its products illustrate this trade card. By 1882, the company was manufacturing 6,000 machines a year. In 1883, Samuel Johnston retired but remained in Brockport after the company had decamped to Batavia.

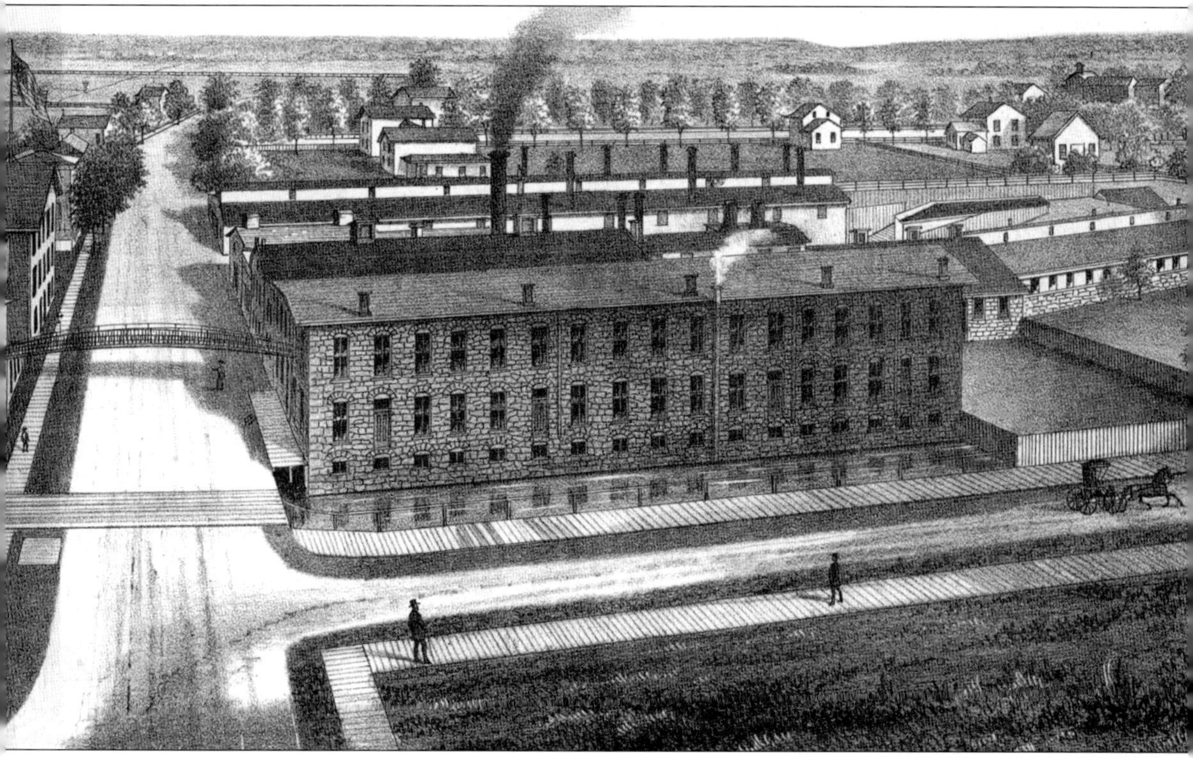

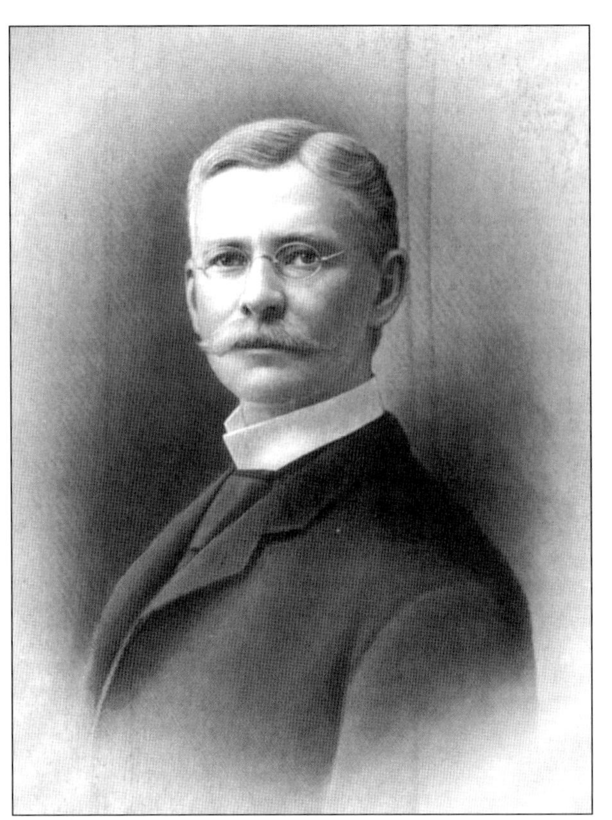

WILSON H. MOORE. Moore (1859–1907) was born in Clarkson. At 19, he founded a newspaper and magazine subscription agency. In 1882, he moved the agency to Brockport, where it succeeded so well that it became the largest such firm in the world. Moore committed suicide in 1907 after failing to prevent construction of a street railway in front of his State Street home. After he died, his agency merged with the D.G. Cottrell agency of North Cohocton, which survived until 1974. He was also a partner in the Brockport Piano Company and the Moore-Kimball hardware store.

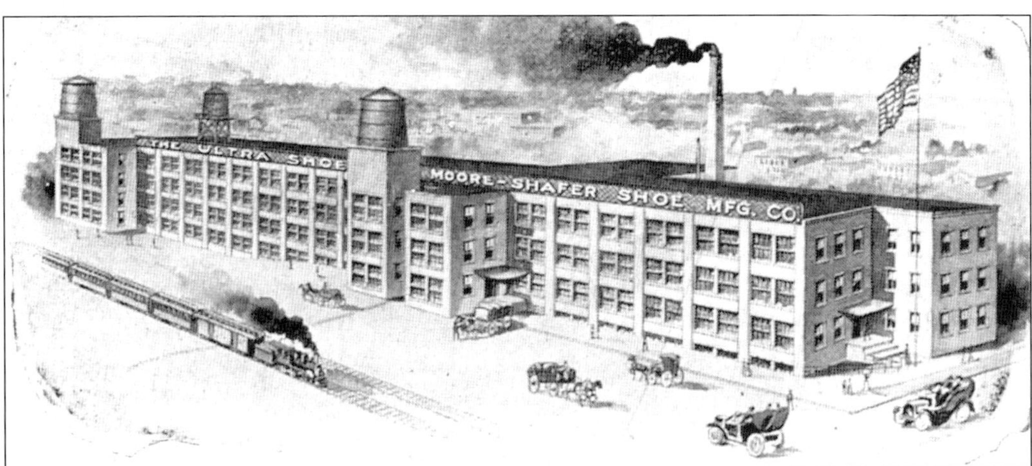

THE MOORE-SHAFER SHOE MANUFACTURING COMPANY. In 1888, Wilson H. Moore, Manley A. Shafer, and some partners bought the bankrupt Ham-Rogers shoe factory on Market Street, reorganized it as the Moore-Shafer Shoe Manufacturing Company, and built a much larger plant at the railroad tracks on Park Avenue. For several decades it was the largest employer in the village, with some 400 workers, but it failed in the late 1920s. The building was occupied later, successively, by a refrigeration company, an upholstery firm, a doll factory, two button manufacturers, and the YMCA. It burned in 1975.

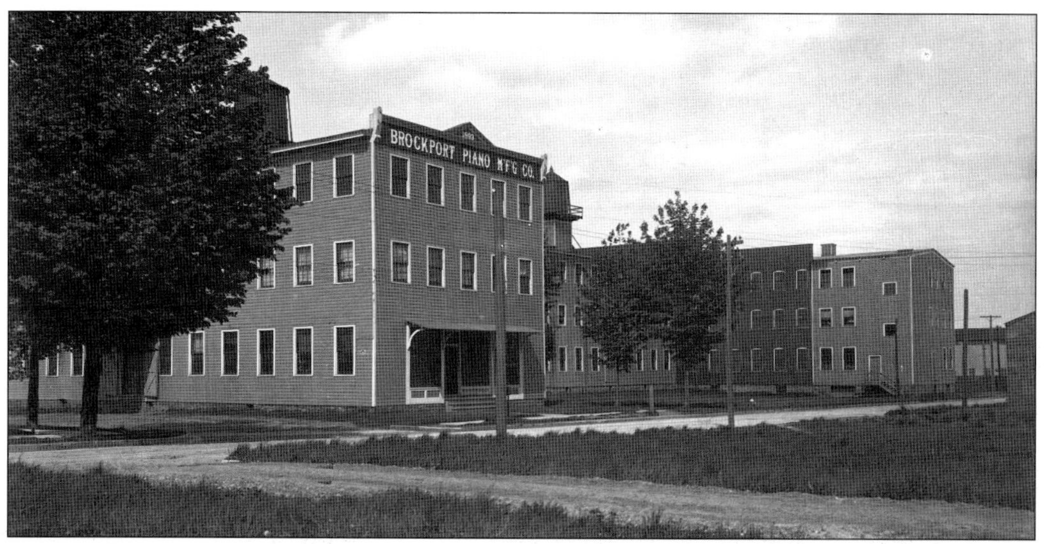

PIANOS, PAILS, AND PAPER BOXES. The Brockport Piano Manufacturing Company produced Capen (page 11) and Metcalf pianos. In 1894, it built on Spring Street "a substantial 3 story structure, fully equipped with the latest and best patterns of delicate machinery and appliances". By 1911, it employed over 100 workers and produced 2,500 to 3,000 pianos annually. The company moved to East Rochester *c.* 1920. Later, the building housed, in succession, the Monitor Clock Company; the stamping works of the McLaughlin Company, which produced galvanized pails, tubs, flour sifters, and so on; the Alderman Paper Box Company; Dynacolor; and the 3-M Corporation; before being demolished in 1979.

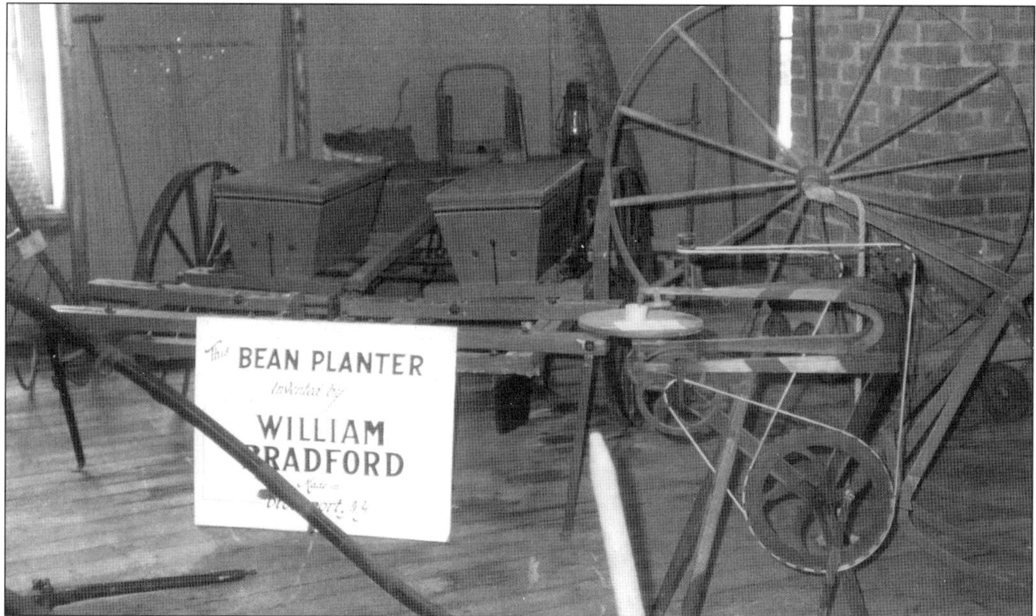

THE BRADFORD BEAN PLANTER. Another farm implement manufacturer in Brockport in the late 19th century was William Bradford, who came from his native England to Brockport in 1851. In 1883, he founded a company to produce the bean planter he had invented. The firm also made potato diggers and cabbage diggers. One of his machines is at the Emily Knapp Local History Museum.

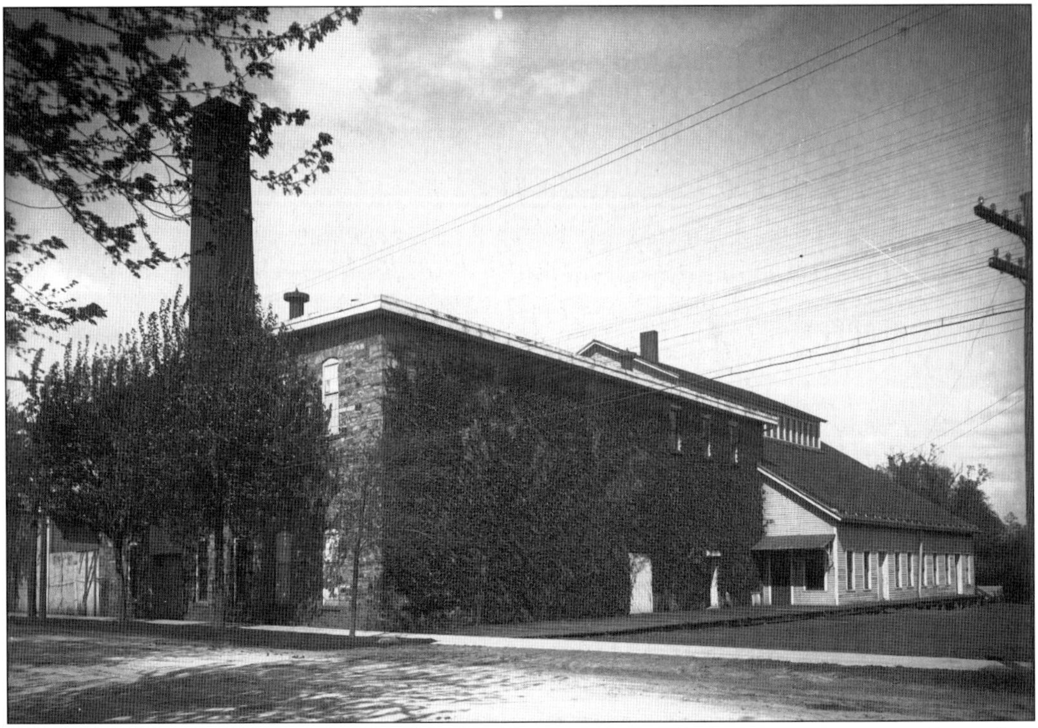

Food Processing. Because of Brockport's location in a rich farming area, a number of its manufacturing plants have been related to agriculture. The Batavia Preserving Company (later the Hudson Canning Company) (above), was on North Main Street in a Johnston Harvester Company building that survived the 1882 fire (pages 48 and 49). This building burned in 1944. The food-processing firm also had plants in Batavia and Middleport. Other Brockport canneries have been on Clinton Street (page 47) and Fair Street. The Agrilink Foods plant on State Street (below) continues that tradition, repacking vegetables and other processed food for retail and institutional sale.

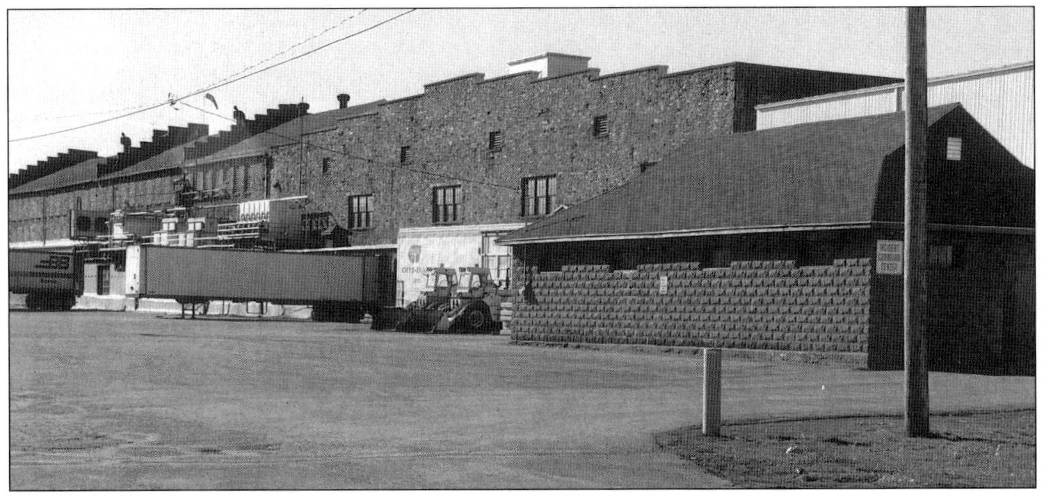

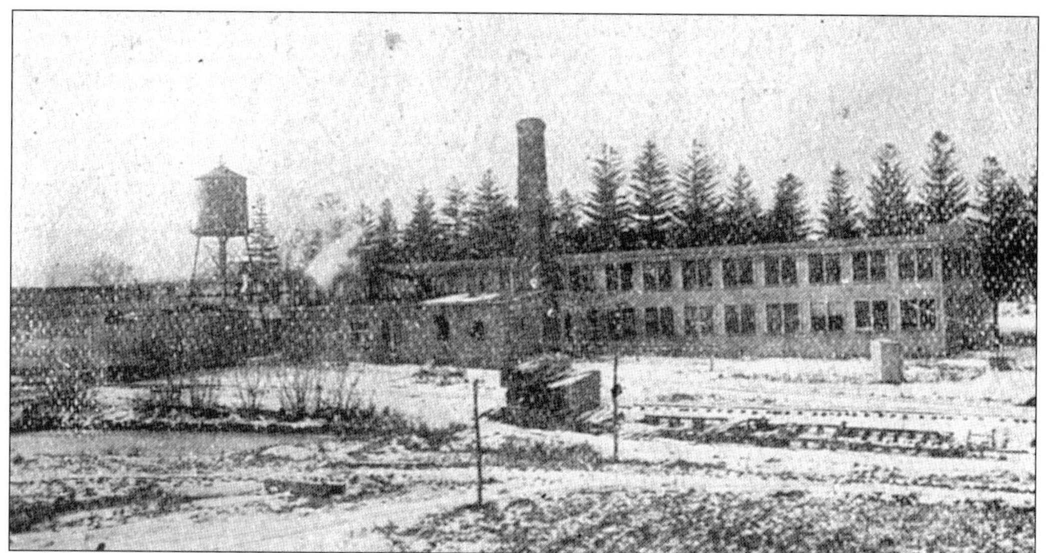

THE A & P PLANT. The Great Atlantic & Pacific Tea Company bought the Dailey Canning Company factory at the east end of Fair Street shortly after World War I. For more than 60 years, it was a Brockport landmark, easily recognized by sight and by the aroma of its chili sauce and other tomato products. In 1982, it closed down and the structure became a Kleen-Brite Laboratories plant (page 54).

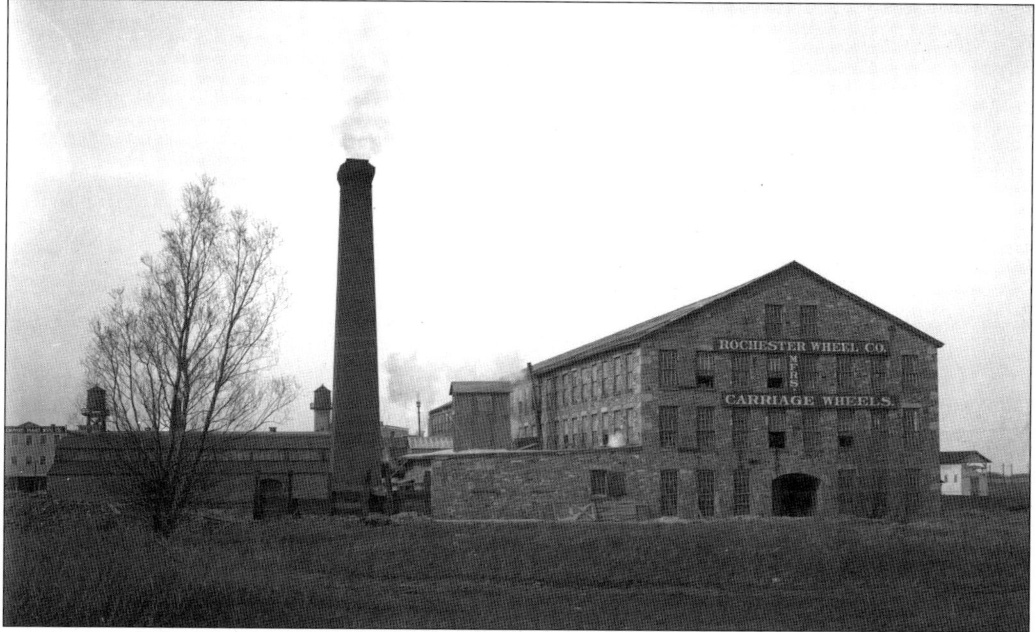

BROCKPORT COLD STORAGE. In 1895, Dayton S. Morgan's son, Gifford Morgan, converted the firm's Plant No. 2 on Spring Street into a Rochester Wheel Company factory (above). Automobiles soon made carriage wheels obsolete, and Morgan installed there one of the first cold storage plants in the country. The company remained in the family until Morgan's grandson, Fletcher Garlock, sold it to Comstock Foods (later Agrilink Foods) in 1986. In the late 1930s, Clarence Birdseye conducted pioneering deep-freeze food-preserving experiments there.

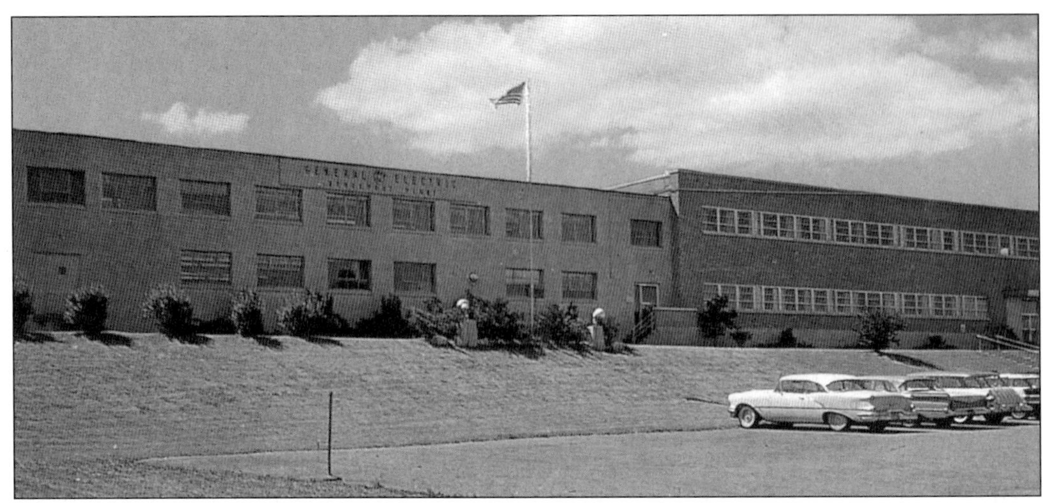

WAFFLES, APPLIANCES, AND CLEANSER. After the county fair (pages 104 and 105) left, its site became a public park. In the middle 1940s, the New York Frozen Food Corporation bought the property and built a frozen waffle plant. The General Electric Company bought the building (above) in 1948 and expanded it to nearly 150,000 square feet in 1958. For 41 years, it (and after 1984, Black & Decker) produced small appliances—mixers, blenders, knife sharpeners, electric knives, can openers, hair dryers—employing as many as 1,100 workers. In 1989, Kleen Brite Laboratories (below), bought the property and made cleansing powders for private labels until 2001, when it closed.

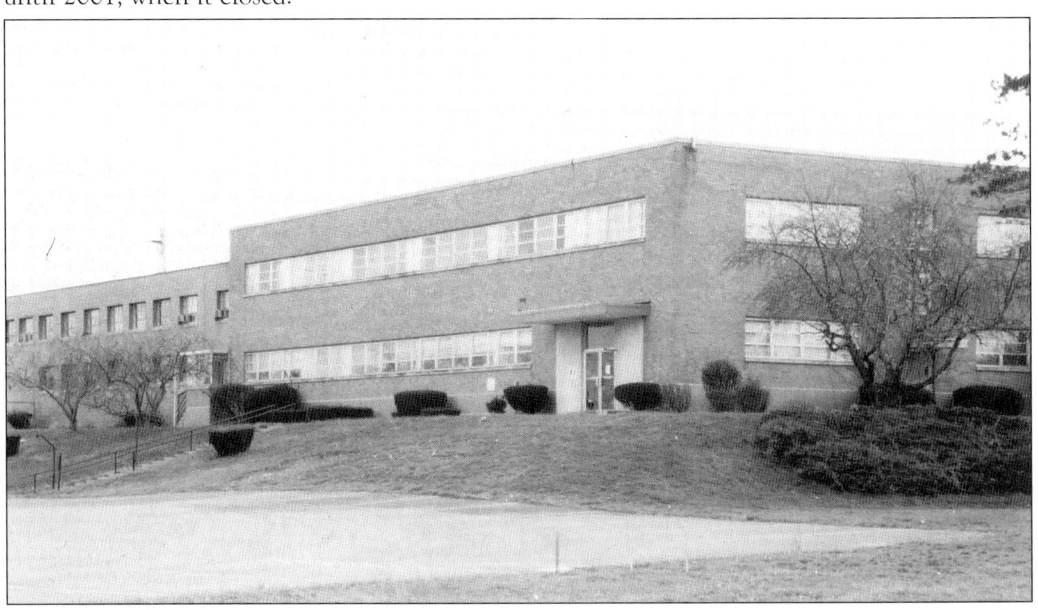

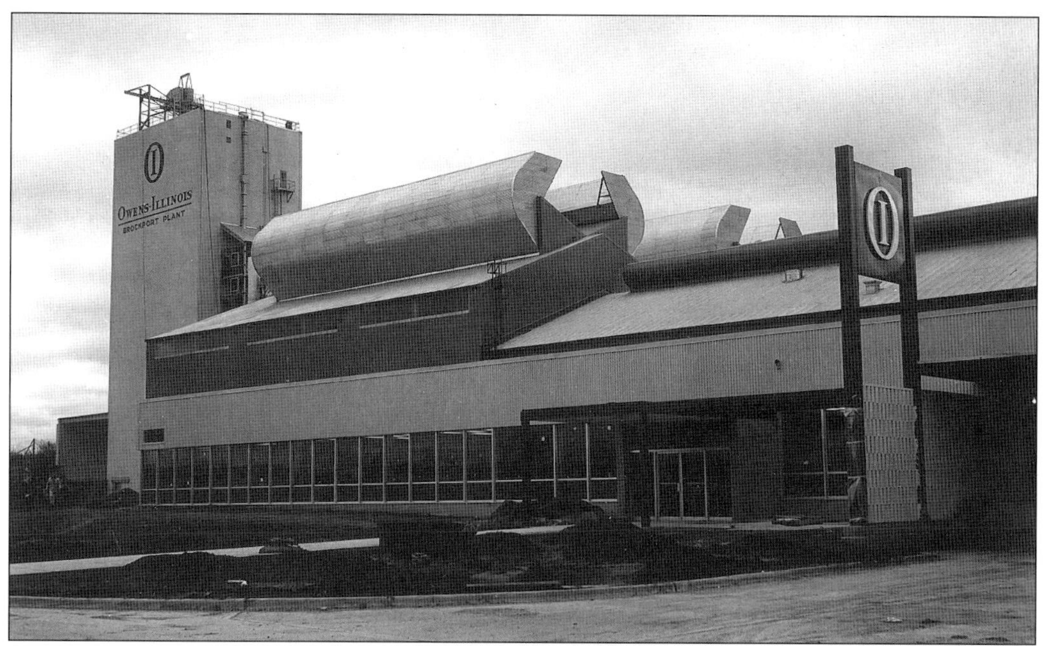

GLASS AND FROZEN STORAGE. In 1961, Owens-Illinois built "one of the most highly automated glass container plants in the world" (above) on Owens Road. The plant employed more than 400 workers and occupied about 350,000 square feet on a 70-acre site. It closed in 1985. The manufacturing plant was torn down in the 1990s and the warehouses were in the process of being sold to Allied Frozen Storage (below) in 2002. The Allied Group also has real estate development, construction, and warehouse businesses in Brockport and Buffalo. It employs some 60 workers in Brockport and has nearly a million square feet of floor space. The company formed in 1955 and entered the frozen-food storage business in 1982.

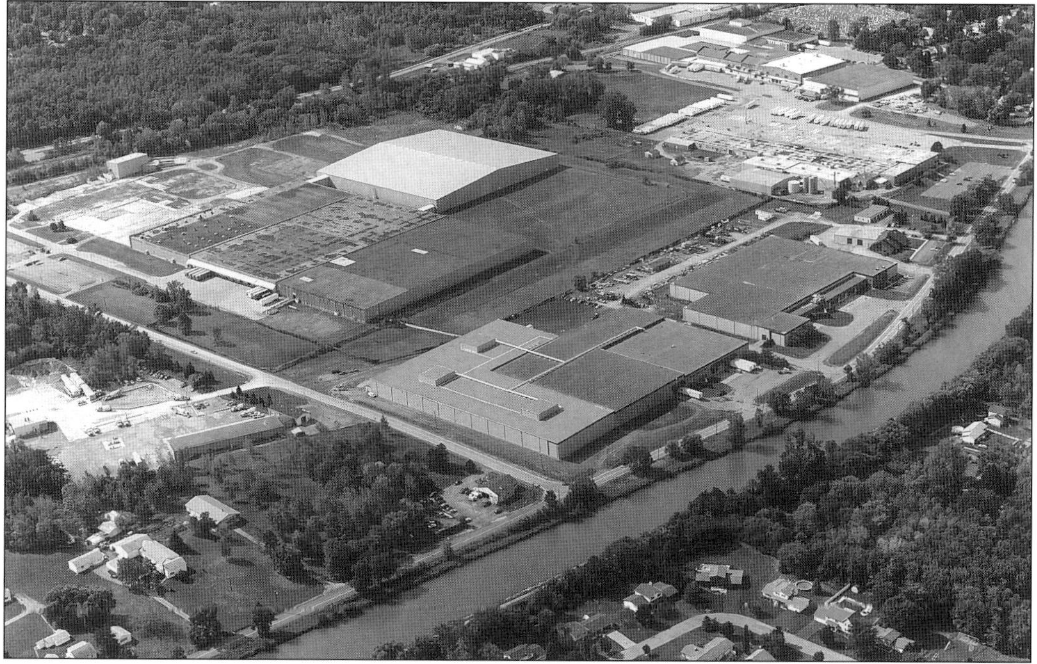

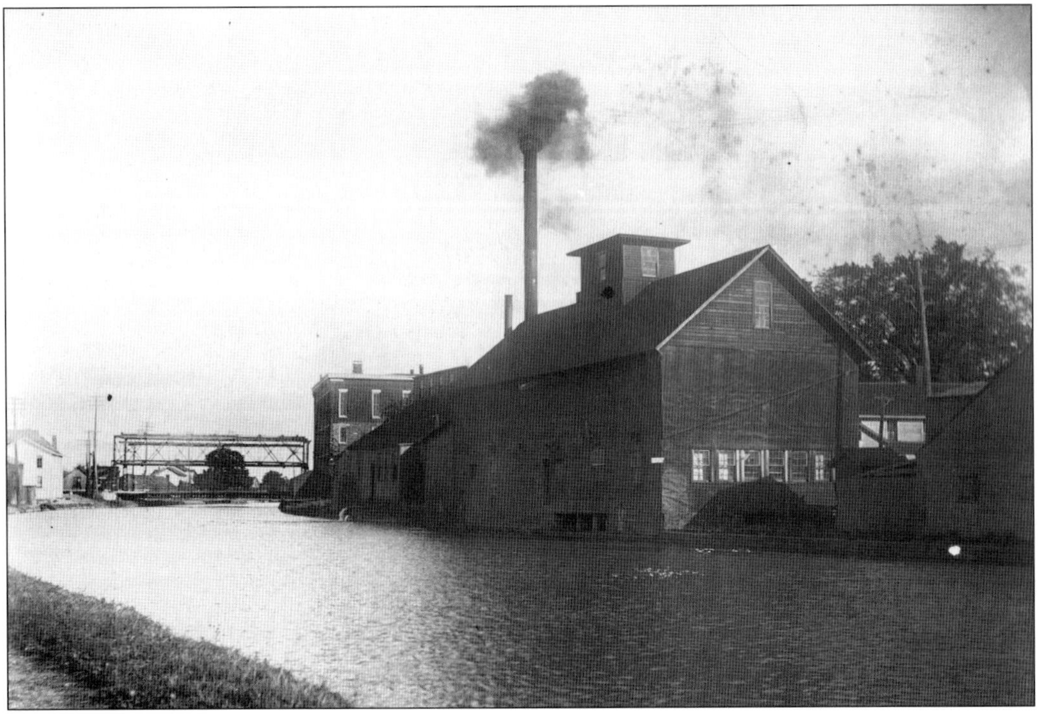

UTILITIES. In 1888, Brockport became the first municipality in New York State, except for the six largest cities, to get electricity, which was generated at the plant (above) between Clinton Street and the Erie Canal. Water was pumped from Holley to Brockport in the late 1880s. A municipal water company was established in 1914, with a pumping station on Lake Ontario (below). The system was sold to the Monroe County Water Authority in 1997.

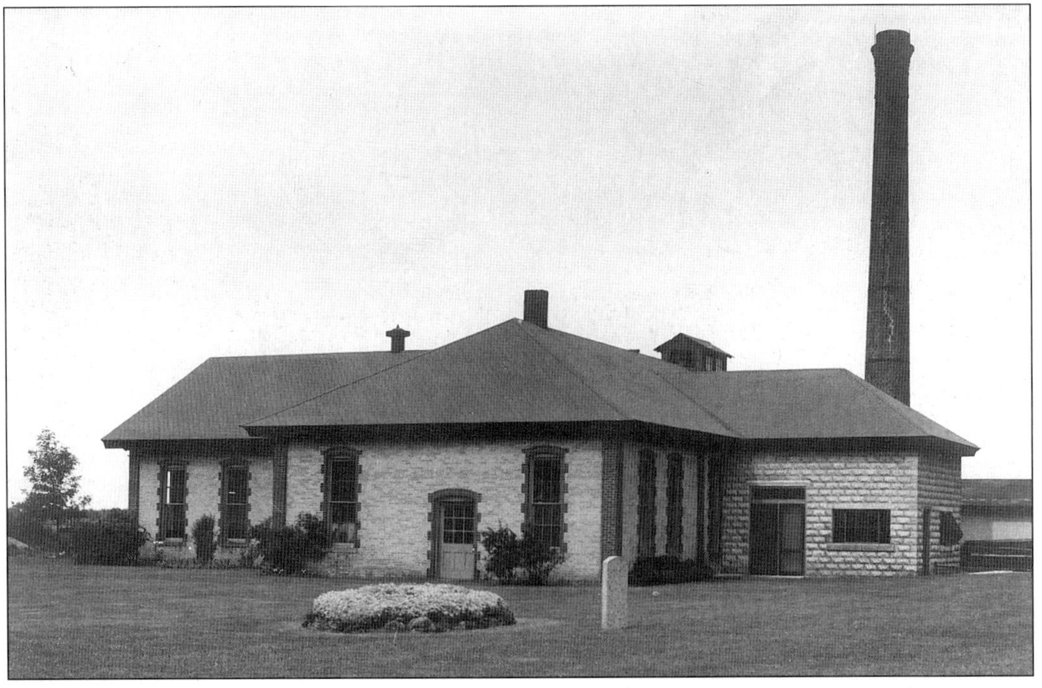

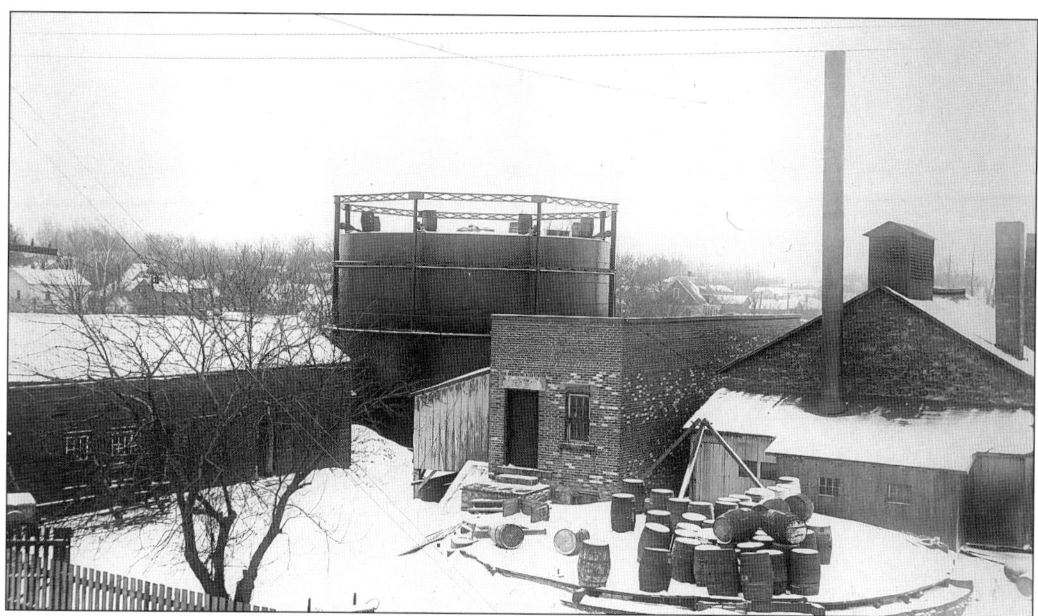

THE GASWORKS. Beginning in 1859, the Brockport Gas Light Company manufactured illuminating gas in the Perry Street plant (above) by heating coal in an oxygen-free environment. This had been the site of the dry dock for Hiel Brockway's packet-building business. On July 4, 1910, a purifier explosion partly destroyed the plant (below). The facility was rebuilt and resumed operation but was idle when the Rochester Gas & Electric Company acquired the property in 1932. A natural gas metering station has occupied the site since 1951. Brockport got local telephone service in 1897 and was connected to the Rochester Home Telephone network the next year. In the early 1900s, the village had two telegraph offices.

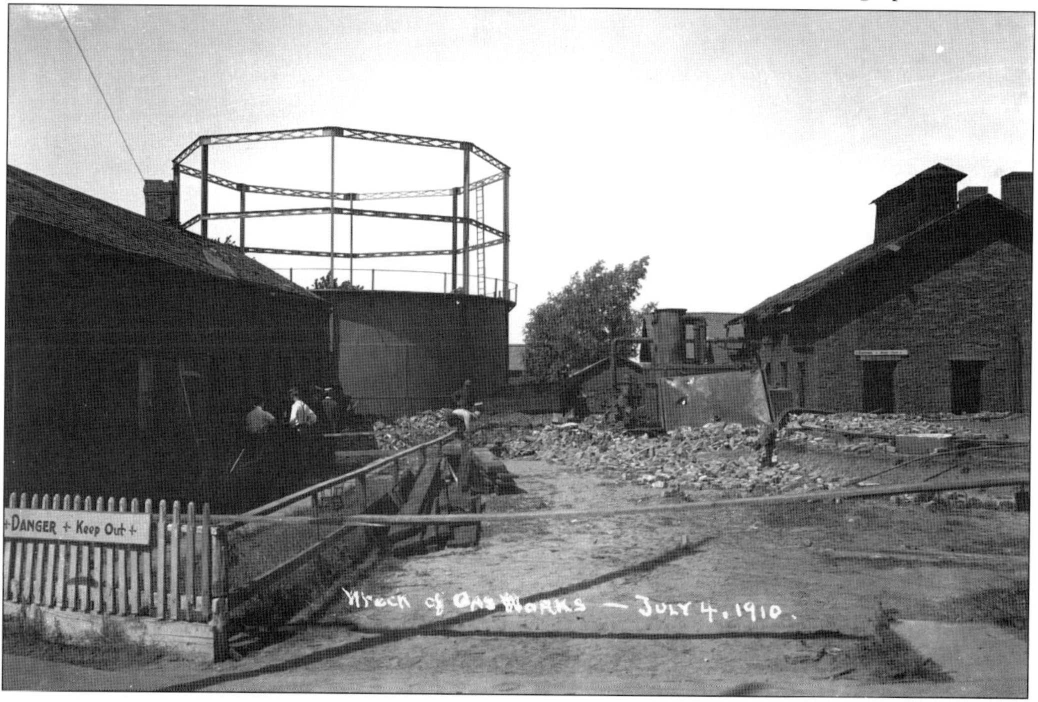

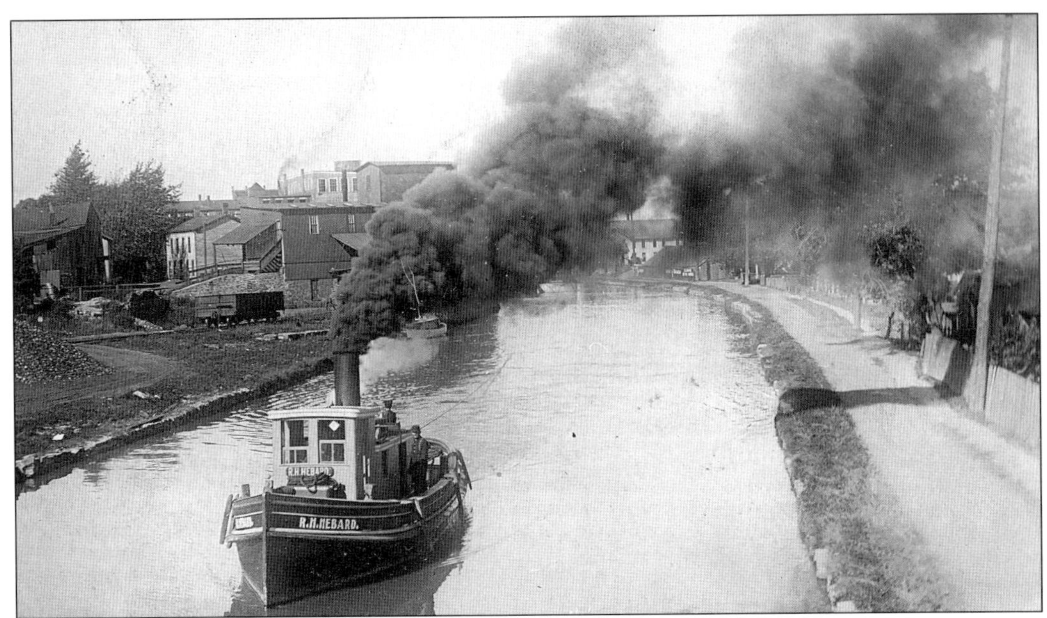

Clinton's Ditch. At Brockport, the United States became a continental power. The village was the western terminus of the Erie Canal from 1823 to 1825, while the locks at Lockport were being built. The canal lowered the cost of shipping a ton of wheat from Buffalo to New York City from $100 to between $5 and $10. For the first time, Americans could live in the Midwest, ship their products to market economically and, thereby, earn a living. This tugboat passed through Brockport near Park Avenue *c.* 1907.

Collector's Office, Brockport Oct. 1 1829

I, T. Sheldon

Master of the Boat Aurora *of* Rochester

Do Certify, that the following is a full and true statement of the present cargo of the said boat, and that I have paid toll thereon as follows:

To J. B. Hill *for original cargo on Clearance No.* 4105 $ 9.18

To *for additional cargo,*

Boat Brockport, Rochester 20 40

1093 28/100 " " 29.5.3.4 8.78

$ 9.18

T. Sheldon

A Toll Receipt. One of the seven toll stations on the canal was located at Brockport near the Main Street bridge until tolls were abolished in 1880. This receipt shows that the master of the boat Aurora paid $9.18 for passage from Brockport to Rochester on October 1, 1829.

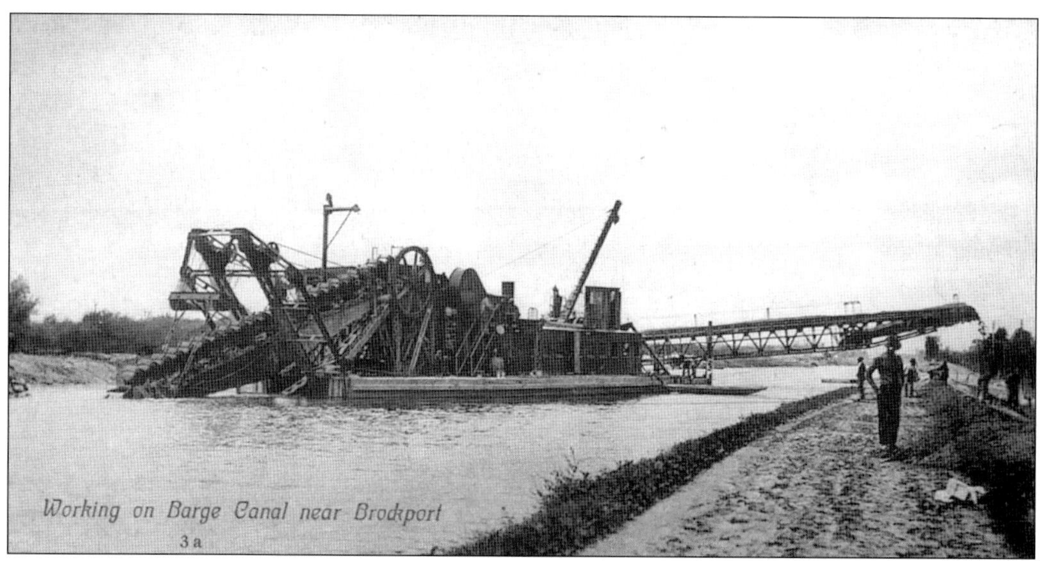

THE BARGE CANAL. The canal was enlarged several times in the 1800s, but traffic declined after 1880. It was rebuilt and converted from animal to mechanical power between 1900 and 1917. This dredge (above) worked on the reconstruction near Brockport. The barge (below) is shown near Park Avenue in 1911. The structures on the right and those on the left bank on the near side of Main Street have disappeared. The building visible above the barge housed the Harrison Bean Company, the largest bean shipper in the country. By the early 1970s, commercial traffic on the canal had ended. In 1990, New York State undertook to revitalize the canal as a major recreation and tourist facility.

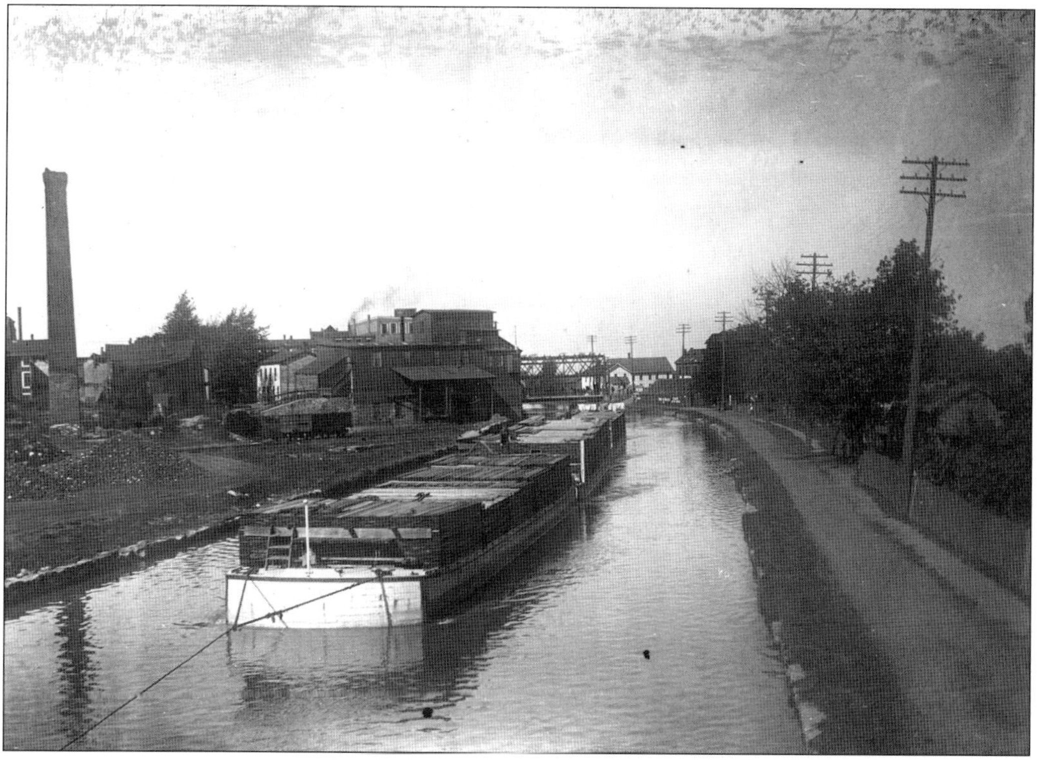

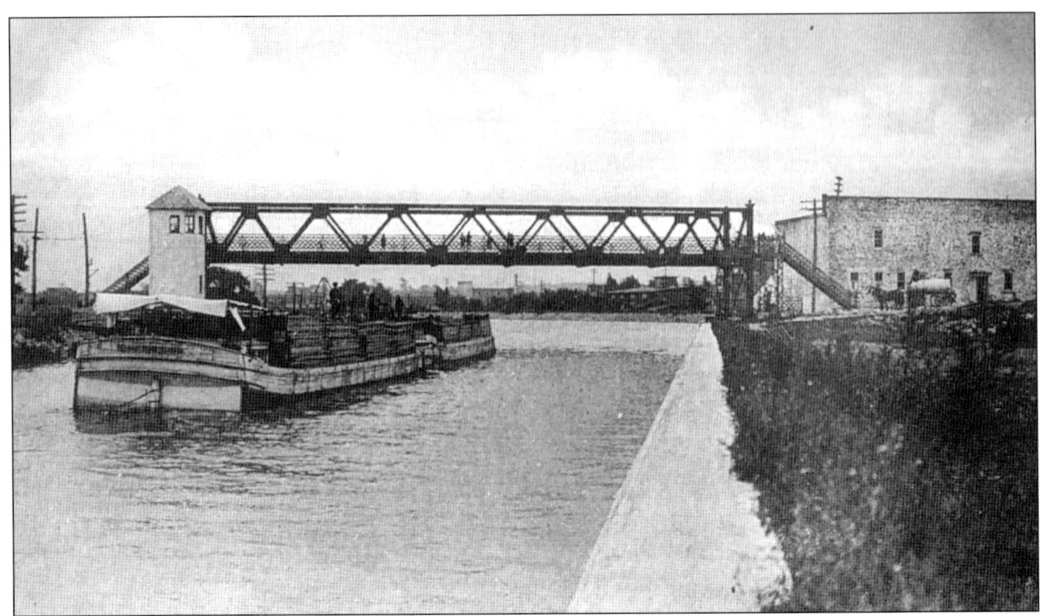

The Park Avenue Bridge. This bridge and the one on Main Street are two of only 16 lift bridges on the Erie Canal. Tradition says that General Lafayette halted at this spot in June 1825 during his triumphal tour of America and greeted Brockporters. The street leaving the bridge to the north was named Lafayette Street in his honor, though the first two letters were dropped later. The building to the right of the bridge housed the reaper factory of Henry Seymour (page 43).

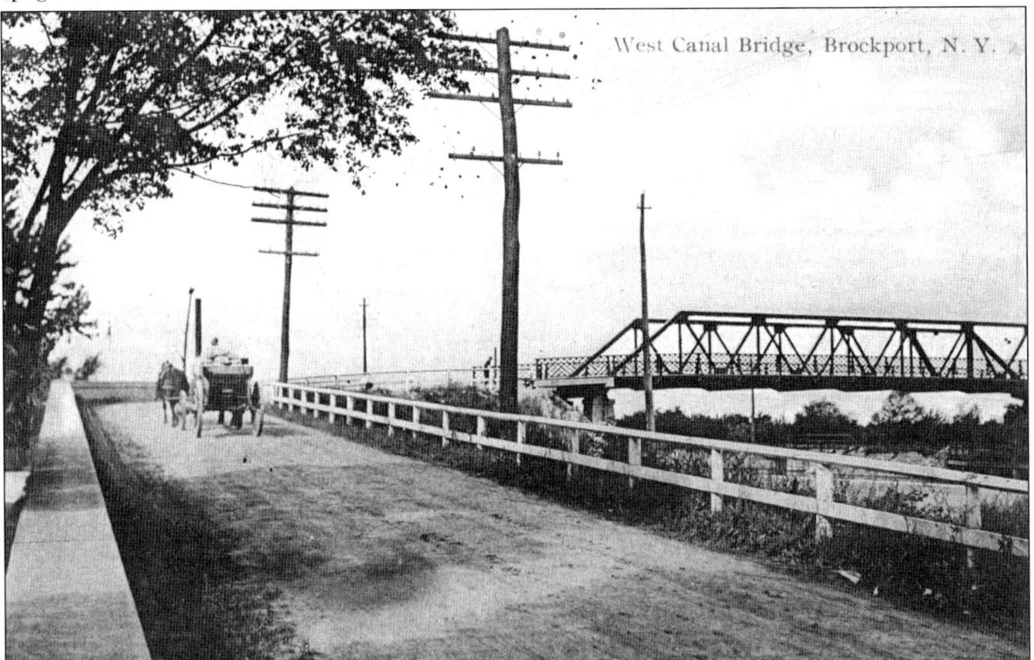

The Smith Street Bridge. Initially, all three canal bridges in the village were high bridges. The Main Street and Park Avenue spans were replaced by lift bridges in the 19th century, but the one that connects Smith and Clinton Streets remains a high bridge.

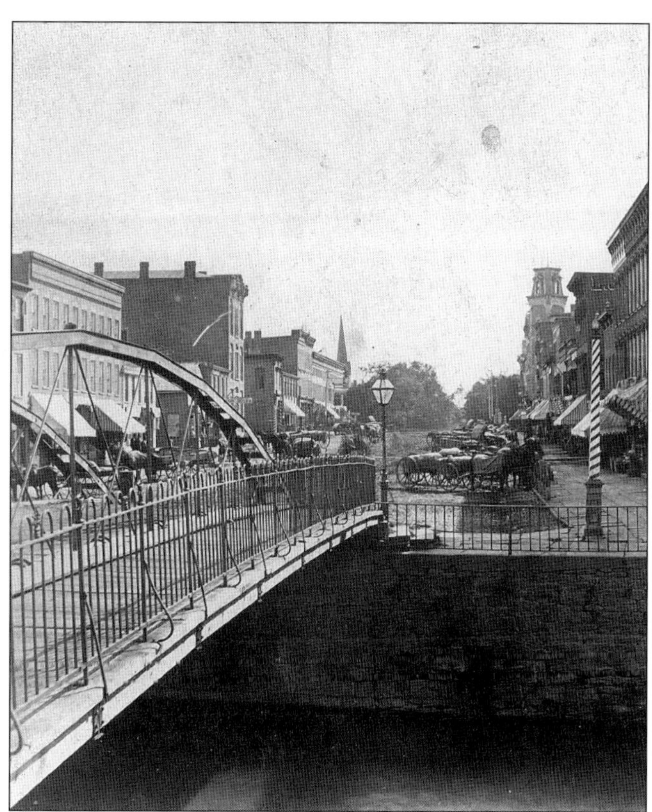

THE MAIN STREET BRIDGE. This stereoview shows the Main Street bridge before the Erie Canal was rebuilt in 1915. The Medina sandstone south canal wall was rebuilt in concrete (below). The concrete lift tower was built in 1913, and the bridge was opened in 1915. It has unusual below the-deck counterweights and is still in use. The American Hotel (page 66 and 72) is visible to the right of the bridge.

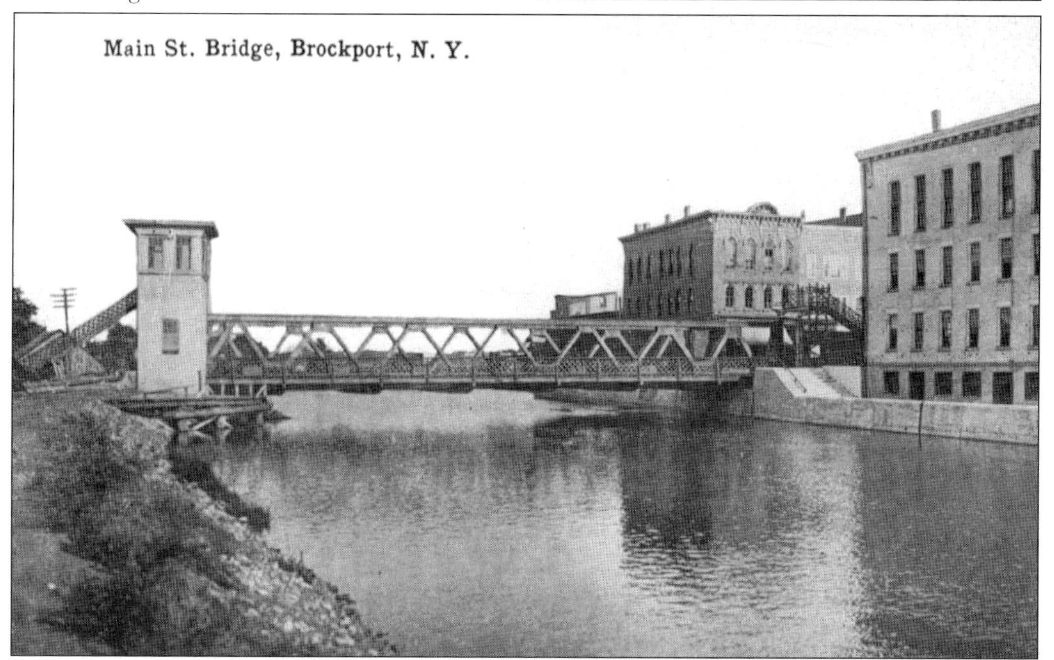

Main St. Bridge, Brockport, N. Y.

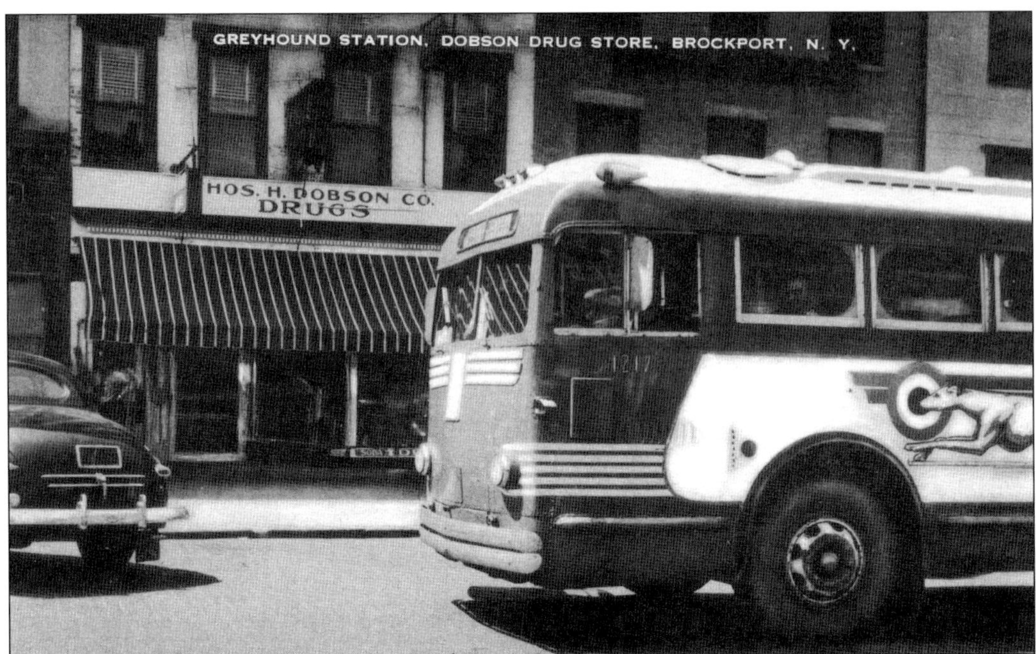

BUS TRANSPORTATION. For several decades, the Greyhound Bus Company provided intercity transportation to Brockport college students and Brockporters employed in Rochester. The Rochester Area Transportation Authority has replaced Greyhound on this route. This bus is embarking passengers who have bought tickets at Dobson's Drug Store on Main Street, which was in business from 1876 to the middle 1960s.

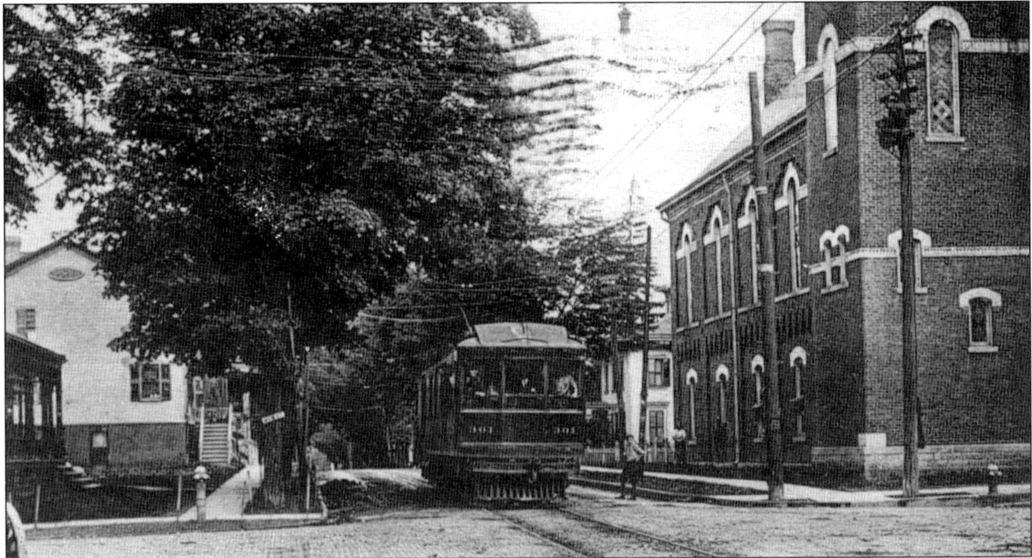

TROLLEY SERVICE. The Buffalo, Lockport, and Rochester Railway (1908–1919) and, as reorganized, the Rochester, Lockport and Buffalo Railroad Corporation (1919–1931) provided interurban electric rail service through Brockport for nearly a quarter century. In 1918, as an example, the Brockport-Rochester one-way fare was 70¢, with 19 or 20 trolleys a day between about 7:00 a.m. and 1:00 a.m. Here, a car travels eastbound car at Erie and Main Streets in 1908 or 1909.

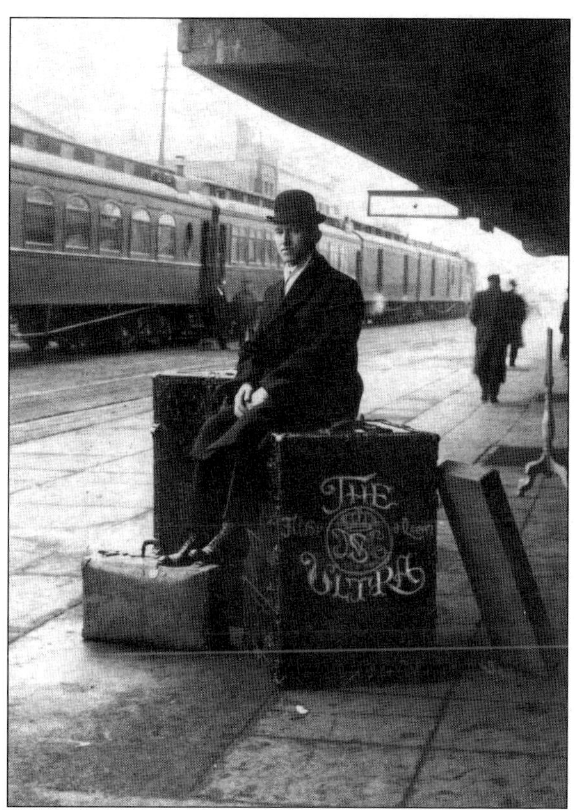

Rail Service. The Rochester and Niagara Falls Railroad (later the Niagara Falls branch of the New York Central) reached Brockport in 1852. Passenger service ended in 1964, when it served only one regular commuter. The Falls Railroad Company continues limited freight service to Brockport industries. The traveling salesman (right) for the Moore-Shafer Shoe Manufacturing Company (pages 11 and 50) peddled Ultra brand shoes "Fit for a Queen." He is shown at the Brockport station in 1911. The depot on Park Avenue (below) is pictured *c.* 1900. Both buildings are now warehouses for the Stull Lumber Company.

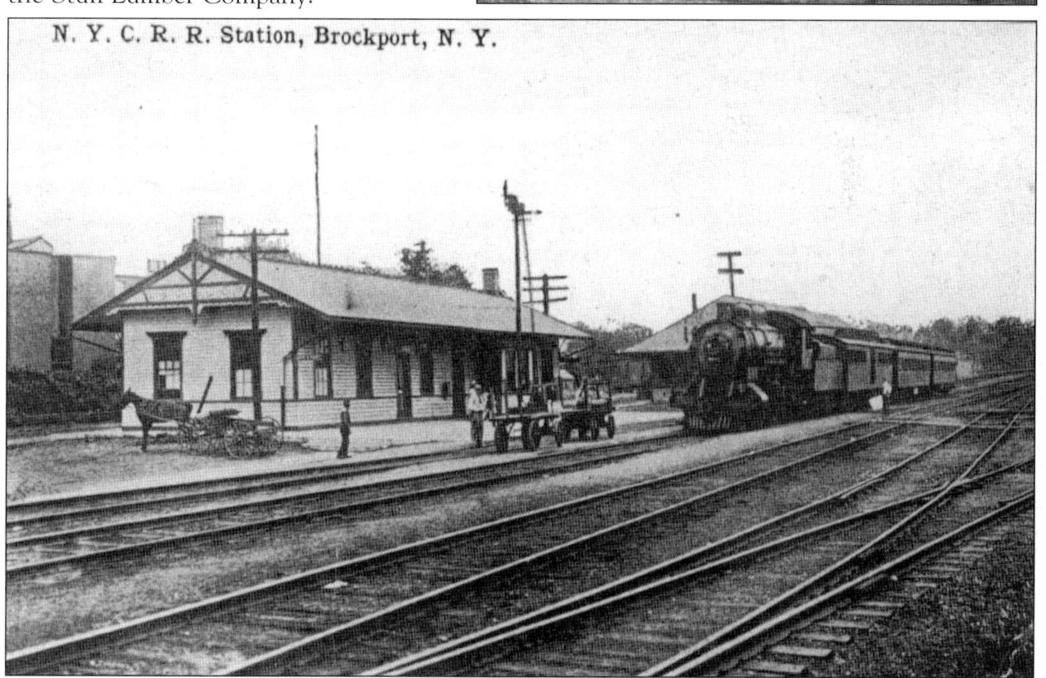

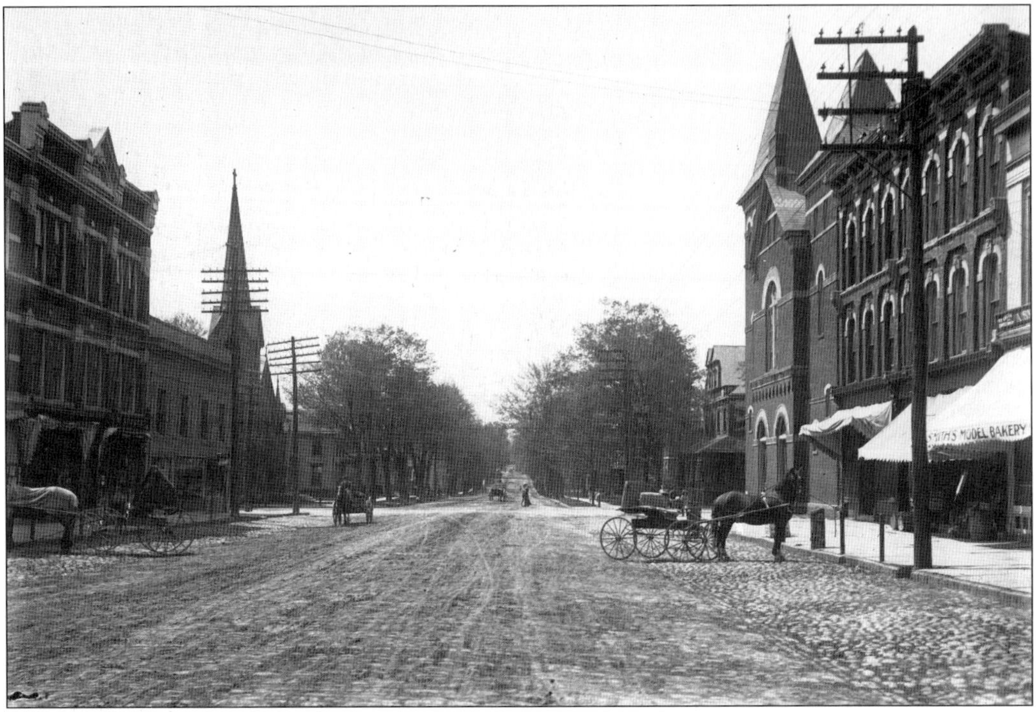

MAIN STREET, FROM KING STREET. Main Street, looking south from King Street, is pictured in 1910 (above) and in 2001 (below). The commercial buildings and churches have survived, though the façade of the last building on the left side was modernized in 1946. The first house on the right side was replaced by a service station and, later, by an optician's shop and Sagawa park.

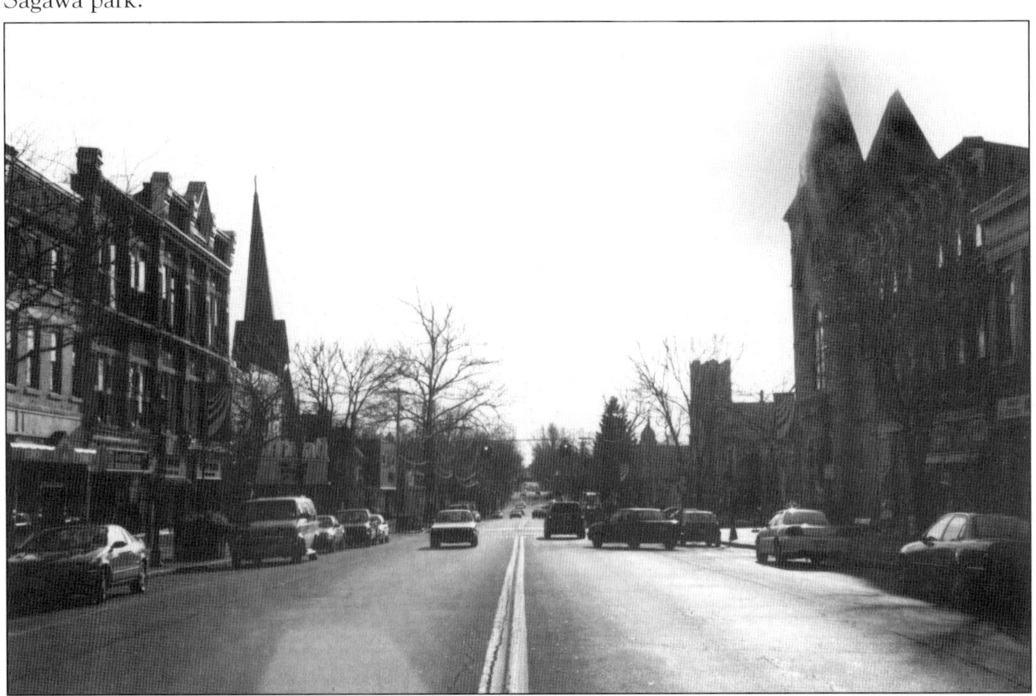

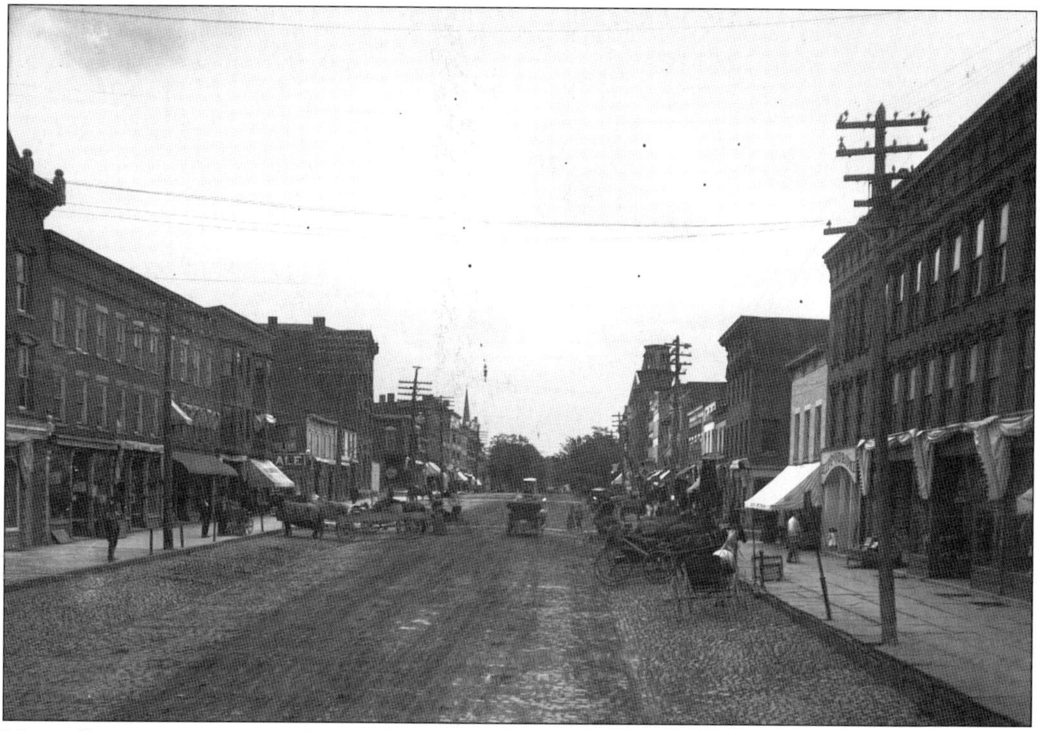

MAIN STREET, FROM THE CANAL BRIDGE. These photographs, taken the same dates as those opposite, show Main Street, looking south from the canal bridge. The structures on the left side have survived with little change, but the commercial buildings on the right from the canal to Clinton Street have given way to an office building and the post office.

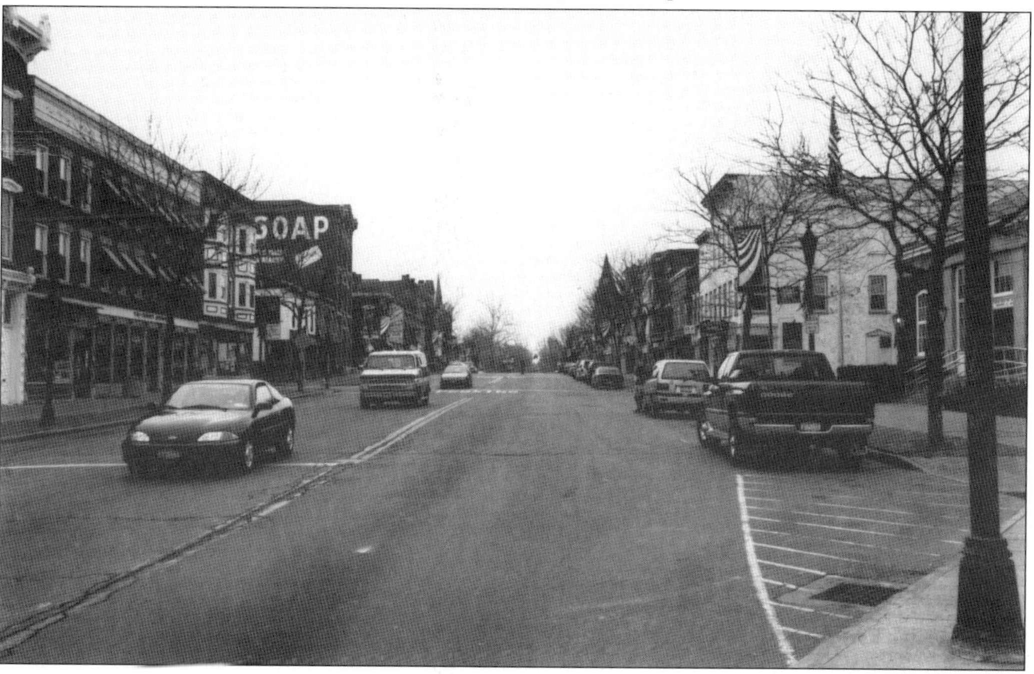

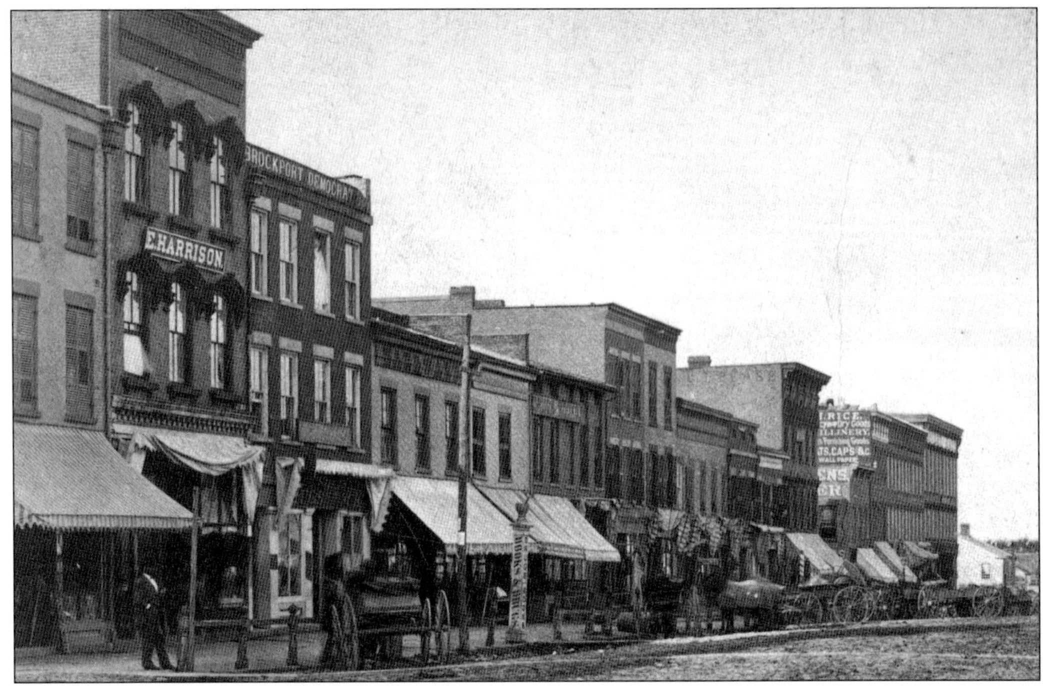

MAIN STREET, WEST SIDE. The 1890s stereoview (above) shows the west side of Main Street from Erie Street north. The building farthest to the left is the dry goods store of Julius Lester (page 70). Next is the clothing store that Edward Harrison (pages 98 and 111) and his son operated from 1858 to 1931. Next to Harrison's store was the weekly newspaper, the Brockport Democrat, founded in 1870. On the far right is the American Hotel. Beyond the Lester building (below) are Hairport and Java Junction.

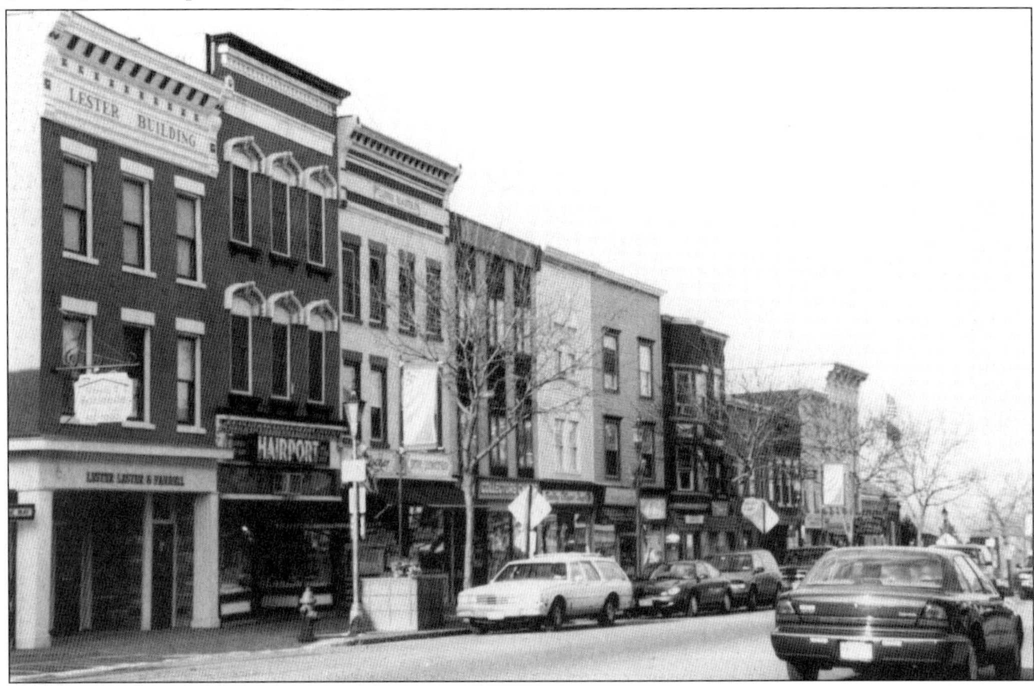

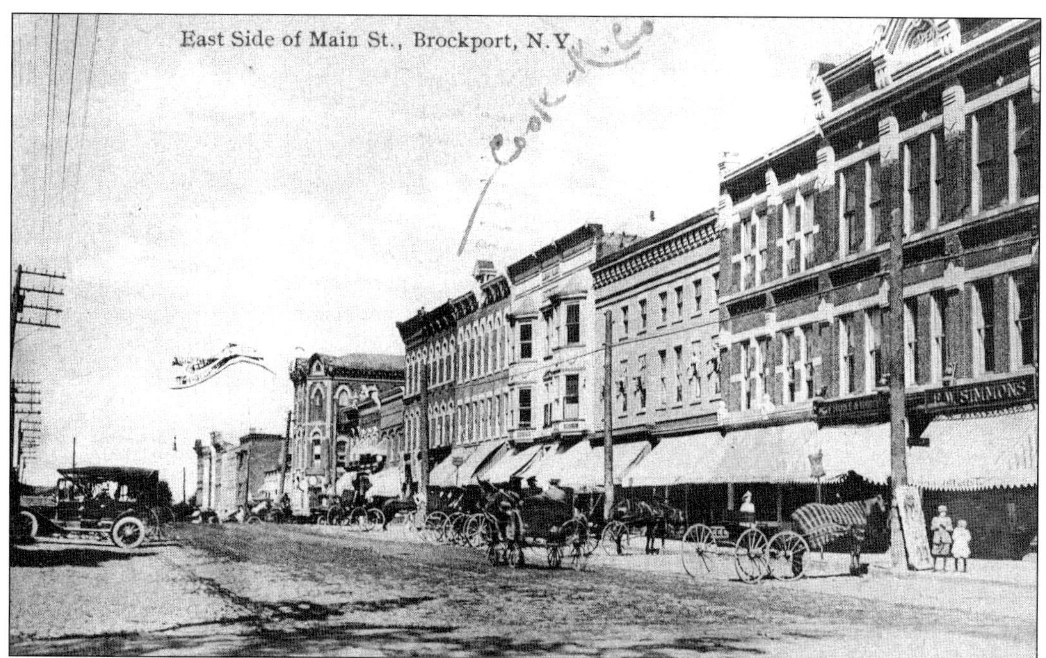

MAIN STREET, EAST SIDE. This is Main Street from State Street north *c.* 1915. E.W. Simmons was a pharmacist. Next door was Frost & Goffe, tailors and clothiers, which also sold "Phonographs, Records and Supplies. Bicycles, Tires, Etc., and Sewing Machines." S.P. Frost came to Brockport at age 34 in 1867 and opened his men's clothing store. Later, J.H. Goffe became his partner and continued the business after Frost's retirement until 1931. In 2001 (below), the same storefronts were occupied by Helen E. Simpson, photographer, and the Mes-Sage Christian bookshop.

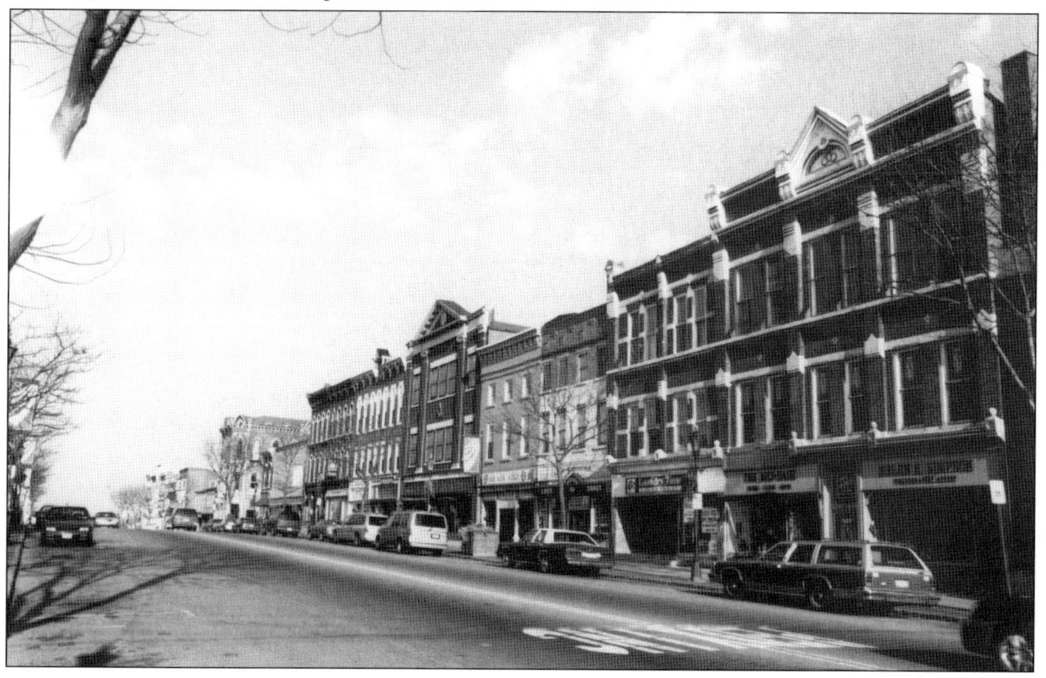

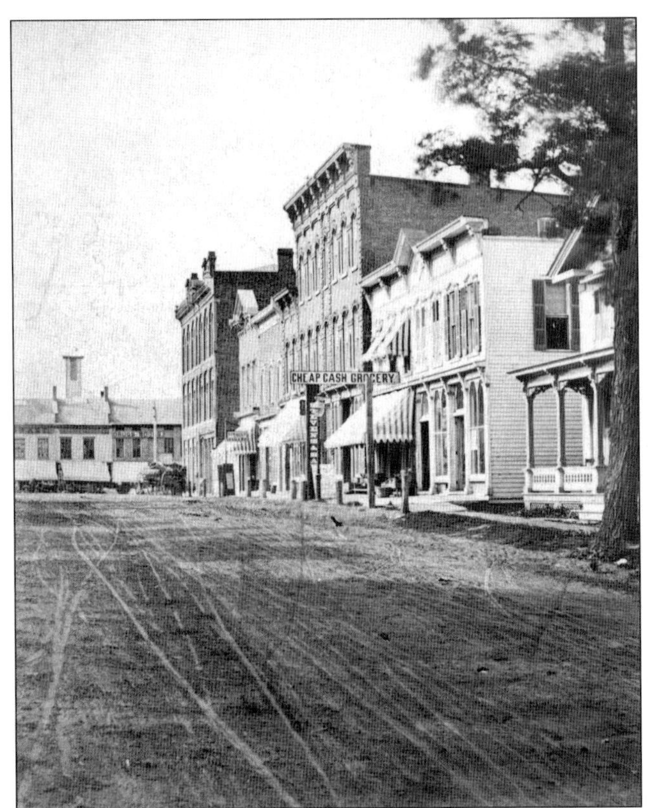

MARKET STREET. The 1890s stereoview (left) shows the north side of Market Street. All buildings facing Market Street were built in 1877, after a fire had destroyed their predecessors. Those structures survived to 2002 with little change.

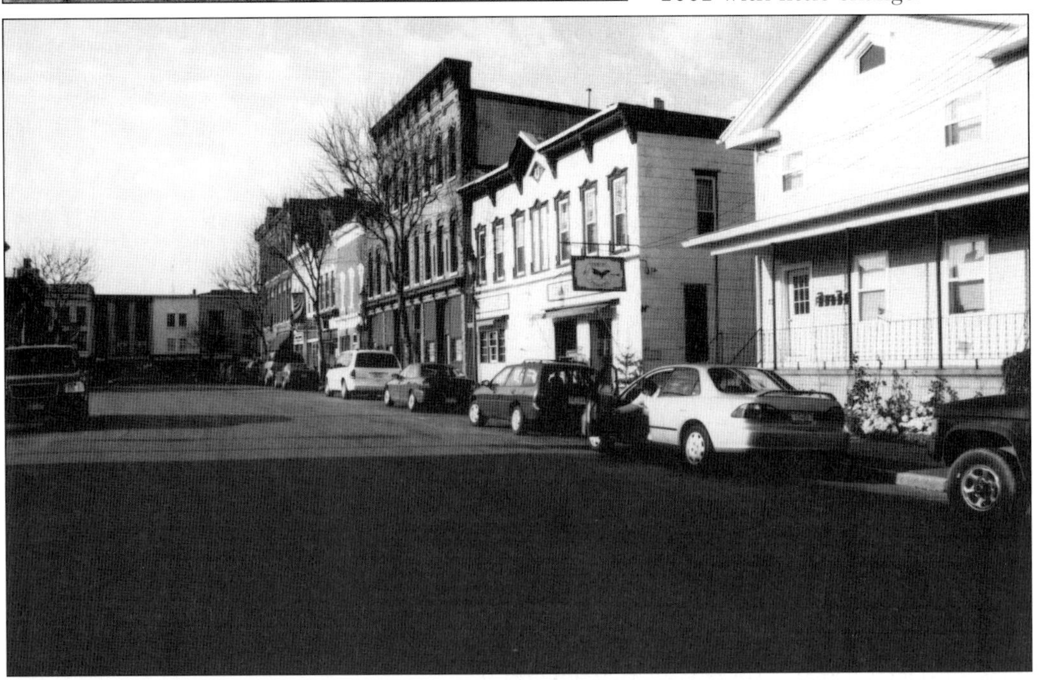

THE DECKER BLOCK. The 1877 book *Rochester and Monroe County* shows the newly completed Decker Block (right), built for J.D. Decker, a local lawyer. It was the only Market Street structure to survive the 1877 fire. The building still stood in 2001 (below). In 1998, architectural historian Paul Malo gave it a "red," the highest rating for a structure in terms of architectural and historic interest.

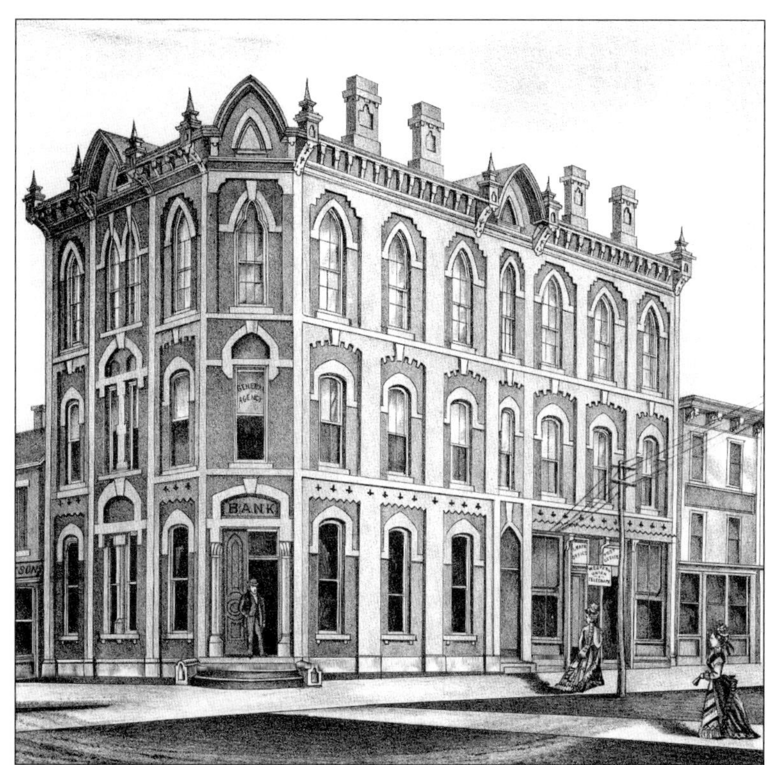

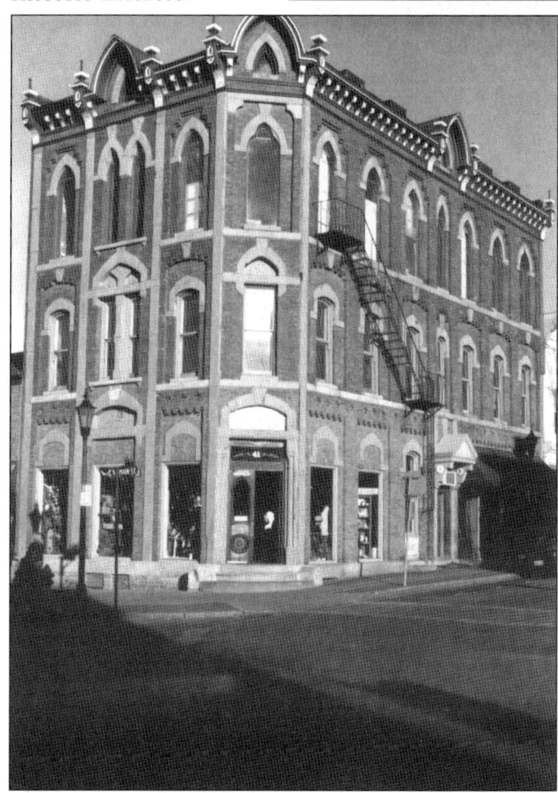

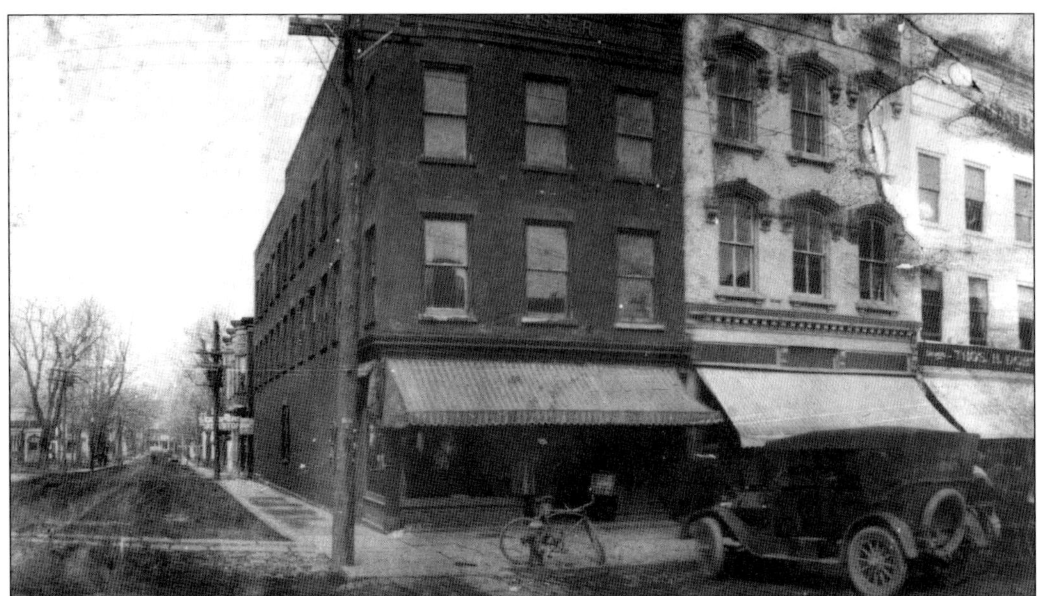

THE LESTER FAMILY. Julius Lester opened a dry goods store on Market Street in 1883 and bought this building at King and Main Streets (above) in 1893. His grandson, Nat O. Lester Jr., owned the building in 2002 and he and his son, Nat Lester III, practiced law there. They have both been town supervisor. Irish-born John Owens, proprietor of a grocery store (below), was in business in Brockport from 1856 (on the Main Street site of the present post office after 1875) until he died in 1920. He sold "imported and domestic fancy and staple groceries" and also carried "a general stock of adamant, cement, plaster and masons supplies." His daughter, Emma T. Owens, married Julius Lester.

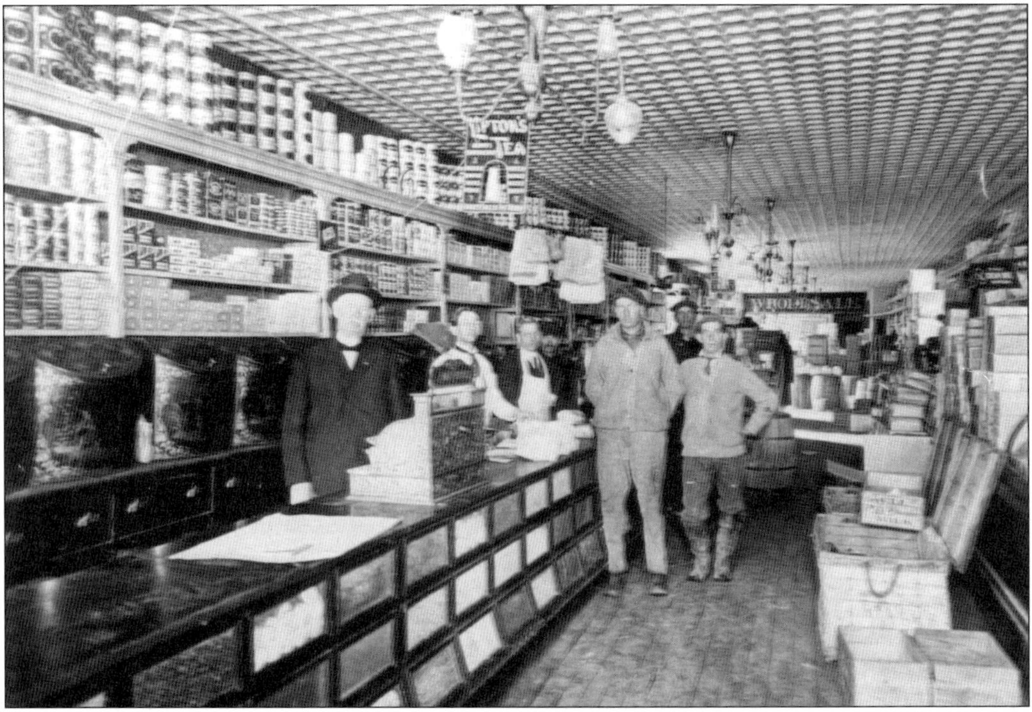

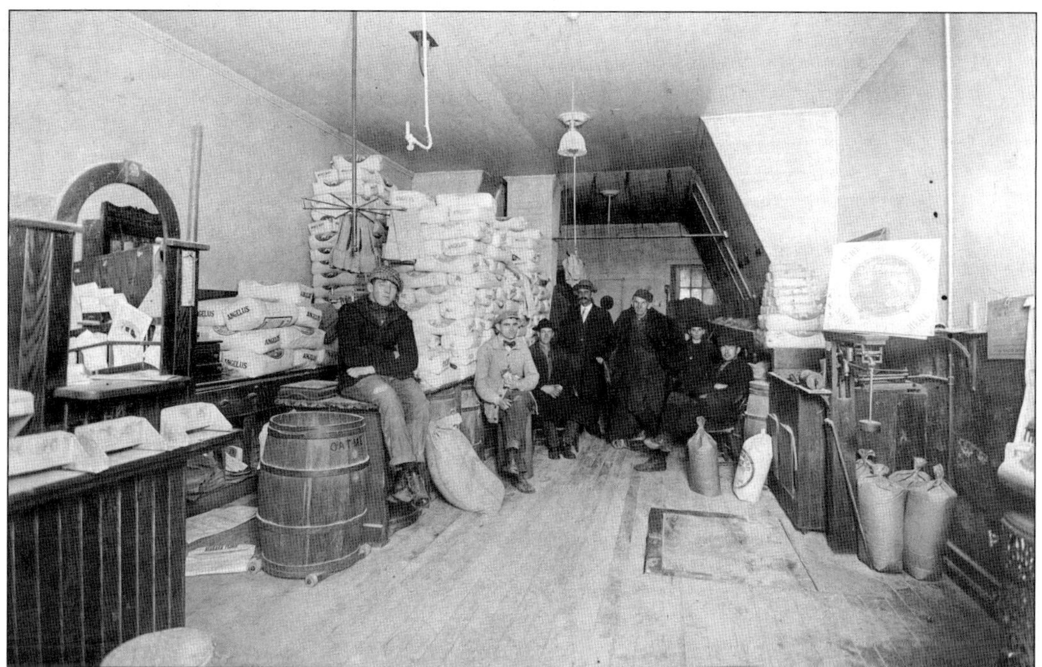

FLOUR, FEED, AND HATS. Fred G. Gillespie (1885–1970) owned this Main Street flour and feed store (above) in 1911. He served as supervisor of the town of Sweden from 1921 to 1922. Katherine T. and Sarah L. Fagan owned the Fagan Store (below), a millinery shop at Main and Water Streets. Meanwhile, Anna, Hannah M., and Theresa R. McDonald sold "Millinery, Fancy Goods and Ladies' Furnishings" at 84 Main Street.

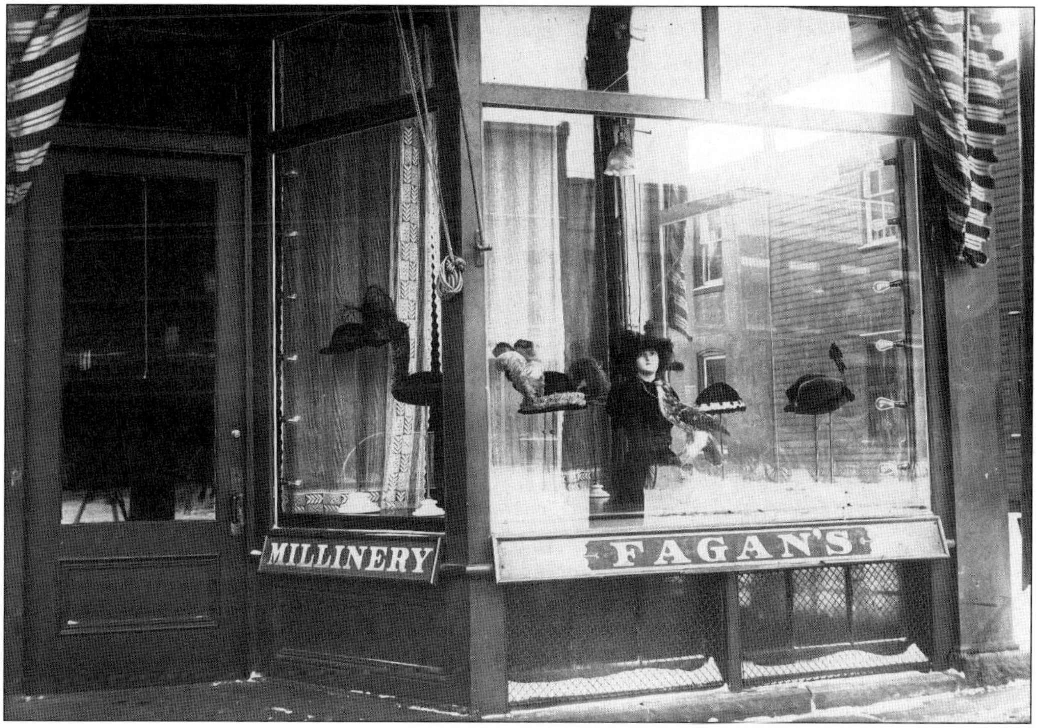

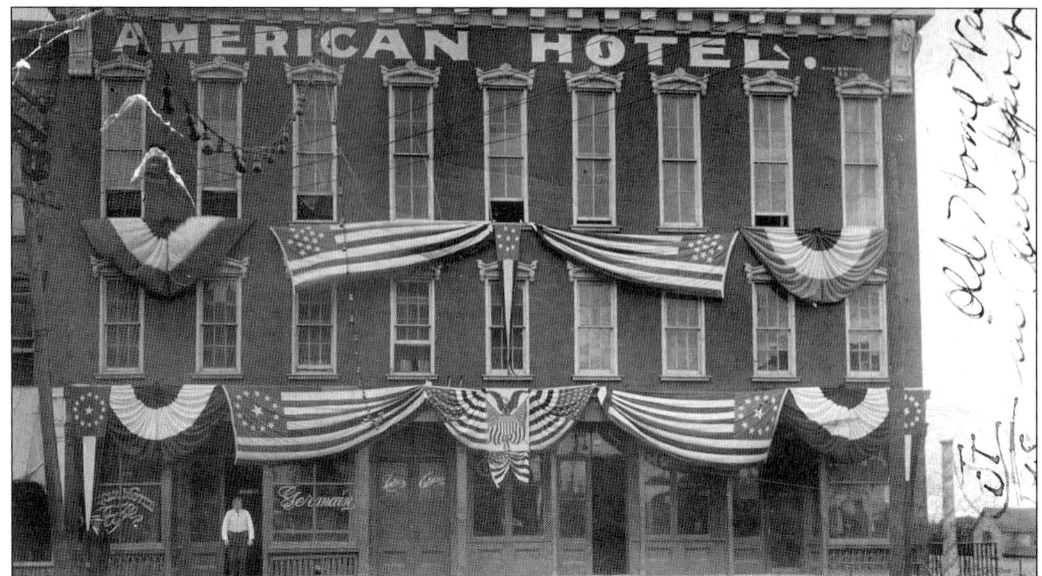

THE AMERICAN HOTEL. This building probably was built in the 1840s immediately south of the canal on the west side of Main Street. Two earlier hotels were on the north side of the canal. Shops were on the ground floor and hotel rooms on the upper two floors. The bunting was decoration for Old Home Week (pages 102 and 103). Later, the building was the Landmark Hotel, the Brockport Hotel, Germaine's Hall, and the Music Hall. The south wing was demolished in 1940 to make way for the post office. The remainder burned in 1955. Frank Sacheli was the last proprietor of the hotel.

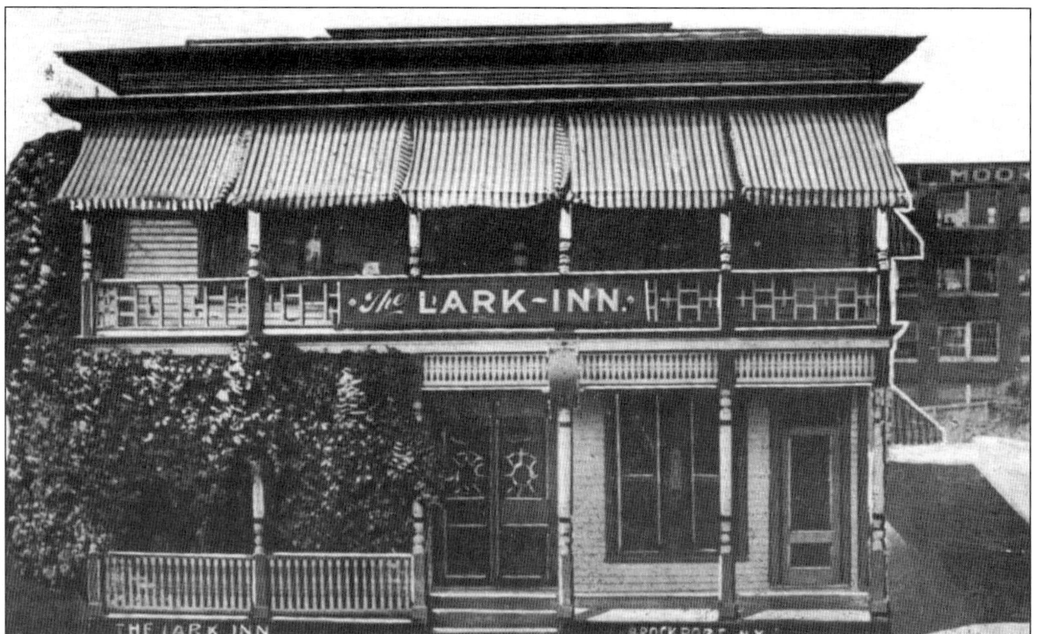

THE LARK INN. During the late 19th and early 20th centuries, travel by rail was popular, and Brockport's hostelries were clustered near the train depot on Park Avenue. The Lark Inn, in that area, was owned by James Larkin, a prominent resident who served as mayor. It burned in a 1913 fire of incendiary origin.

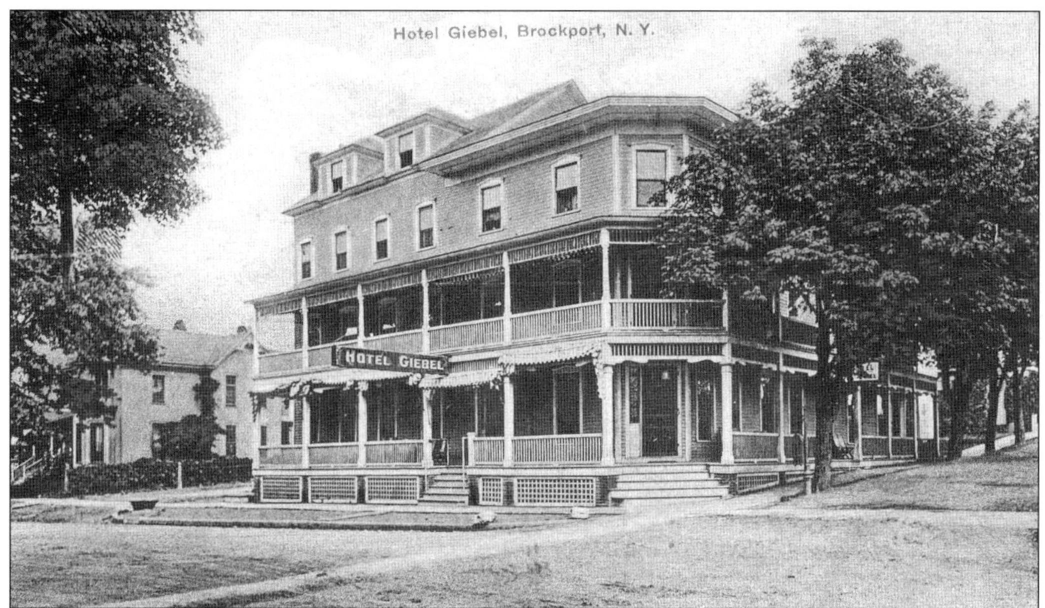

HOTEL GIEBEL. The hotel at Main Street and Railroad Avenue (above), immediately adjacent to the Lark Inn, survived the fire that destroyed the Lark Inn. The Giebel's barroom (below) was very elegant. Railroad Avenue no longer exists. Other Brockport hotels at various times (some only name changes) were Heinrich House, Tremont Hotel, Porter's Hotel, and Getty House.

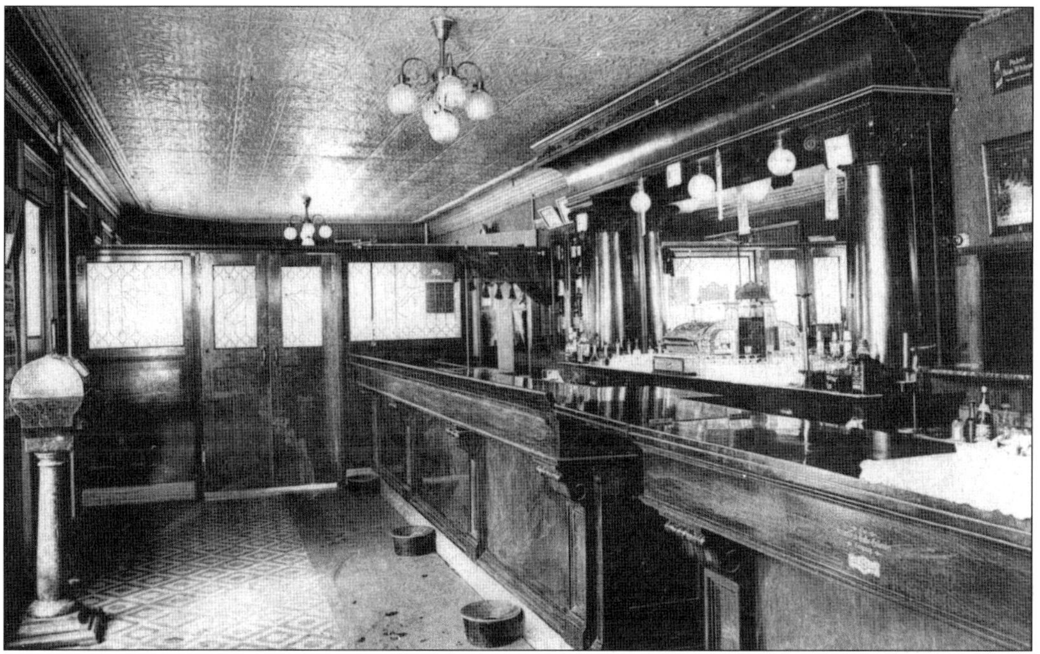

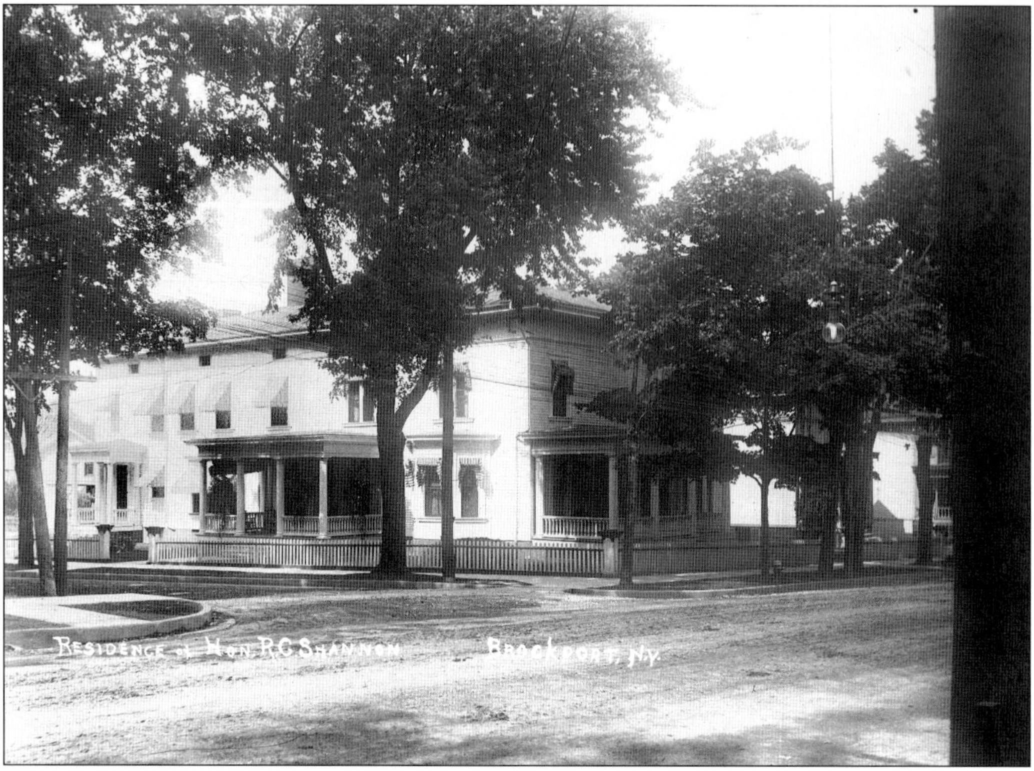

THE SHANNON HOME. The residence of Richard Cutts Shannon (1839–1920) was at College and Main Streets (above). Pictured in 1911, the home was built by Dr. R. Thatcher, "physician and surgeon" *c.* 1860. Shannon bought it in 1902, after the 1901 death of his wife, and remodeled it extensively before occupying it in 1903 . Shown is the landscaping on the College Street side of the residence (below).

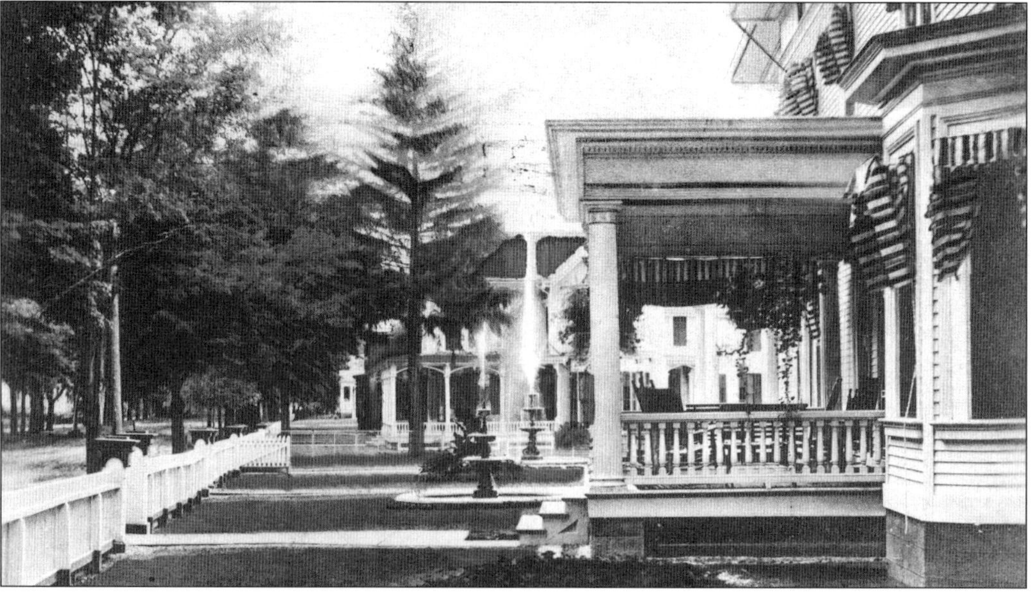

R.C. SHANNON. Shannon served in the Union army and, in 1871, was a diplomat in Brazil. There, he met Charles Backus Greenough of Brockport and his wife, Martha Ann Spaulding, of Clarkson. In 1874, he joined Greenough in the street railway business in Rio de Janeiro, which became very successful. Greenough died in 1880, and Shannon married his widow in 1887. Shannon was a lawyer, minister to three Central American republics, and represented New York City in Congress from 1895 to 1899. Later, his home became an upscale restaurant and inn, the Casa Loma, and, from 1931 to c. 1970, the Roxbury Inn (below). It was then a bar and is now student housing owned by Norman Giancursio. The Shannons were noted philanthropists. Martha Shannon spent $250,000 to save a relative's bank from insolvency.

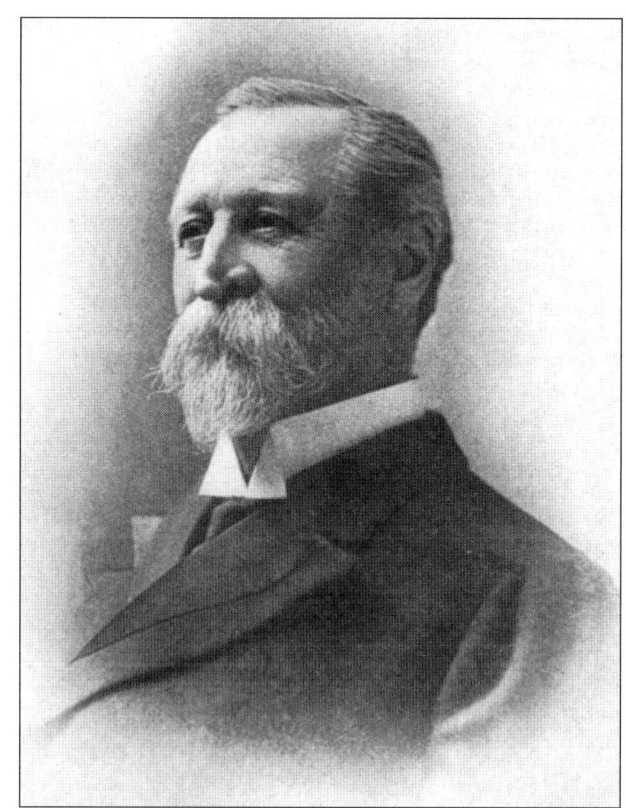

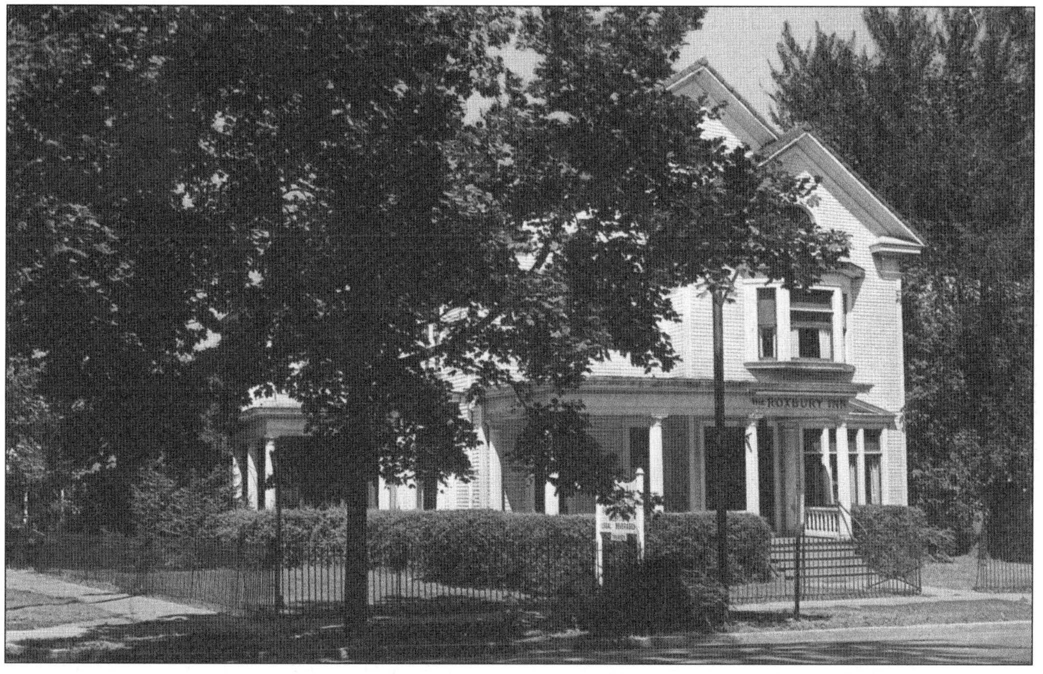

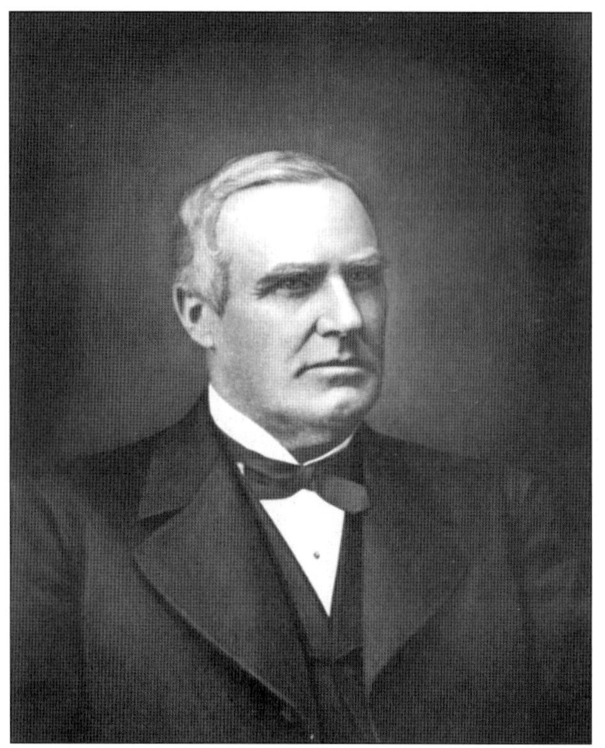

LUTHER GORDON. Gordon (1822–1881) arrived in the village in 1856. He owned a wholesale and retail lumber business, with sawmills in Brockport, Holley, Olean, and Michigan. In 1864, he founded the First National Bank, the repository for canal tolls collected at Brockport. He and a brother owned extensive timberlands, including 7,000 acres in Michigan. In 1858, he built a house (below) directly across South Street from the Morgan-Manning house (page 44) and across Main Street from the Shannon house (page 74). His only child, George C. Gordon, succeeded his father in his business interests.

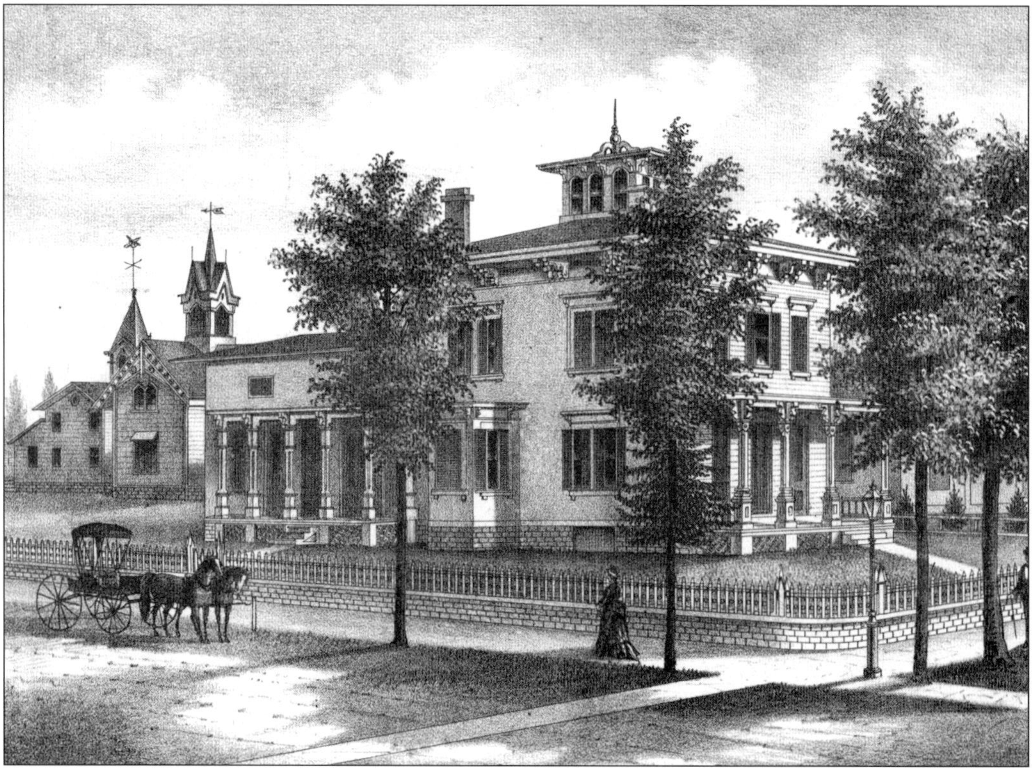

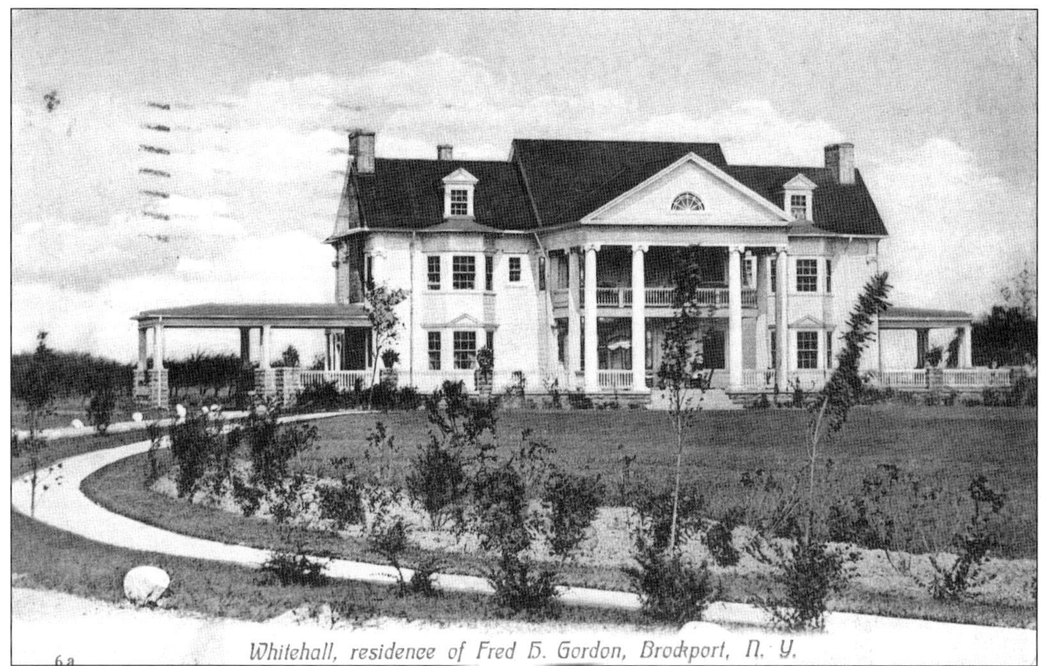

FRED GORDON. Three sons of George C. Gordon were prominent Brockporters. Fred Gordon owned the Whitehall Farms in Clarkson, just north of the village. His home was one of the finest in the area. Luther Gordon Jr. succeeded his father in the banking and lumber business. In 1927, the family sold the lumber business and, in 1932, the firm's former manager, W.E.B. Stull, continued the business on his own. Stull Lumber remains in operation on Park Avenue.

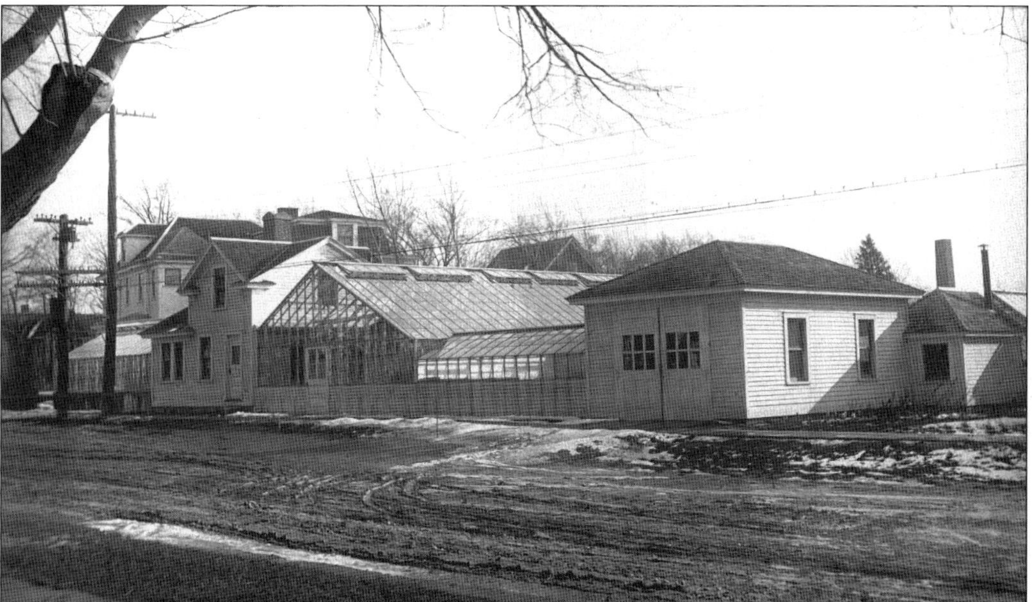

THOMAS GORDON. Thomas Gordon became bank president when Luther Gordon Jr. died. He replaced the 1873 building at Main and King Streets with the present neoclassical structure that houses the Chase Manhattan Bank. He built the greenhouses at his home on West Avenue as a hobby and, later, business. Today, they are the Rogers Flower Shop and Greenhouses.

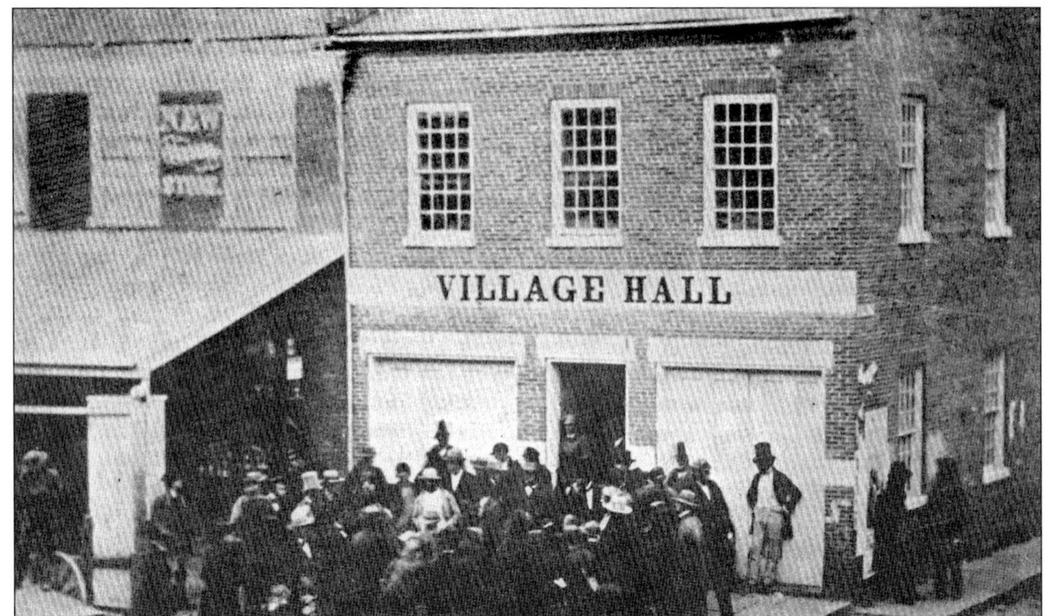

THE FIRST VILLAGE HALL. This 1844 King Street building is the earliest known structure devoted exclusively to village business. At times, fire companies occupied the ground floor and offices were upstairs. Also, the town of Sweden held occasional board meetings there.

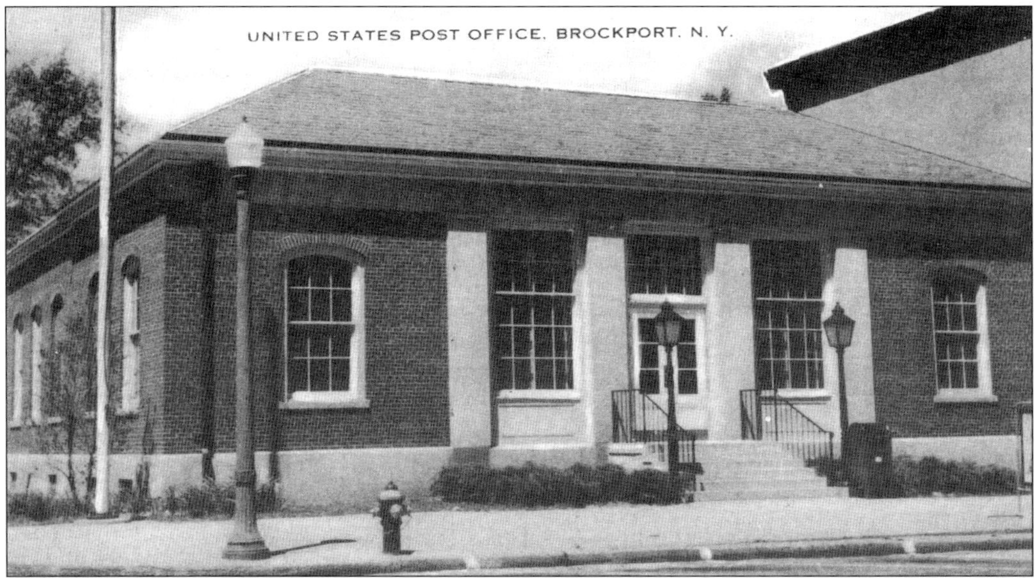

THE POST OFFICE. Sweden's first post office opened in West Sweden in 1819. Brockport's first office opened in James Seymour's general store, on the northeast corner of Main and Market Streets, in 1823. The post office has moved six times, never more than 100 yards away from its first location. It shared quarters with groceries, telegraph facilities, and a bank until it acquired its own space on the ground floor of the Decker Block (page 69) in the 1890s. Later, it occupied the ground floor of the Masonic Block and the present site of the Tri-County Advertiser. In 1940, this structure was built expressly for postal purposes. In 1999, the U.S. Postal Service agreed to provide full service there "for no less than 20 years" while operating a sorting annex elsewhere.

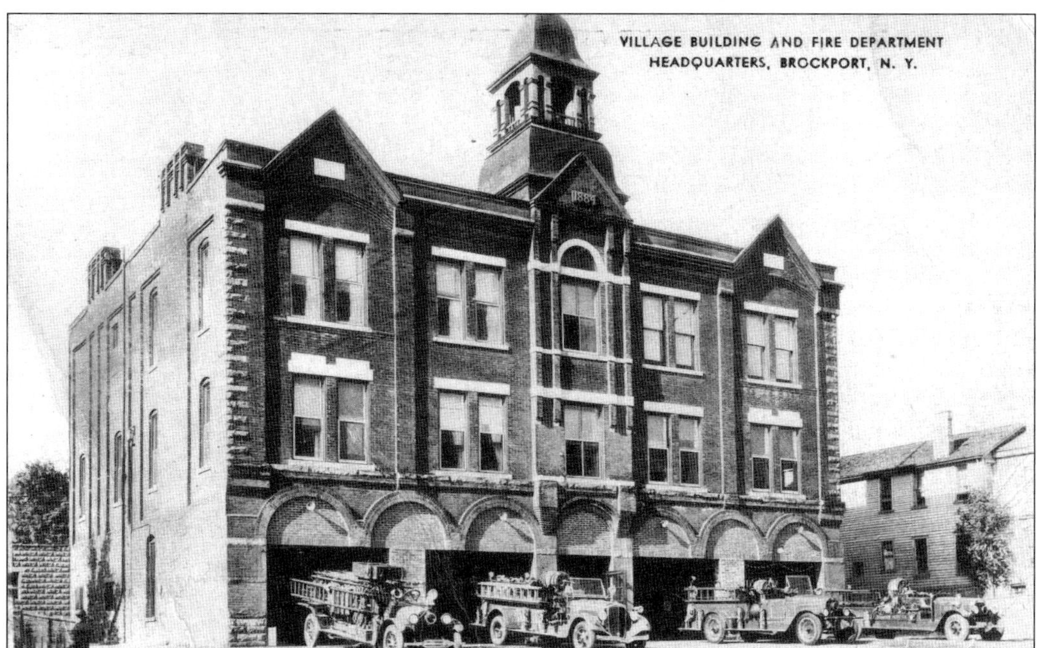

THE MARKET STREET BUILDING. This was the village hall from 1884 until 1969. The ground floor garaged fire engines, and the upper floors were village offices. The ground floor façade was remodeled *c.* 1930 to accommodate more modern motor-powered fire engines.

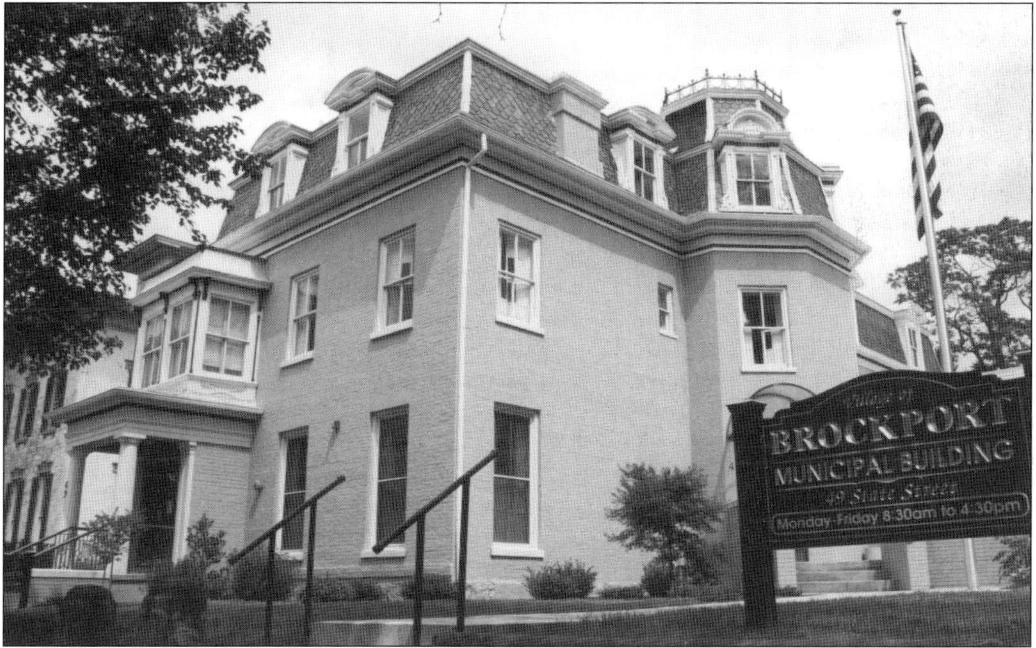

THE SEYMOUR BUILDING. In 1969, the village of Brockport demolished the Market Street building and the town of Sweden vacated its offices on Erie Street. The town acquired and remodeled a former supermarket at 18 State Street, occupied part of it, and rented the rest to the village. In 1996, the Seymour Library moved from the former Seymour residence, at 49 State Street (page 43). The village renovated that structure and moved its offices there in 2000.

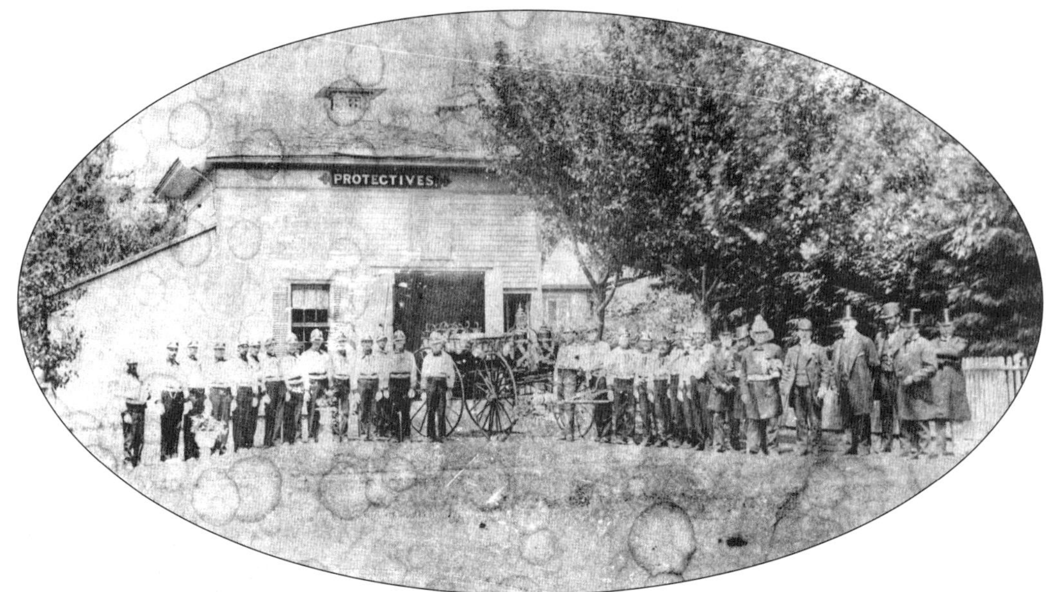

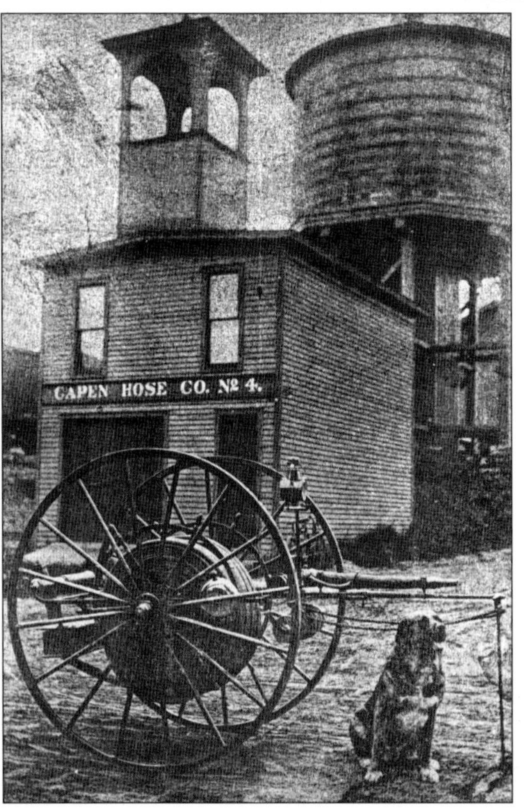

EARLY FIREHOUSES. Brockport's first fire company, Water Witch Engine Company No. 1, organized in 1832, three years after the village was chartered. The Conqueror Engine Company No. 2 formed two years later. No information about their firehouses survives. The first village hall (page 78) served as the first known firehouse. In 1877, the Protectives built a structure on Monroe Avenue (above), where the Catholic rectory now stands. The 1884–1969 village hall (page 79) housed several companies. The first Capen Hose Company No. 4 firehouse (left) was built on Main Street just south of the railroad in 1893–1894. The background shows a railroad water tower.

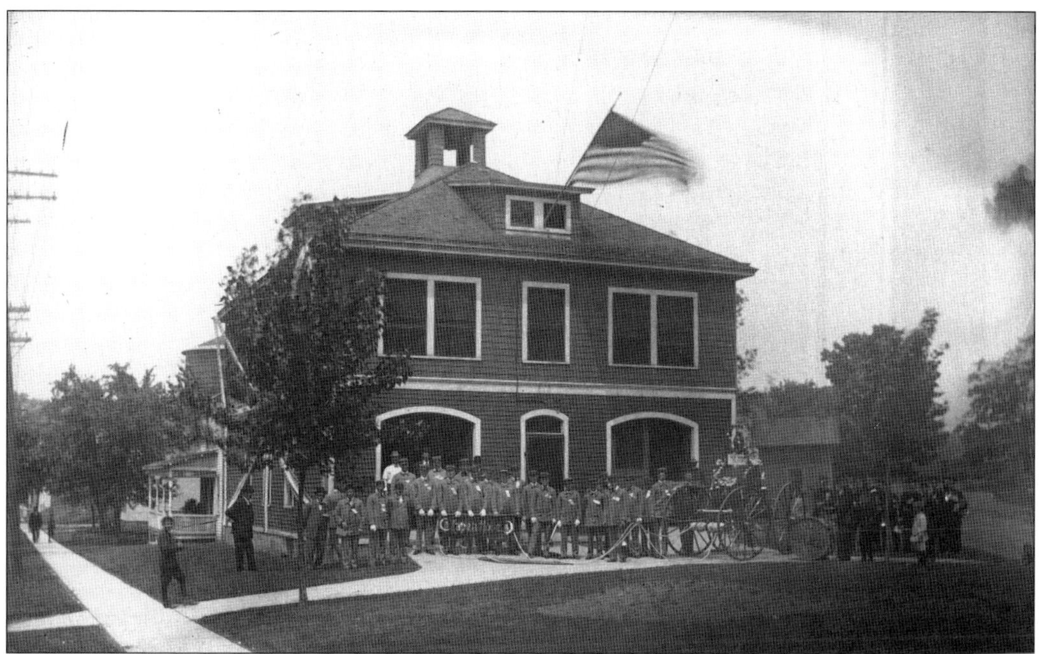

FIREHOUSES TODAY. Brockport now has four firehouses. The 1894 Capen Hose Company building was replaced in 1904 by the one at Park Avenue and South Main Street (above). It remains in service, with relatively minor changes, as one of the oldest fire stations in western New York. In 1967, the village converted an auto repair shop on West Avenue into a firehouse. This firehouse (below) opened in 1971 on the site of the 1884 village hall. The fourth firehouse, on Lake Road in Clarkson, opened in 2000.

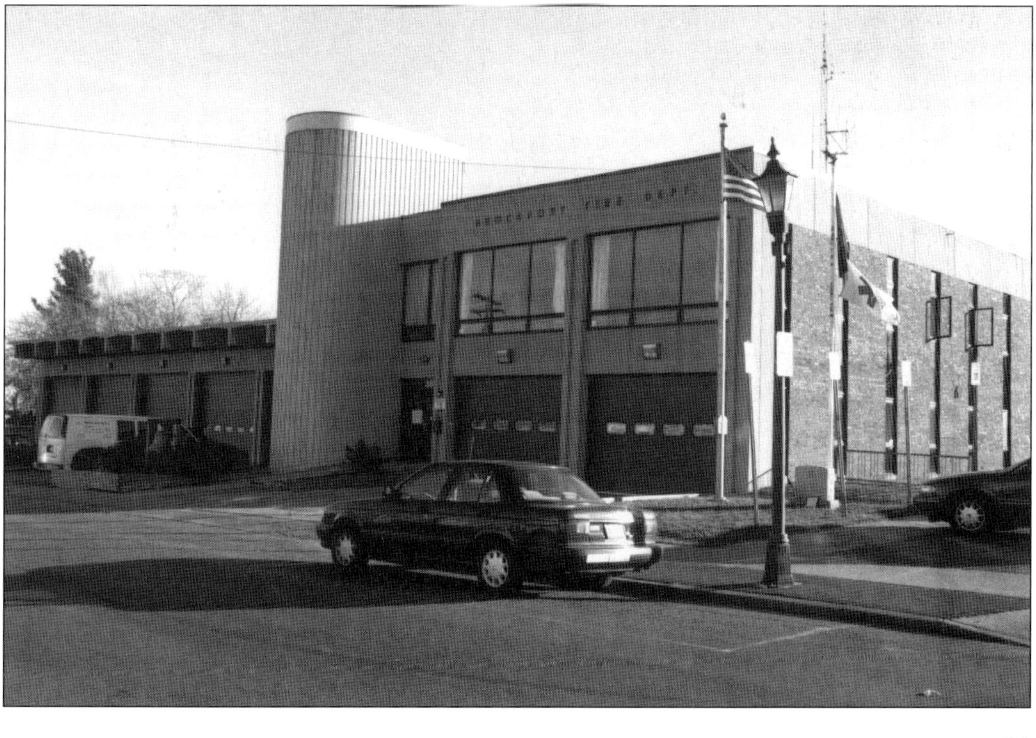

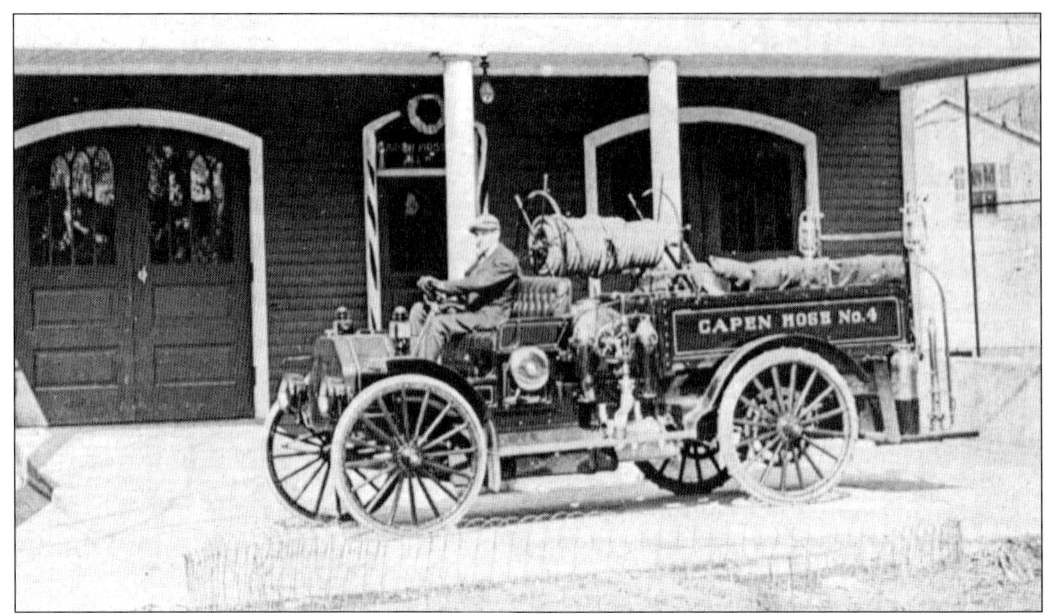

MOTORIZATION. The International chain-drive chemical and hose truck was the Brockport department's first piece of motorized equipment. It enabled the Capen Hose Company to respond to alarms outside the village. The hand- or horse-drawn ladder truck (below) was in service from 1877 until the first motorized hook and ladder truck was bought in 1924. It is shown here as the C.W. Dewey Hook & Ladder Company leaves the Market Street fire hall, responding to an alarm.

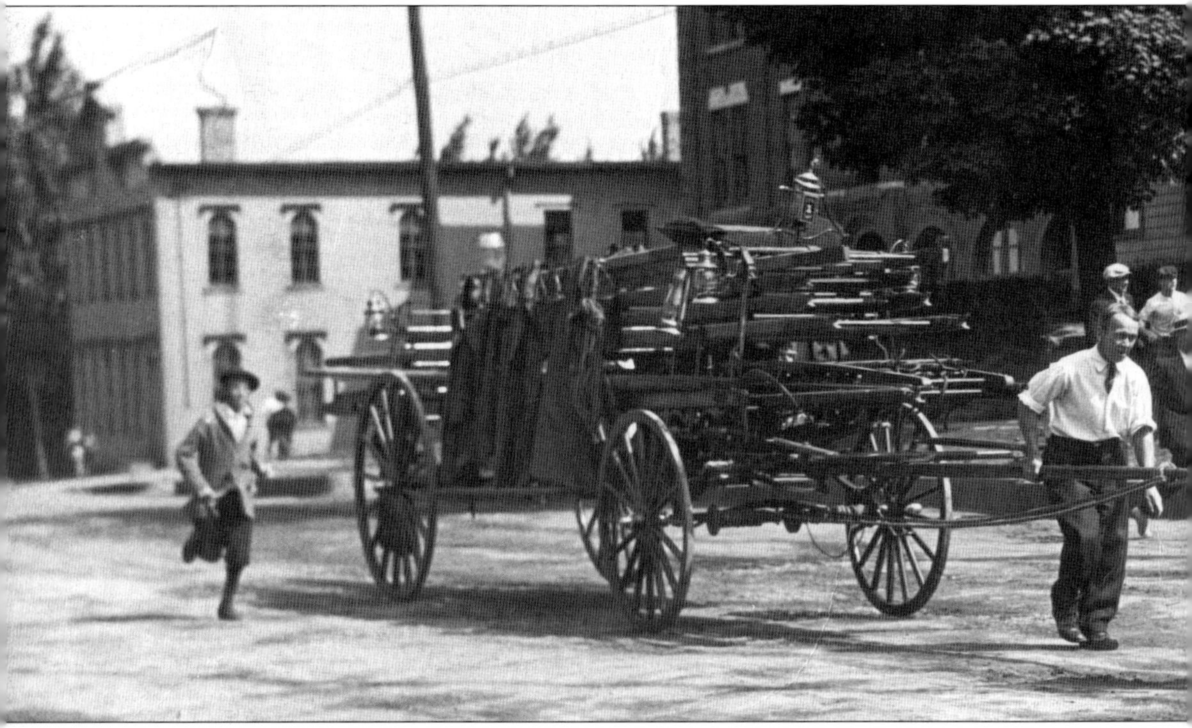

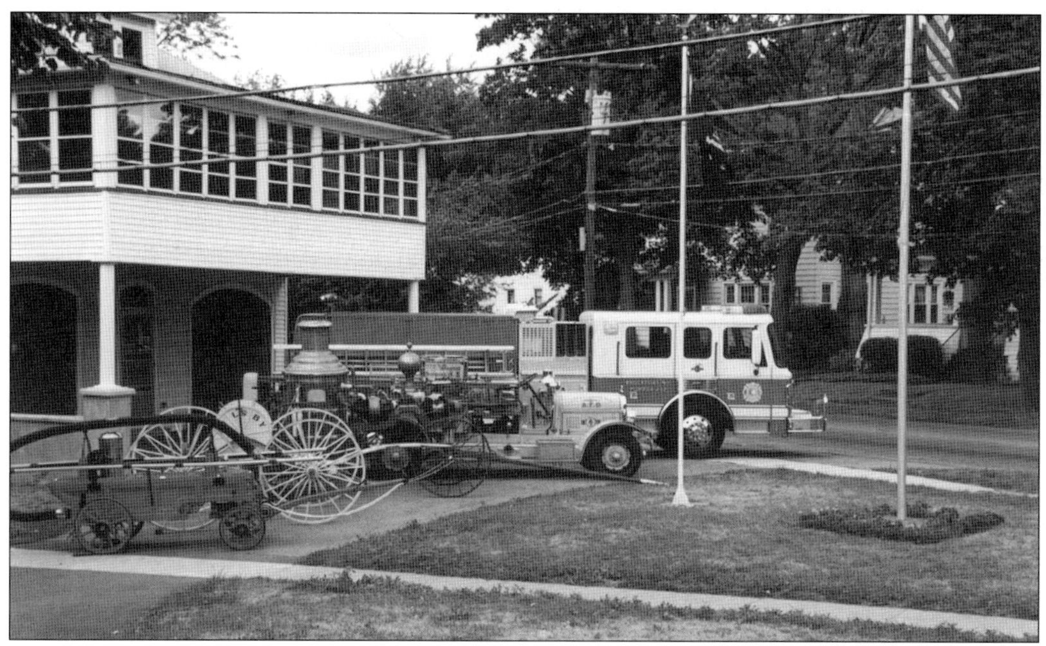

FIREFIGHTING MUSEUM. The Capen Hose Company building houses an extensive firefighting museum. Brockport fire companies own some 20 antique fire engines, including (above), from left to right, an 1847 Selye & Porter hand pumper, an 1880 S.M. Stewart hose carriage, a Silsby steam fire engine that was the manufacturer's display model at the 1876 Philadelphia Exposition, a prizewinning 1930 Seagraves, and a 2000 American LaFrance pumper.

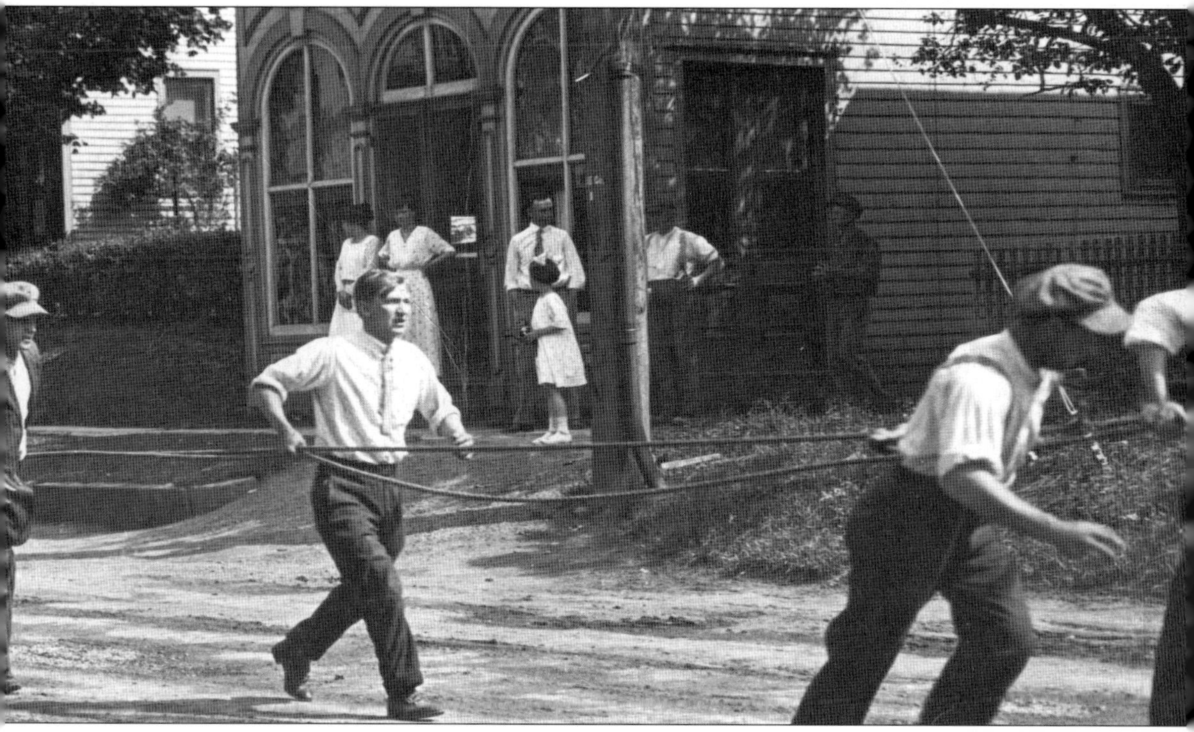

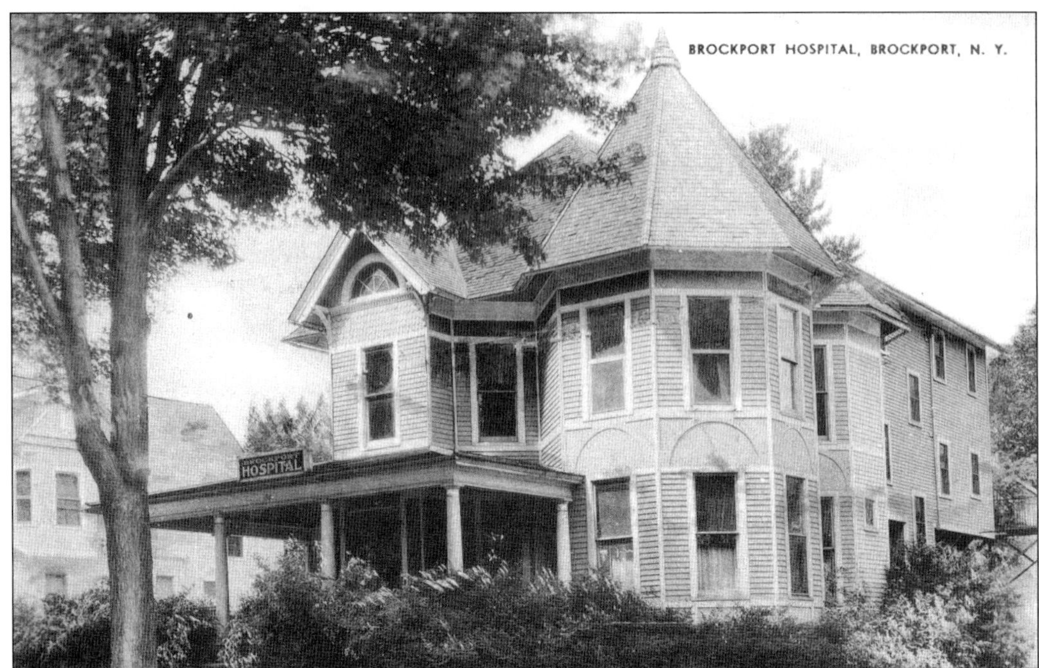

THE BROCKPORT CENTRAL HOSPITAL. Brockport's first physicians were Andrew Millican (1823) and Davis Carpenter (1824). In 1924, George Cochran opened Brockport's first hospital in a home on North Main Street. In 1927, he moved it to a building (above) on South Main Street that had been the Manley Shafer home. It soon failed, but in 1932, the village rented and later purchased the building and established there the Brockport Central Hospital. In 1947, its name became Lakeside Memorial Hospital to honor Brockport's World War II veterans. In 1951, a new building (below) was constructed on West Avenue and occupied by Lakeside.

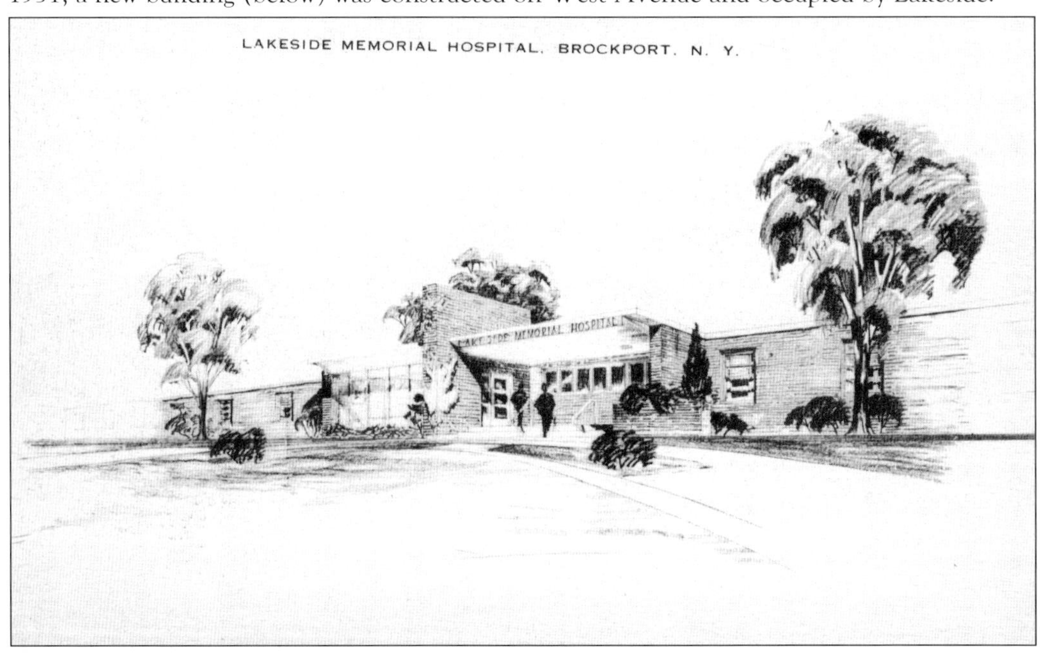

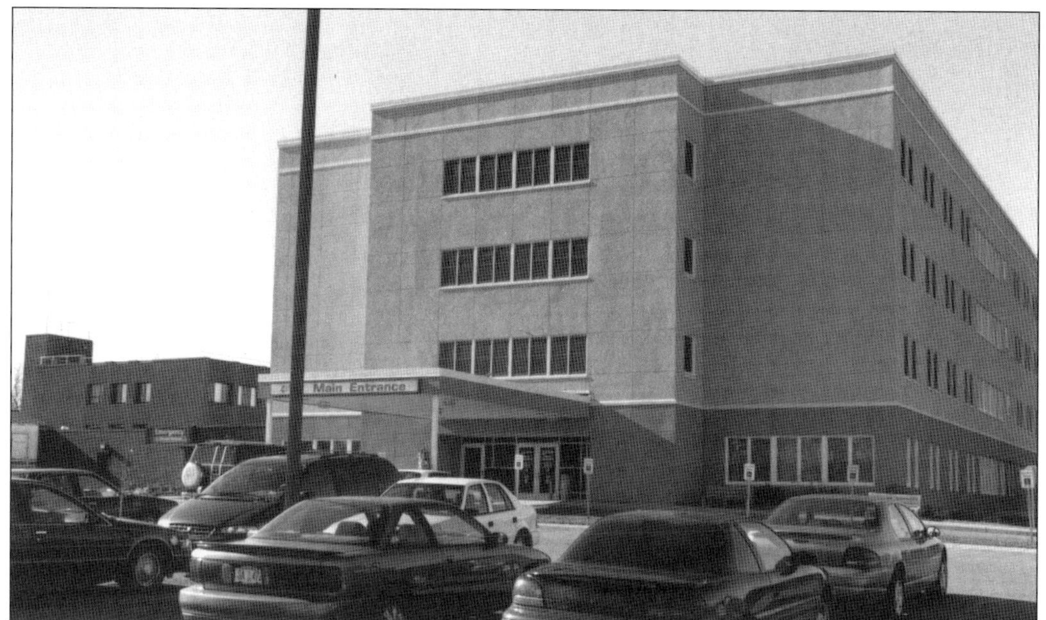

THE LAKESIDE MEMORIAL HOSPITAL. The 1951 building has been expanded several times and now includes a 61-bed full-service hospital, the 120-bed Lakeside-Beikirch skilled nursing home, a 118-capacity child care center, and a 20-office professional building. A Twig Association offers support for patients and staff.

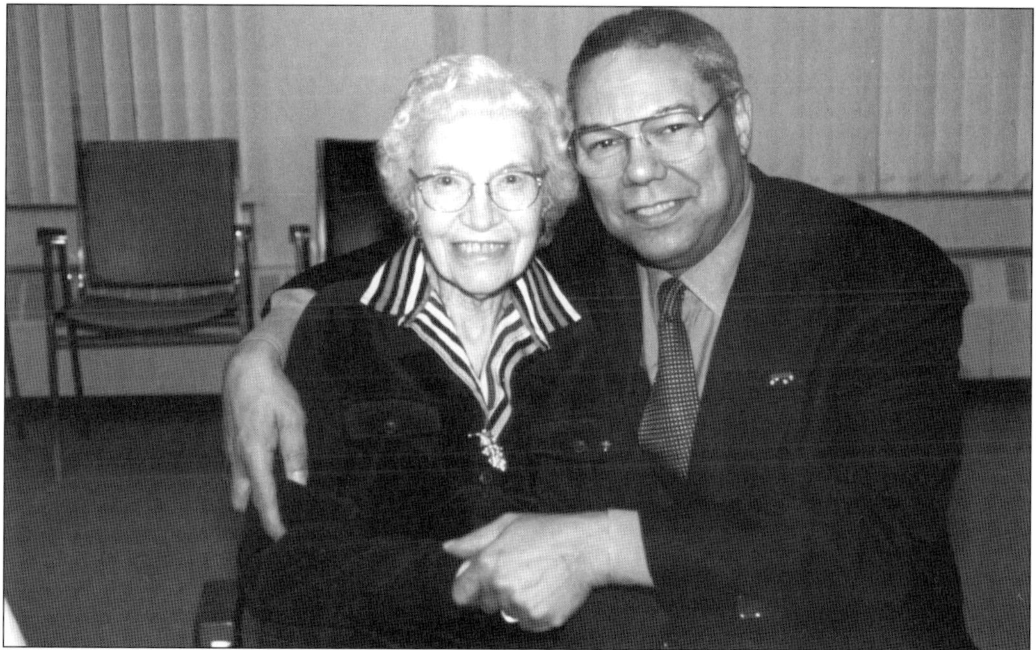

MAY EPKE. When Gen. Colin Powell attended Lakeside's annual fund-raiser in 1998, he greeted May Epke, who had been a nursing supervisor at Highland Hospital in Rochester for 20 years. She became administrator of Brockport Central Hospital in 1944 and supervised the name change and the move into the West Avenue structure. She retired in 1964 and died in May 2001 at age 102.

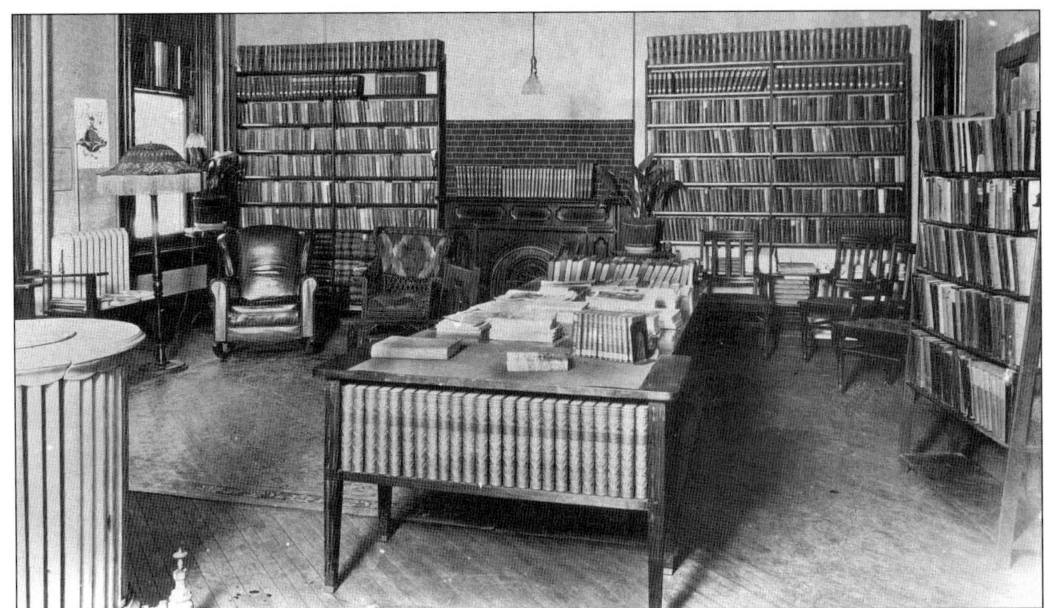

THE READING ROOM. Some village women and newspaper publisher Horatio N. Beach founded Brockport's first library above Smith's bakery *c.* 1872. The library moved several times, finally settling as a Reading Room in the Community Center in the Masonic Block on Main Street in 1920. Dobson's Drug Store (pages 62 and 99) rented books during the same period and donated 50 books to the Reading Room. Others came from the First Presbyterian Church Sunday School. The Reading Room moved twice, to the Decker Block and the Winslow Block on State Street.

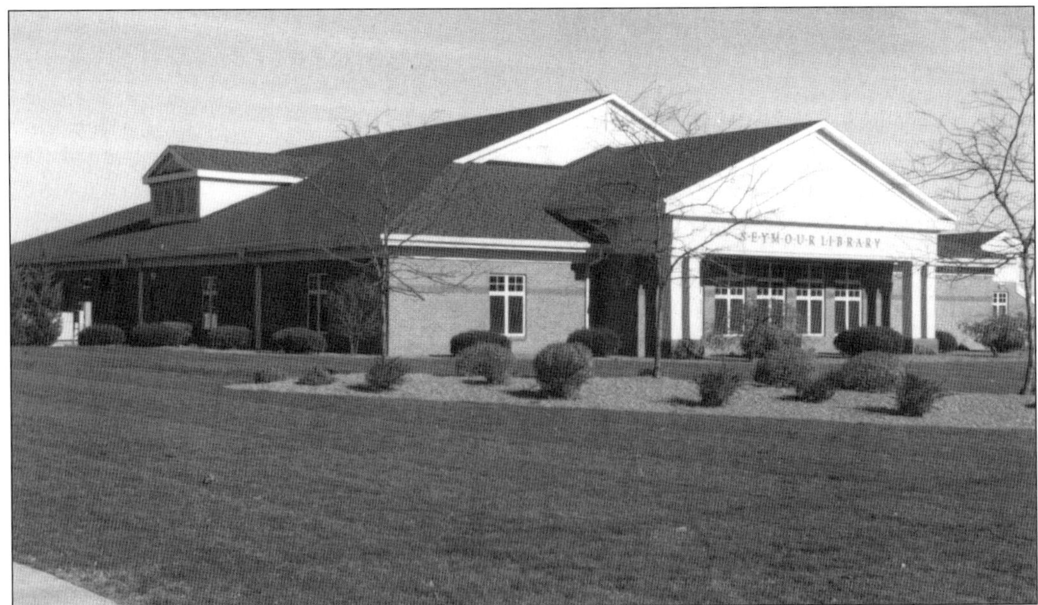

THE SEYMOUR LIBRARY. Over the years, the Seymour Library was expanded and was used and supported by residents of Sweden, Clarkson, and Hamlin, as well as Brockport. By the 1990s, the State Street building had become overcrowded. A bond issue financed a handsome new structure on East Avenue, which opened in 1996, with Mark Jacarino as director.

JAMES H. SEYMOUR. James Horatio Seymour, William H. Seymour's younger son, moved to Sault Ste. Marie, Michigan, where his older brother, Henry Seymour, had a reaper factory and, later, lumber and farming business. When William Seymour died, his daughter, Helen Sylvester, inherited the family home. When she died, the house went to James H. Seymour. He resided in the home only in summers, California then being his residence. When he died in 1930, he left the property and a $15,000 endowment to the village for a library. In 1936, the 1,400 books in the Community Center were moved to the Seymour building and the Seymour Library (below) opened, with Florence Coller as the first librarian. The structure is pictured before a large one-story wing replaced the open side porch in 1958. The Emily Knapp Local History Museum occupies the top two floors.

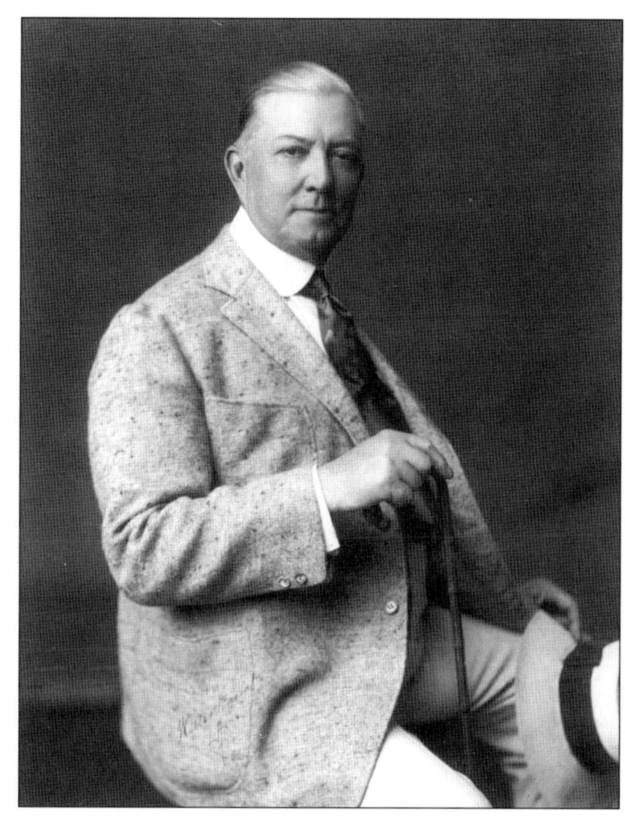

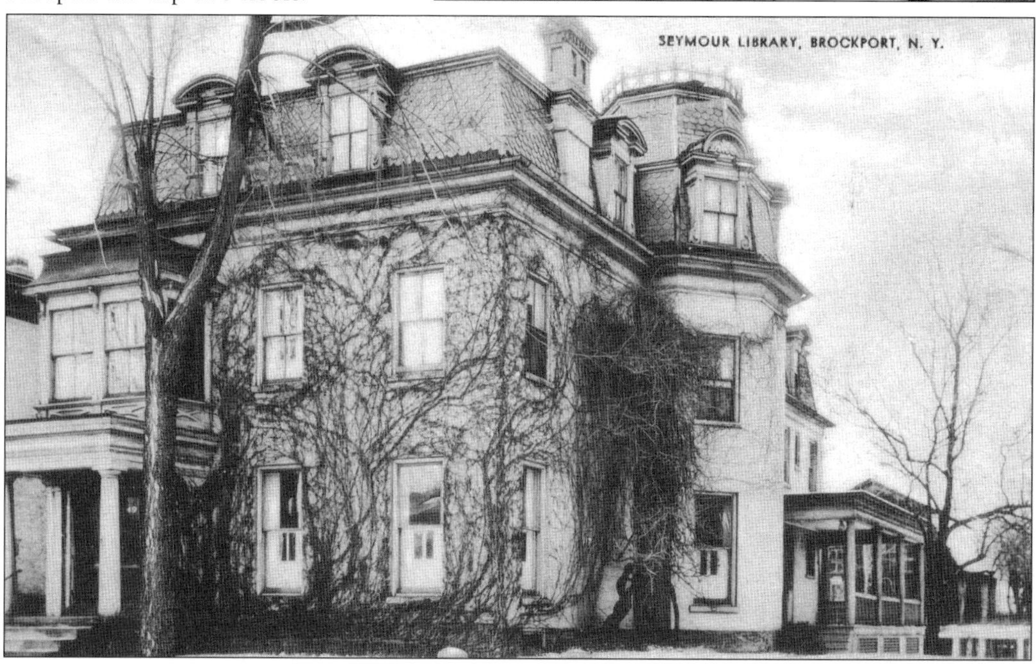

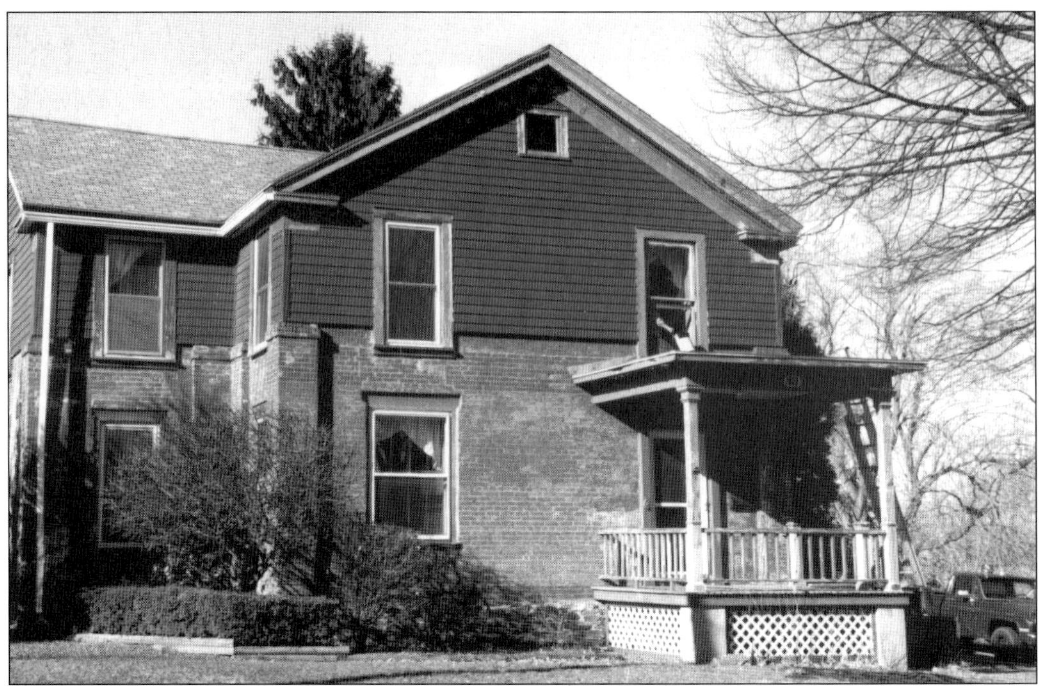

Elementary Schools. Early Brockport had a public school, and several small private schools were conducted in teachers' homes. Three district schools were built *c.* 1850. The only survivor, as a private residence, is on Fayette Street (above). In 1915, the Grammar School (below) replaced the others on the site of a district school at Utica and Holley Streets. That lot had been donated by Hiel Brockway. The Grammar School was succeeded by the Barclay (1956), Ginther (1961), and Hill (1990) schools on Allen Street. Also, Brockport has had Catholic schools (page 92), a grade school at the normal school and its successors (page122) from 1867 to 1981, and classes for kindergarten through eighth grade at Christ Community Church, on Allen Street, since 1982.

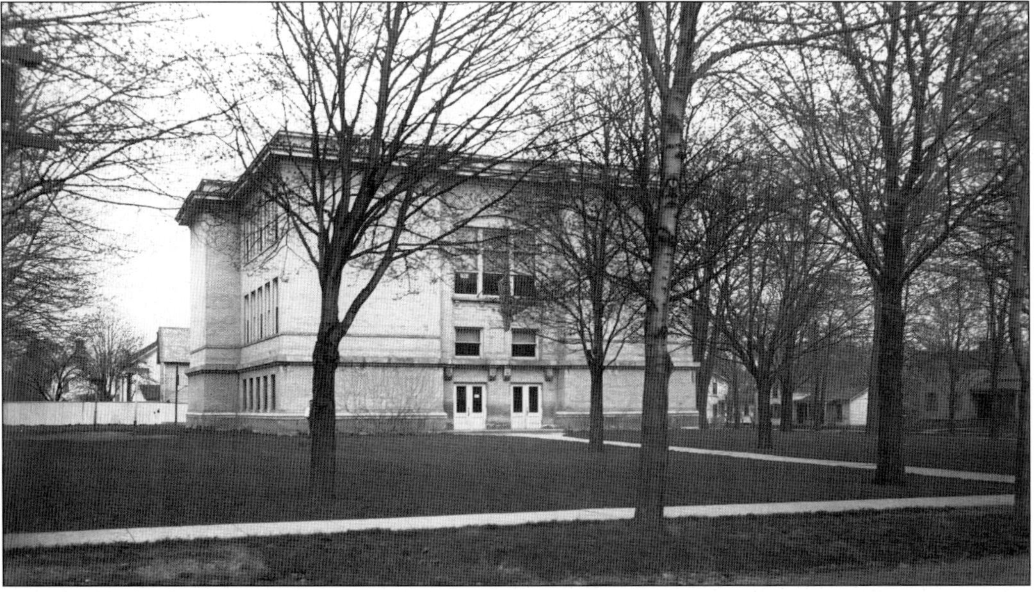

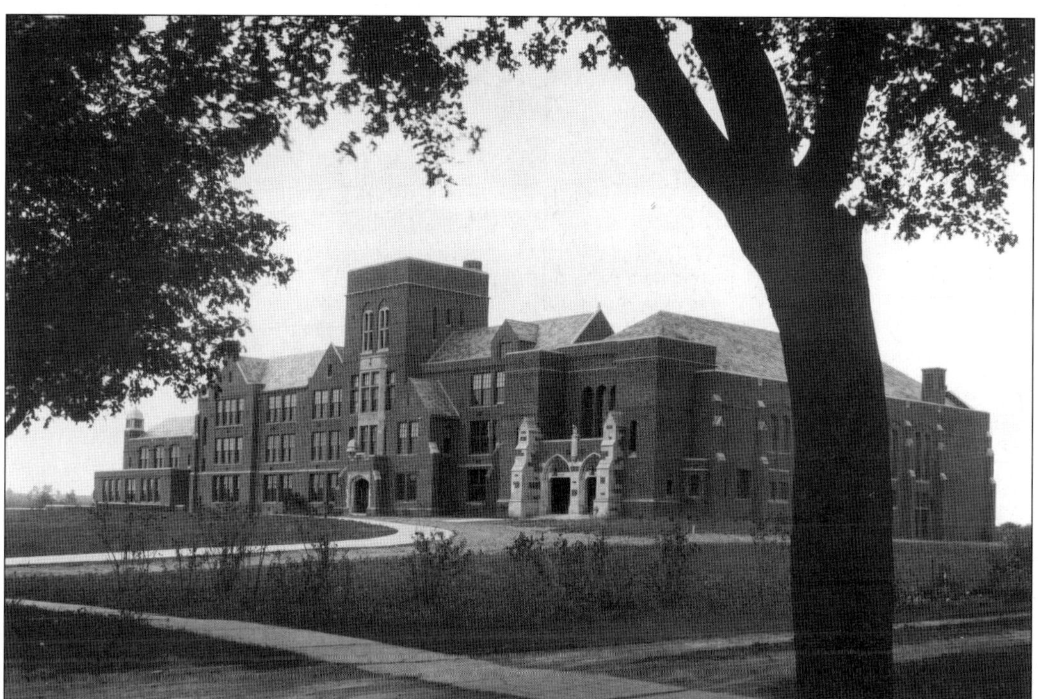

Secondary Schools. The Baptist college in 1835, the Brockport Collegiate Institute from 1841, and the normal school after 1867 provided secondary education to village residents. In 1925, the state ended the high school program. In 1927, the village organized the first consolidated school district in the county and the second in the state, and built a handsome neo-Gothic structure (above) on Allen Street. It opened in 1934 and became a middle school when a new high school building opened in 1967. The high school with later additions (below) is pictured in November 2001.

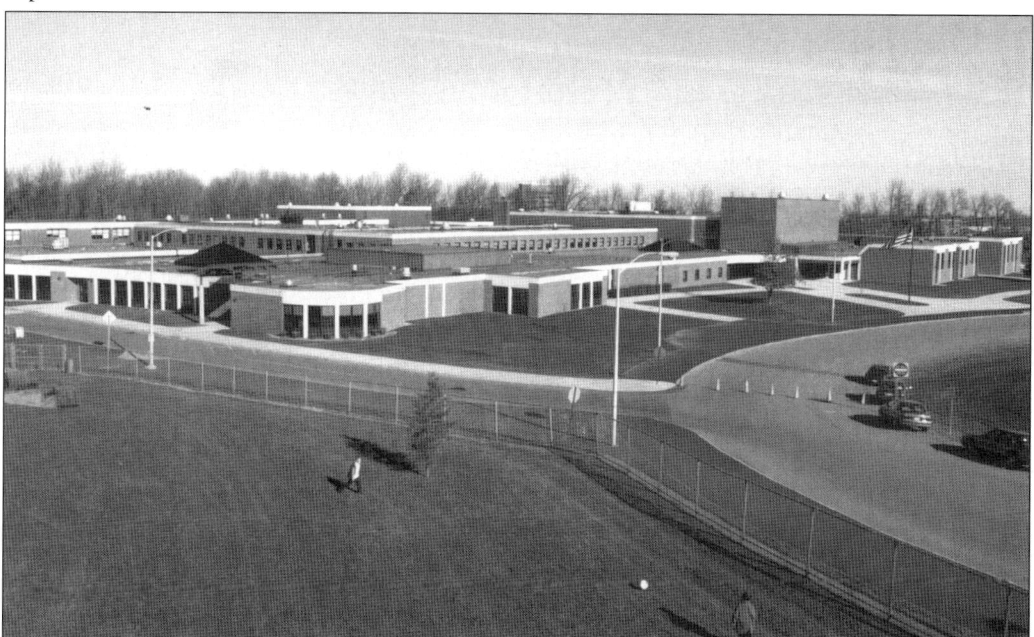

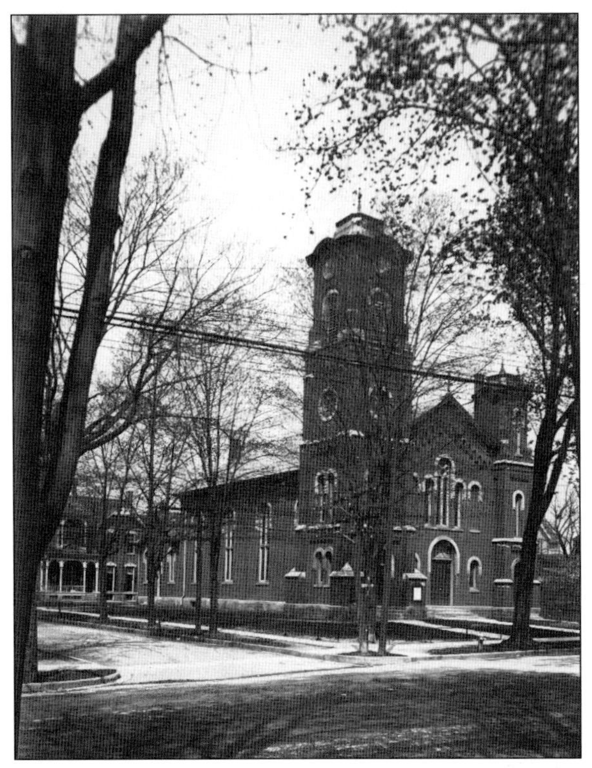

BAPTISTS. The First Baptist Church of Brockport, at Main and Holley Streets, was one of the three earliest churches in the village. Its first home was a former schoolhouse on the same site, in 1828. The current building was erected in 1863. A south tower spire was removed in 1911–1913. Extensive remodeling was done in the 1920s, and the main entrance was moved from Main Street to Holley Street. A parsonage behind the church on Holley Street was built in 1878 and razed in 1998.

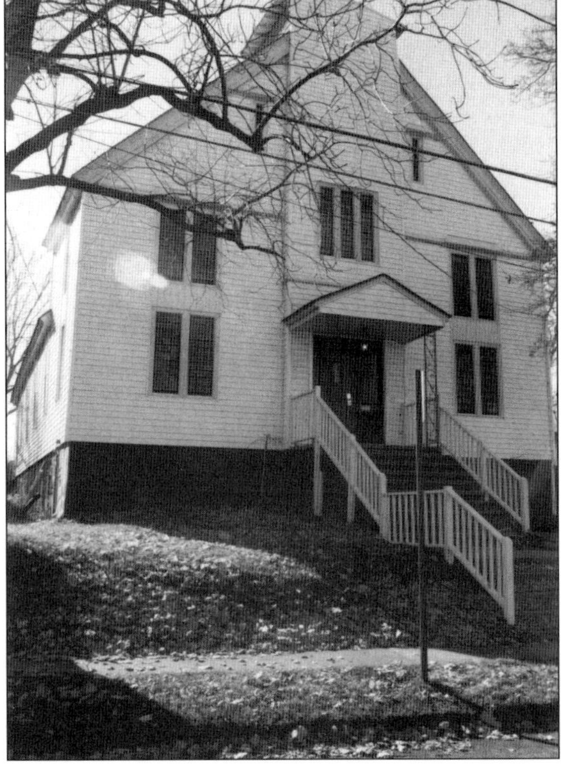

LUTHERANS. An Evangelical Reformed Lutheran Society of Brockport organized in 1862 and built a church on Monroe Avenue where Lathrop Hall now stands. The structure was enlarged in 1871. It was renamed the German Evangelical Association in 1874 but was dissolved in 1909, and the structure became a residence. In 1886, the First German Evangelical Lutheran Concordia formed in Brockport and built a church on Spring Street in 1887. It acquired a parsonage across the street in 1925 and remodeled the church in 1942. In 1960, it bought six acres on Fourth Section Road, built a modern church, and moved there in 1975. The Spring Street structure is now home to a Church of Christ congregation.

METHODISTS. Methodist Episcopal circuit-rider ministers held services in private homes and hotels in the Brockport area as early as 1820. A congregation formed in 1827 and built a church on the north side of Market Street in 1829. The present Romanesque Revival structure at Main and Erie Streets was designed by western New York's leading architect, Andrew Jackson Warner, and was built by Honeoye Falls contractor George S. Wilkinson in 1876. The local Daughters of the American Revolution chapter donated the 1914 clock, which still keeps time.

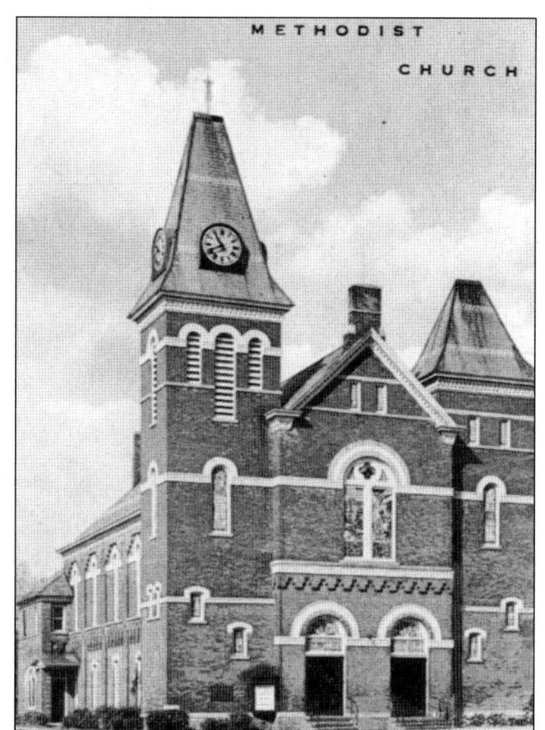

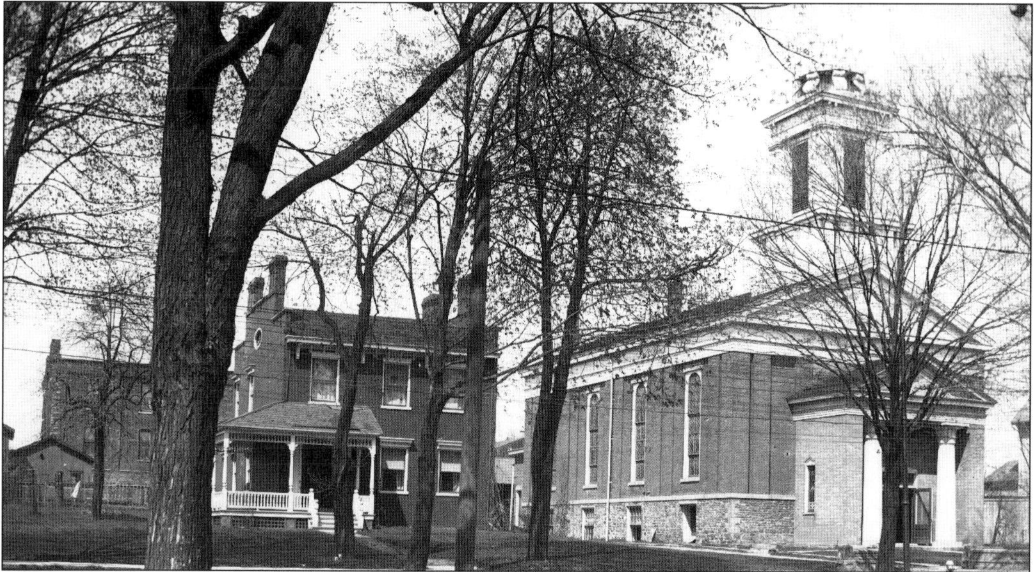

PRESBYTERIANS. A First Congregational Society formed in Brockport in 1827, became a church organization in 1828, and from 1830 to 1831, built a church on the State Street site of the present First Presbyterian Church on a lot donated by James and Mira Seymour (page 26). In 1841, it became "strictly Presbyterian." The original church was replaced by the present Greek Revival structure, erected in 1852. An 1823 house immediately west of the church served as a manse from 1904 until demolished in 1965. An organ chamber was added to the church in 1891, and the structure was enlarged in 1901, 1947, and 1958. The building was listed on the State and National Registers of Historic Places in 1999.

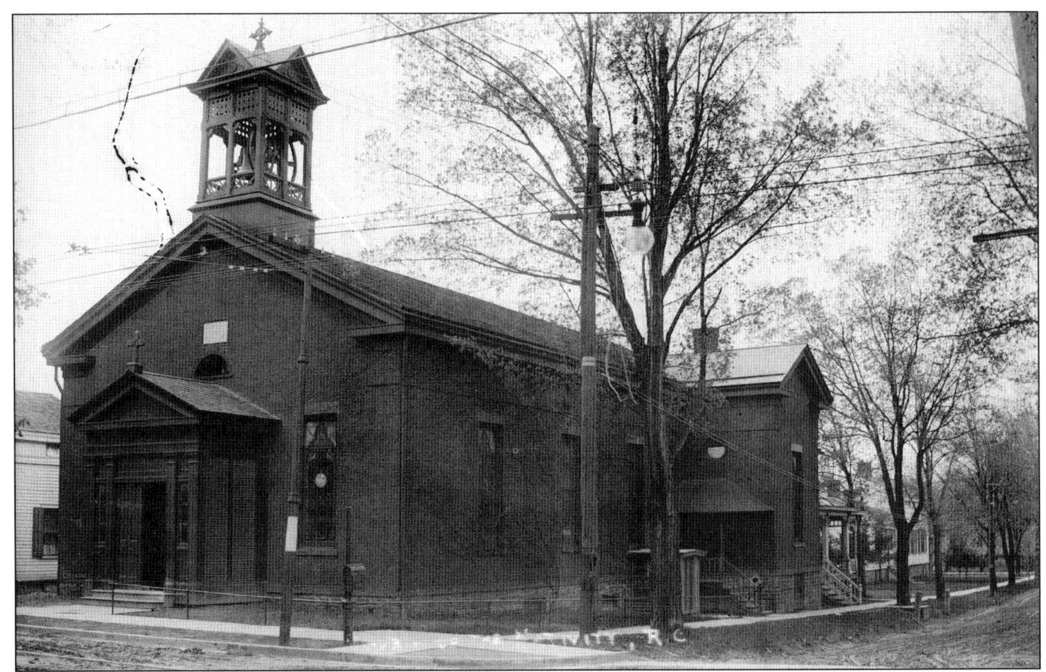

CATHOLICS. A mass was celebrated in Sweden Center in 1843, and the first Roman Catholic congregation was formed in 1848. In 1854, the Nativity of Our Blessed Virgin Mary Church was built at Erie and Utica Streets (above). Directly across Utica Street was the convent and school (below), founded in 1876. Those buildings gave way to a playground in the early 1930s. The original church is now part of the school. The school added a wing in 1915.

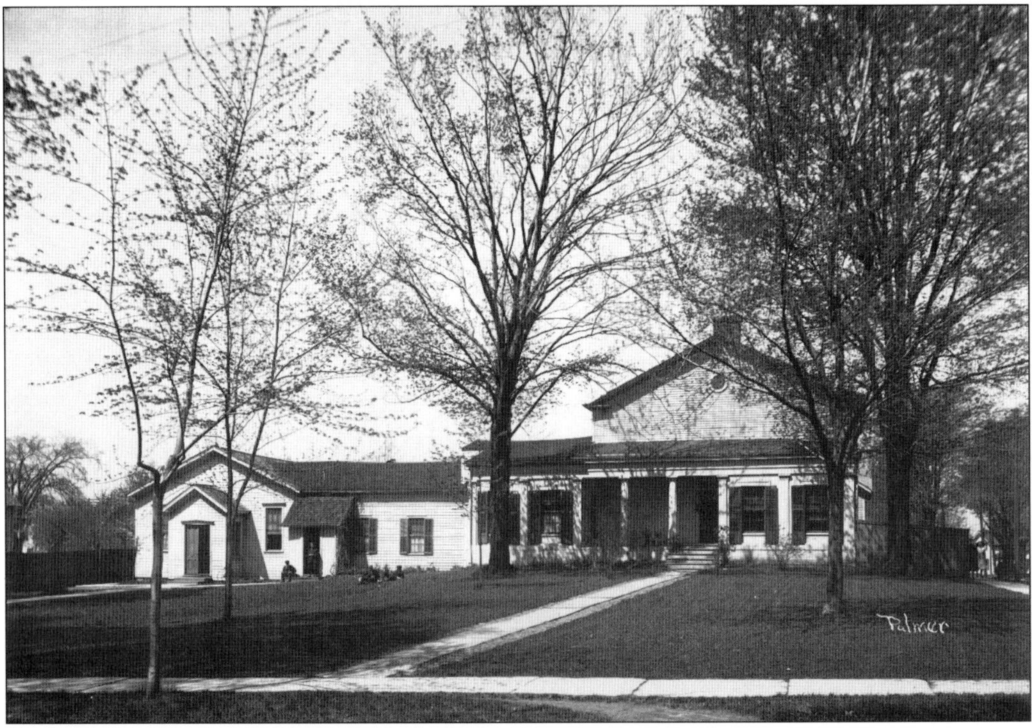

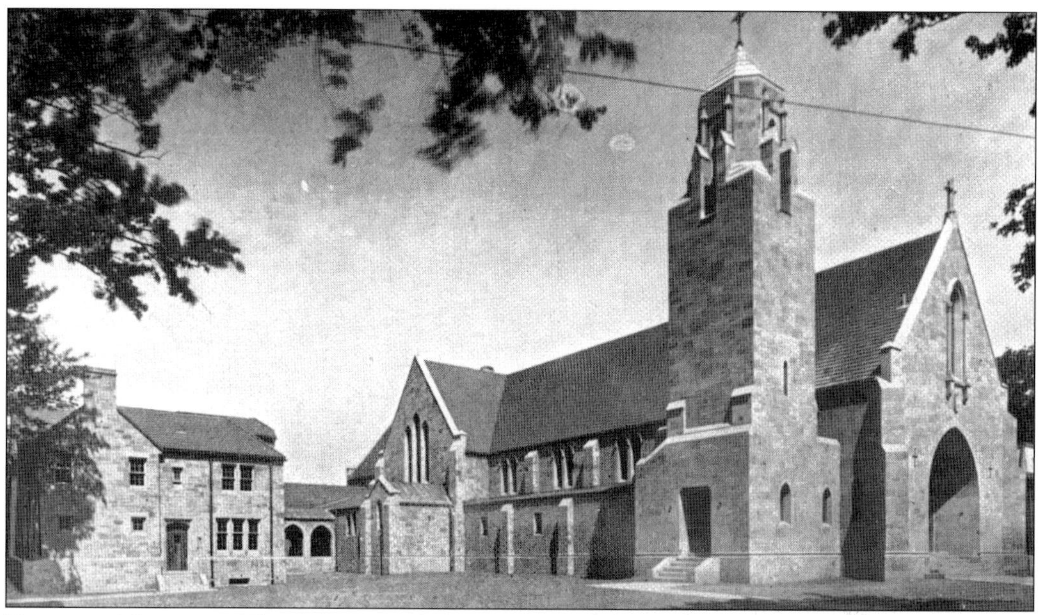

THE 1926 CHURCH. The present English Renaissance–style Catholic church was built in 1926 at Main Street and Monroe Avenue. Also, a Newman Oratory, especially serving State University of New York at Brockport students, is at Adams and Kenyon Streets, adjacent to the campus.

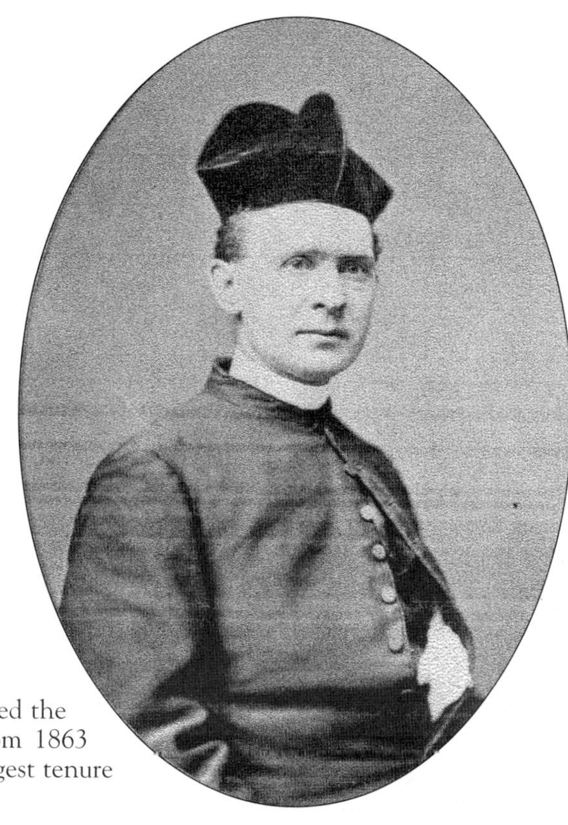

FATHER STORY. Fr. Richard J. Story served the Brockport congregation for 51 years, from 1863 until his death at age 81 in 1914, the longest tenure of any priest in Brockport.

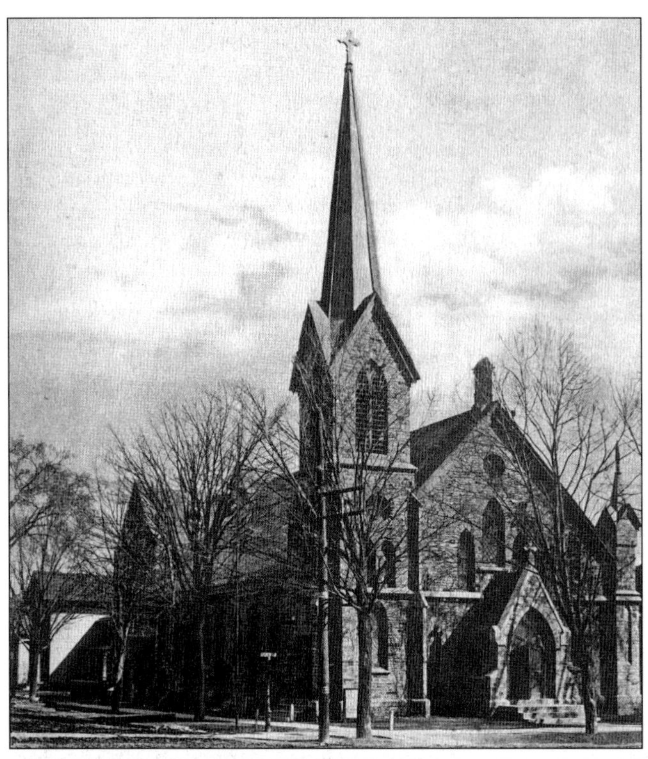

EPISCOPALIANS. St. Luke's Parish formed in Brockport in 1838 and met in the village hall or the Free Will Baptist Church. In 1855, the present limestone and Medina sandstone structure was erected at Main and State Streets. It was remodeled in 1873, and the front door was painted red in 1956 in accordance with widespread Anglican and Episcopalian practice. A parish house, built with money donated in memory of Mrs. Richard Cutts Shannon (pages 74 and 75), was added to the rear of the church in 1903 on land given by Jane E. Cary.

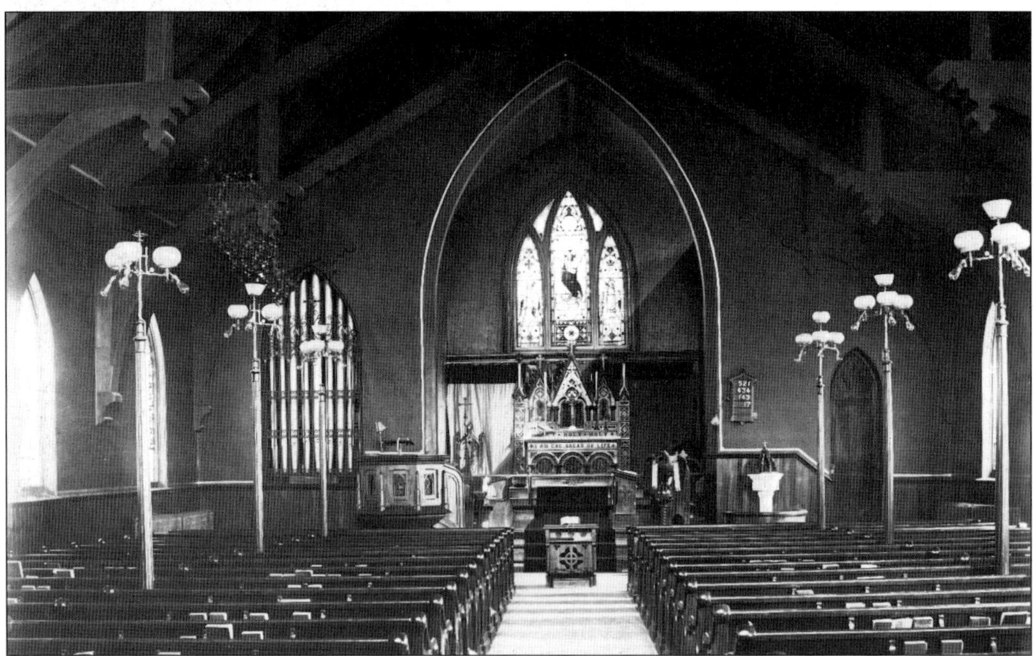

AN INTERIOR VIEW. The gothic interior of the church reflects the exterior Neo-Gothic architecture. The organ was a gift from the estate of Mrs. Richard Cutts Shannon. In 1990, the church was listed on the State and National Registers of Historic Places. Among other churches in Brockport have been a Free Methodist congregation on Perry Street, which moved to Fourth Section Road, and Christ Community Church, on Allen Street.

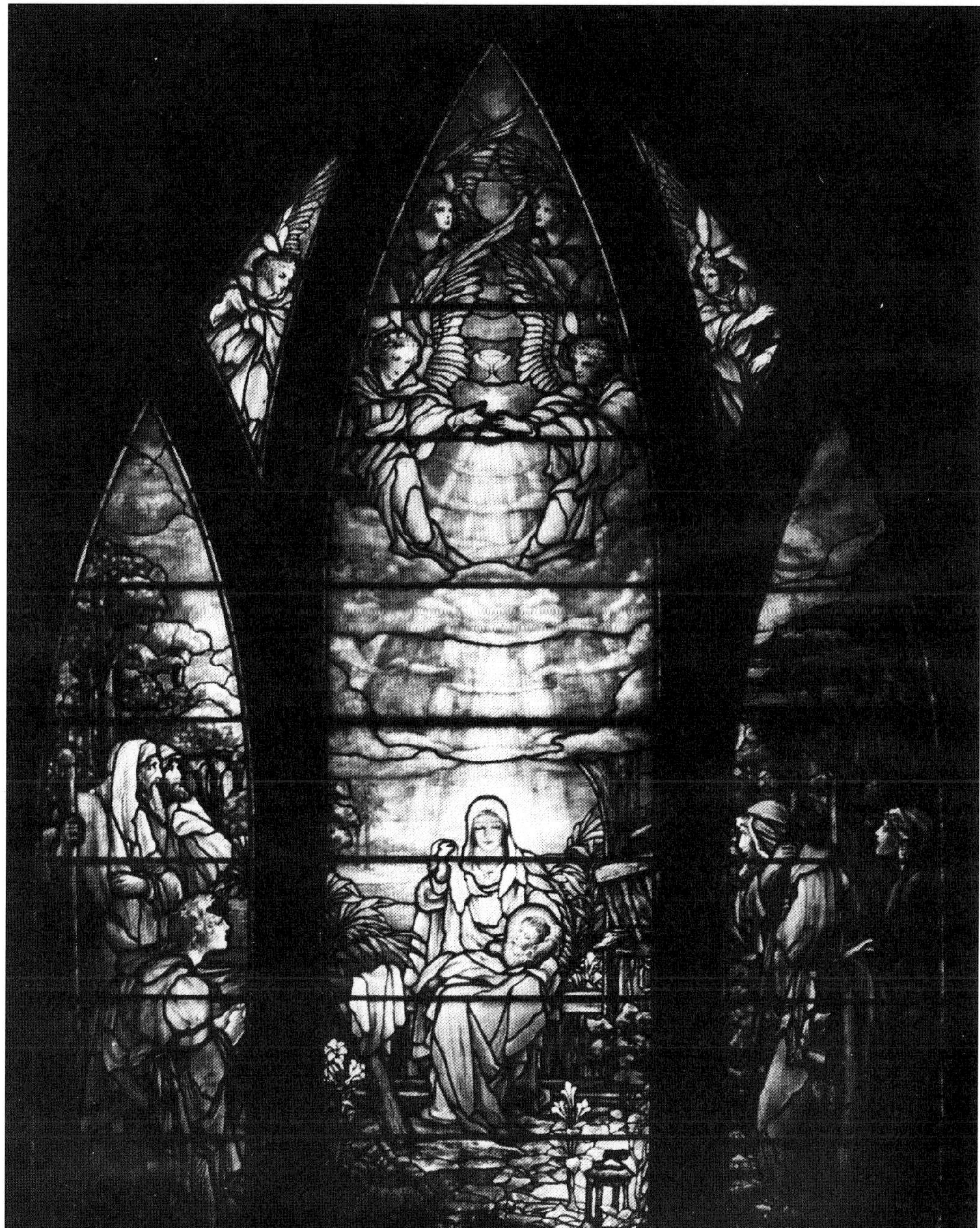

TIFFANY WINDOWS. St. Luke's has six stained glass windows from the L.C. Tiffany studios. The largest of them is this nativity scene in the east wall above the altar. Sara Morgan Manning gave it as a memorial to her son, Arnold Morgan Manning, who died in 1916 at age 21. A reproduction of it was the centerpiece of the Eastman Kodak Company Christmas display at New York City's Grand Central Station in 1955.

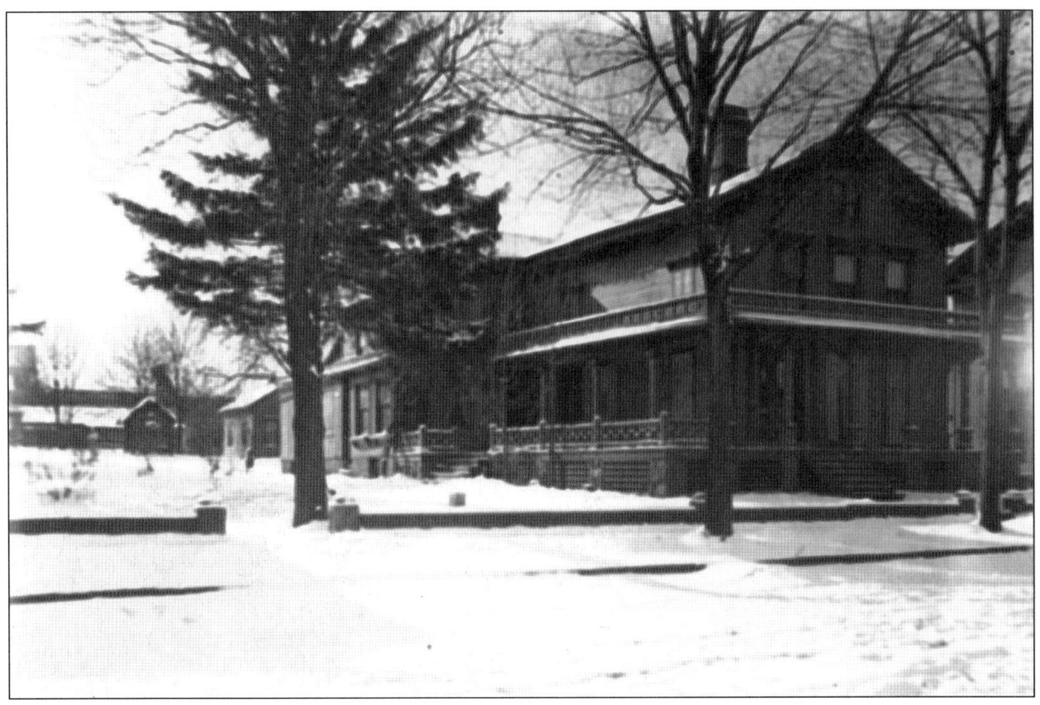

THE BROWN COTTAGE. Popular literature came to American women from Brockport. Mary Jane Holmes (1828–1907), who lived in this College Street house for more than half a century, was one of the first novelists to write a large body of fiction especially for the average American woman. She attained such national celebrity that her home became a tourist attraction, drawing travelers to the village. Postcards such as these were souvenirs. Her husband, Daniel Holmes (1828–1917), was a lawyer, village clerk for 20 years, justice of the peace for 30 years, and secretary of the normal school board for 50 years.

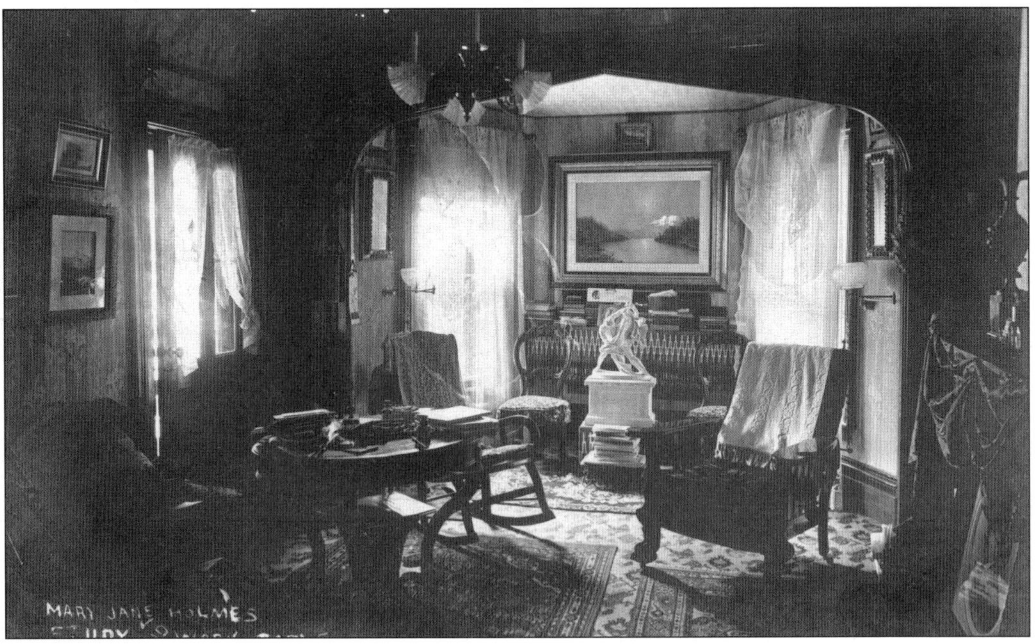

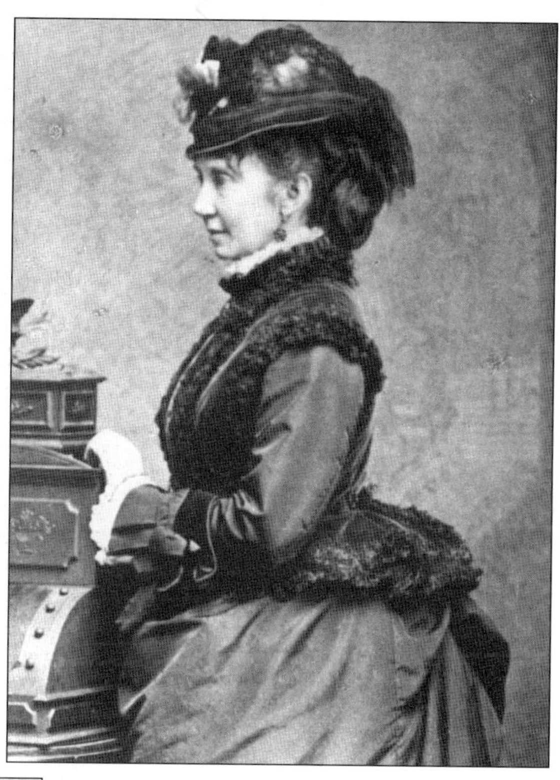

Mary Jane Holmes. From 1854 to 1905, Brockport's famous authoress (right) produced some 40 novels and collections of short stories, which had sold over two million copies by the 1890s. Her works were published under numerous titles in some 900 editions by more than 40 different publishers. They were popular, sanitized romances with moral lessons, contrived plots, and invariably happy endings. Their tone is reflected in the *'Lena Rivers* book cover (below).

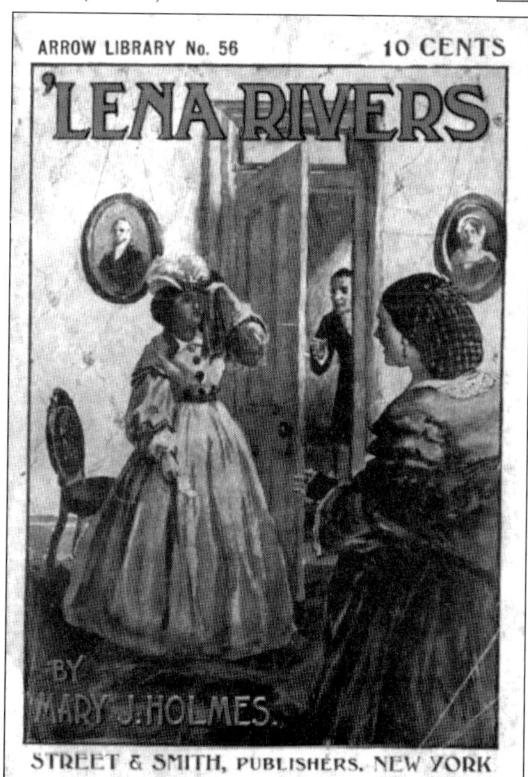

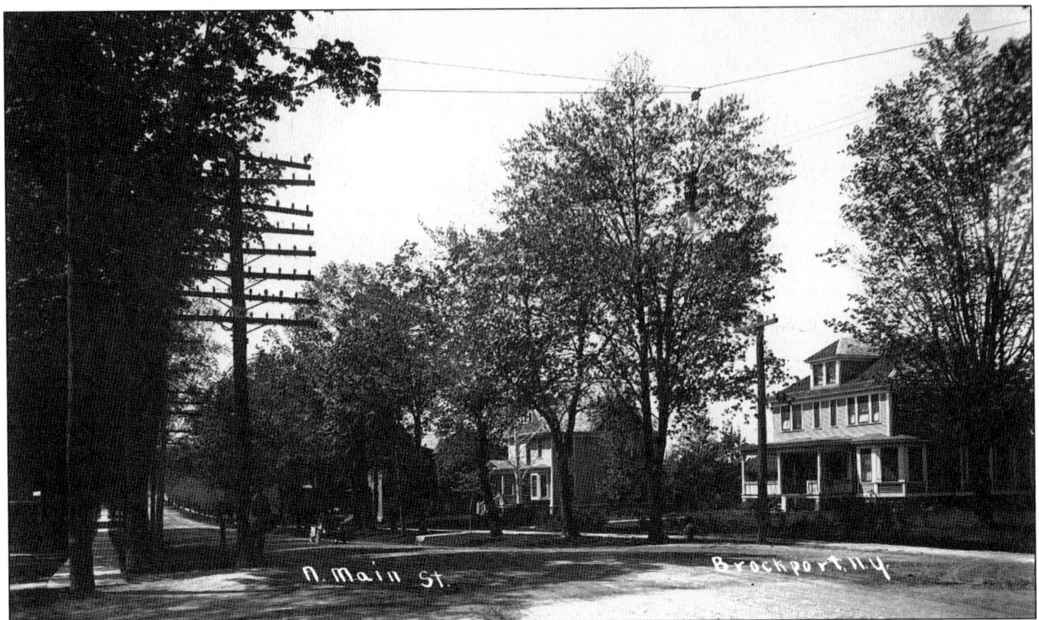

MAIN STREET. Pictured above is North Main Street in 1910, looking south from East Avenue. Clark Veazie, a traveling salesman, lived in the third house across the street. In 1962, these homes were replaced by commercial buildings. Pictured below is Main Street in 1910, looking north from the railroad tracks. The nearest house on the left was the home of Manley Shafer, partner in the Moore-Shafer Shoe Manufacturing Company (page 50). The second house was owned but not occupied by Edward Harrison (pages 66 and 111). The third house was on the site of Hiel Brockway's home (page 41) and was built by John D. Burns, a Civil War veteran and lawyer. Later, it belonged to John Hazen, a physician, and is now the Webster Funeral Home. The houses on the right belonged to harness maker Christian Neidthardt, Mary Raleigh, and Susan Cornes, widow of a leading Brockport businessman.

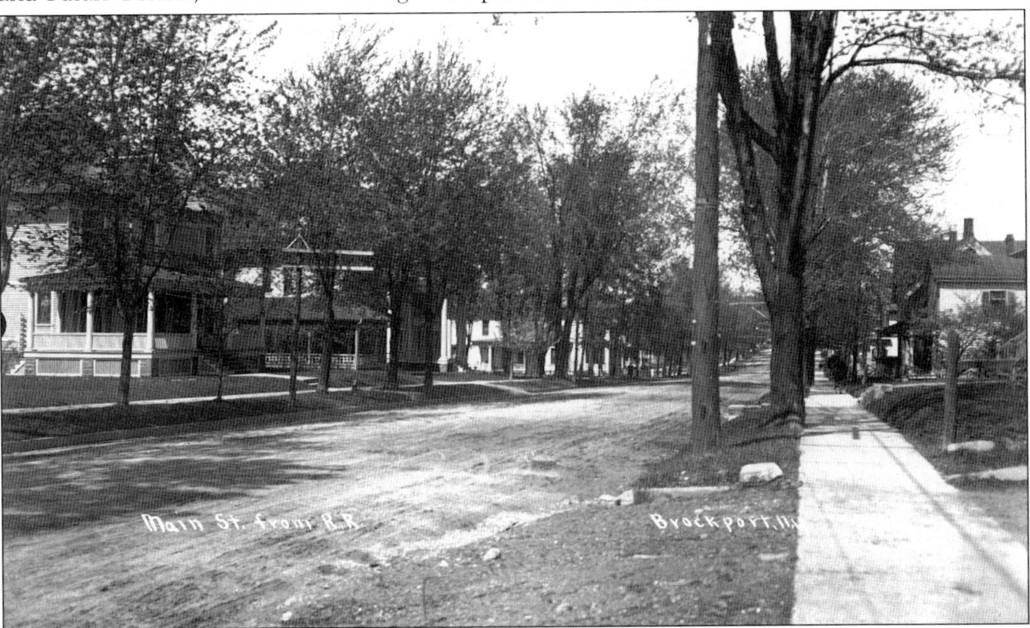

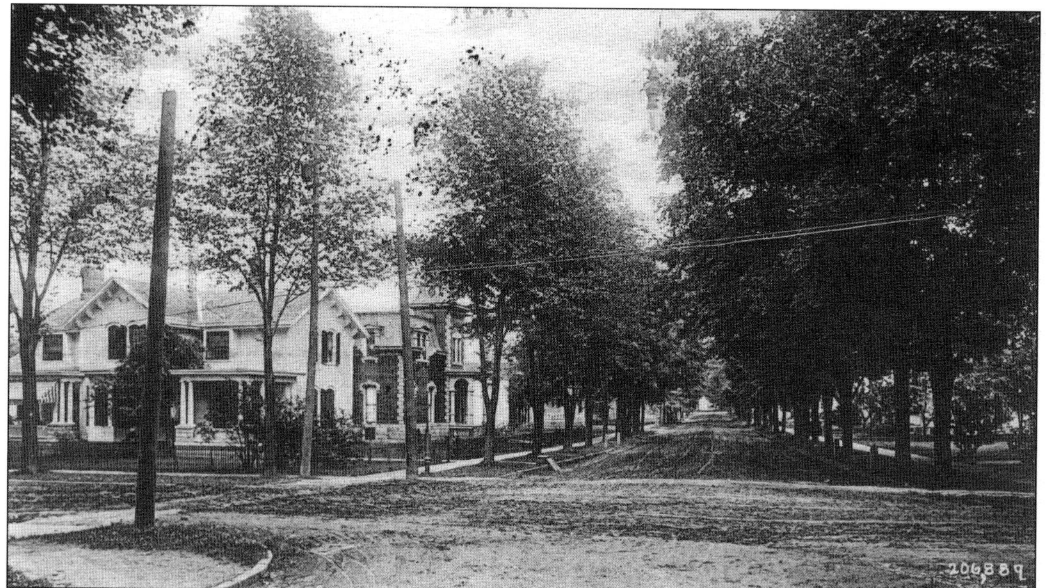

College and South Streets. Pictured above is College Street, looking east from Utica Street in 1908. The nearest house was the home of Thomas H. Dobson and, later, his son, Harold Dobson (pages 62 and 86). Next door was Lucius T. Underhill, who built both houses, owned a lumberyard and a roller flour mill, developed real estate, and built homes. Also, he served as town supervisor and village trustee. The third house was owned by Daniel Holmes (page 96), who lived near the far end of the street. These structures still stand. Below is South Street c. 1910, looking west from Park Avenue. The houses on the left were the homes of Mrs. Charles Baker, Elizabeth Brown, and Ida M.Gordon, widow of G.C. Gordon (pages 76 and 77). Those on the right belonged to Biencia Miller, jeweler Hiram D. Randall, and H.A. Metcalf, an officer of the Brockport Piano Company (page 51).

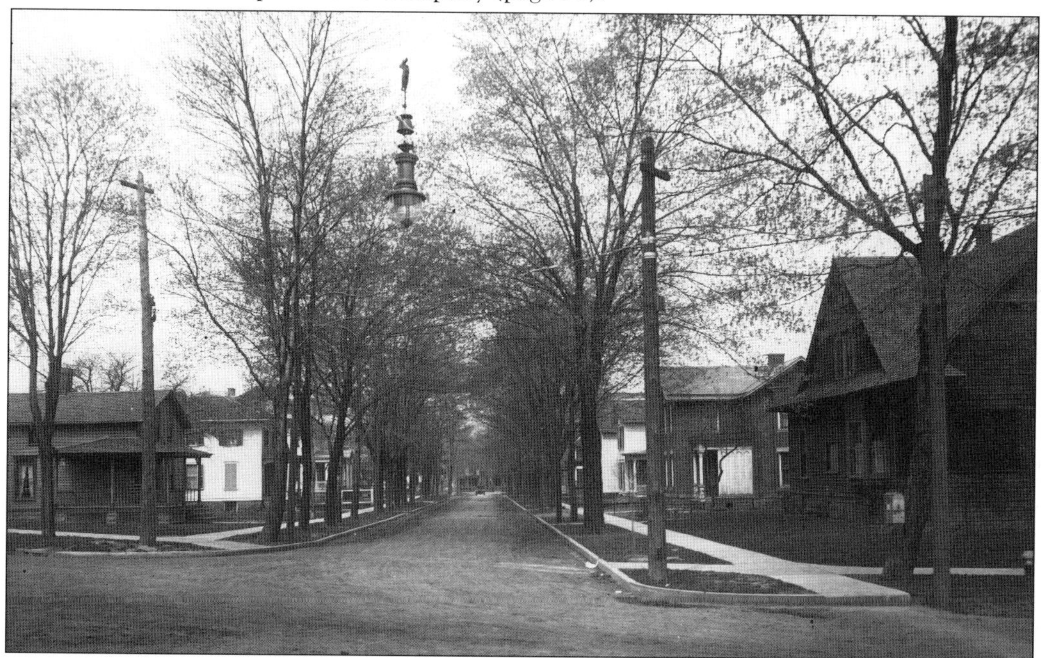

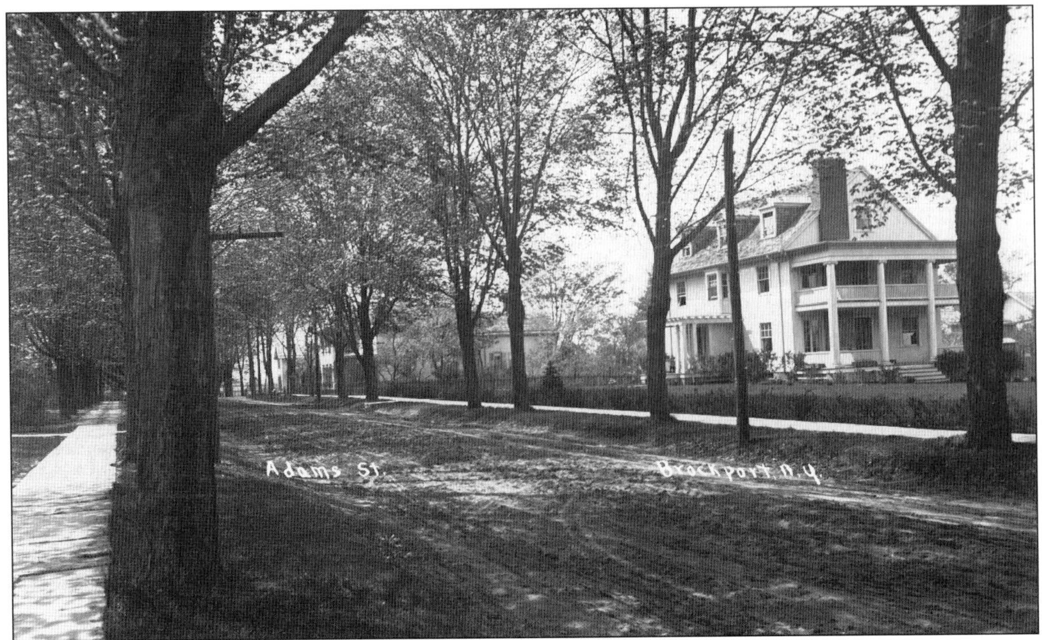

Adams Street. This 1910 photograph looks west along Adams Street in southwestern Brockport. The home of Milo Cleveland, a civil engineer who helped build the reconstructed Barge Canal, is on the right. It was built by his father, Merritt A. Cleveland, a contractor and chief engineer in the construction of several U.S. and Canadian railroads and canals. It now serves as the Newman Center, with rooms and a religious and social meeting place for Catholic college students. The houses in the background have been replaced by Cooper Hall, on the college campus.

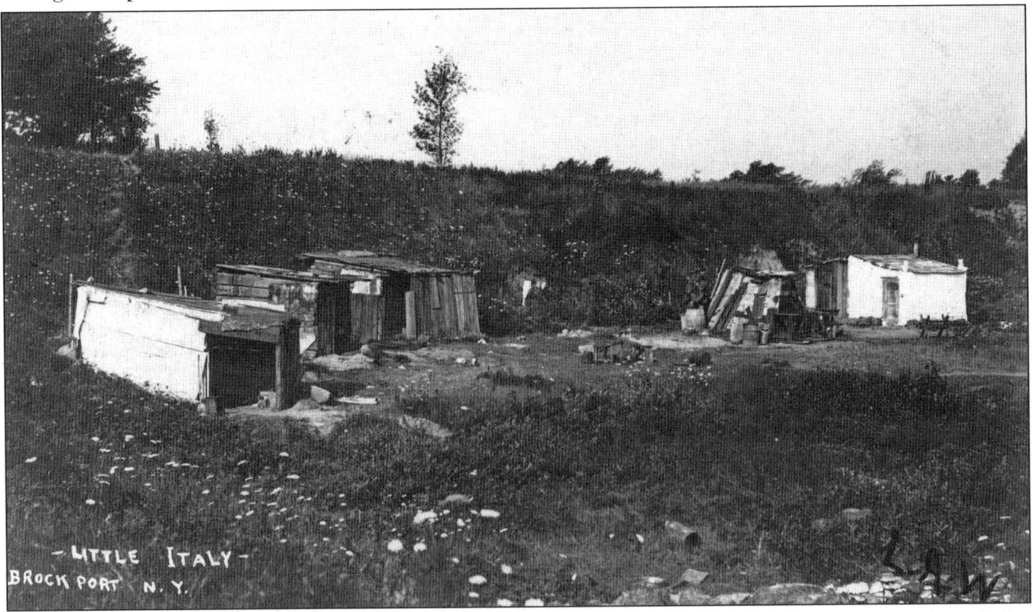

Little Italy. This 1907 postcard shows five hovels near the canal bank on the edge of the village. They probably were occupied by Italian immigrant manual workers employed in the reconstruction of the canal that was under way at that time.

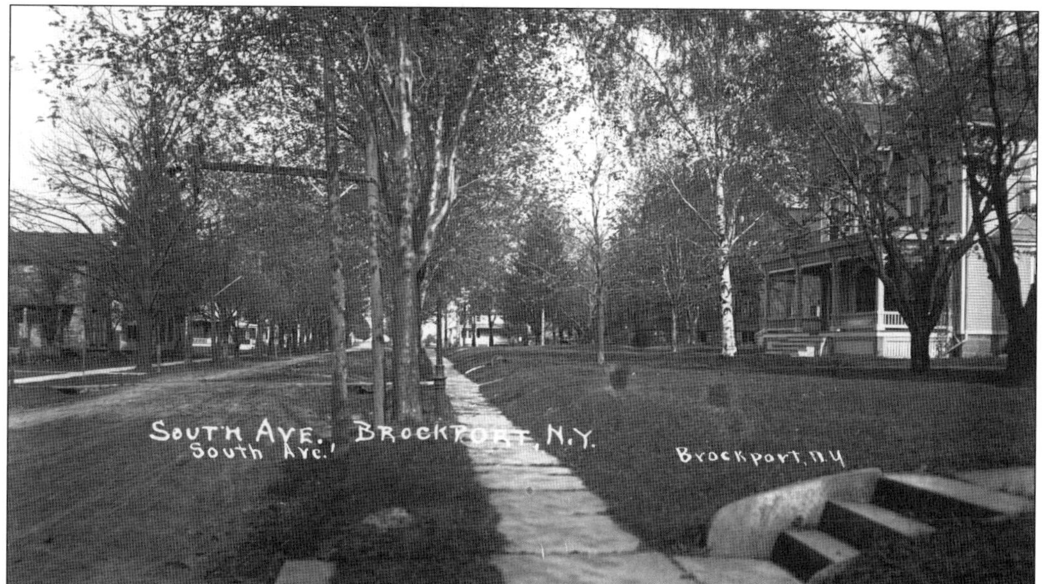

SOUTH AVENUE. This 1910 photograph shows, at the time, the most southerly street on the east side of Main Street. A.T. Wells, a salesman, lived in the house on the far right. Next door was William D. Dailey, owner of the Dailey Canning Company (page 53) and one of the largest coal and produce dealers in western New York. One son, Vincent Dailey, was a top aide to Governor Lehman *c.* 1940 and New York State Democratic party chairman. Another son, Donald Dailey, was commissioner of public safety and postmaster of Rochester. Two other sons were state golf champions. The Dailey house was demolished *c.* 1995.

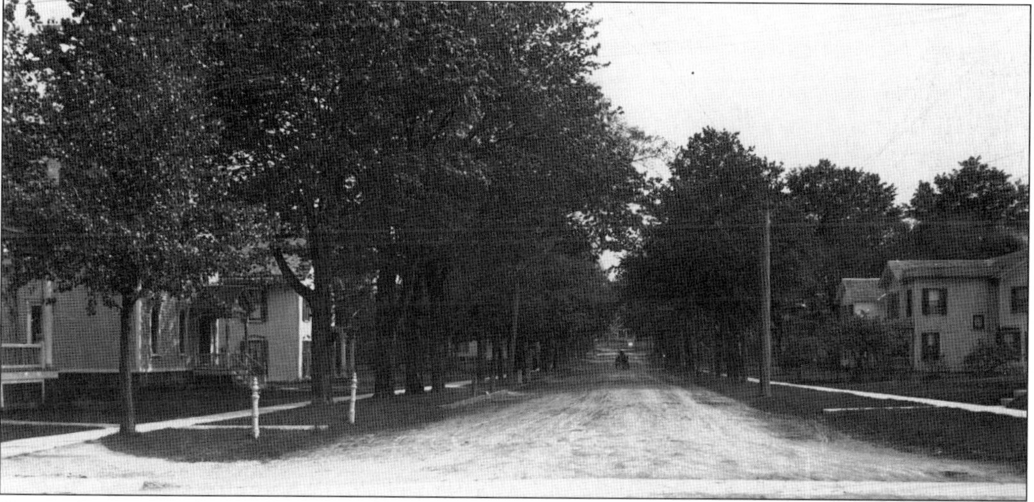

PARK AVENUE. This 1910 photograph of a fashionable east side street shows the Dauchy family house on the right. O.W. and Oscar Dauchy farmed near the village. J.F. Dauchy had a furniture and undertaking business on South Main Street. The porch on the extreme left was on the home of Dr. Willis C. Cook, village health officer and a leading physician. His grandfather Lemuel Cook died in Clarendon in 1863 at age 107, the last surviving veteran of the Revolutionary War. The next house belonged to F.T. Sparlin, who owned farmland on South Lake Road and West Avenue. The third house was the home of John R. Davis, proprietor of a Main Street grocery store.

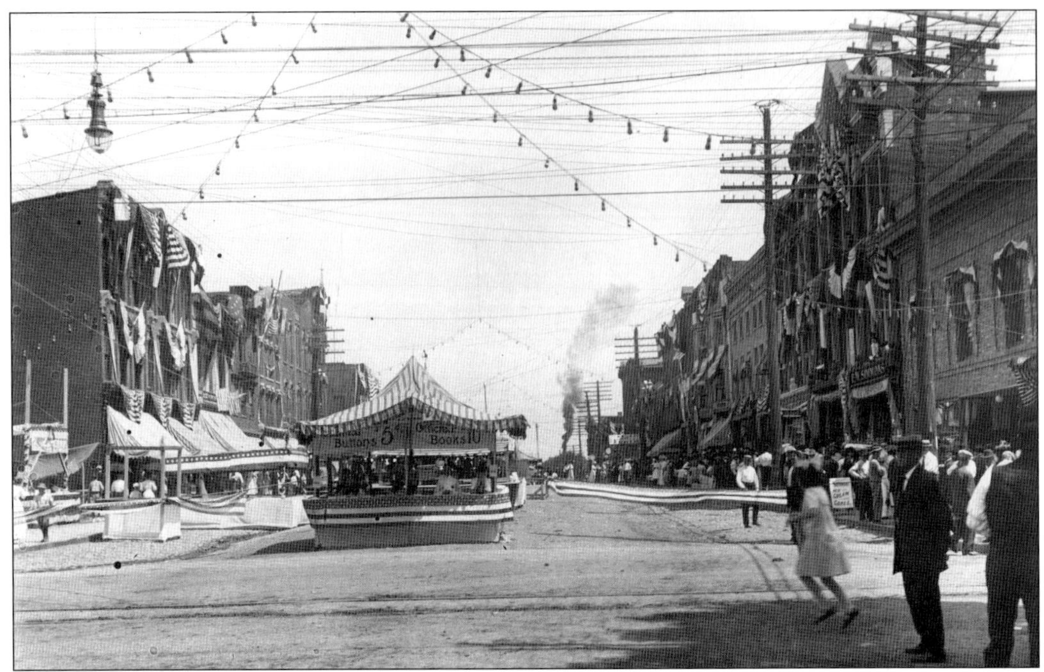

A CELEBRATION. Brockport's greatest celebration was Old Home Week, July 2–9, 1911. Vending booths occupied Main Street. On Sunday, all churches had special services. Monday featured a parade, sports, and games for 3,000 children. Tuesday's highlights were "a grand military and civic parade" (below), concerts, sports, a keynote address, and fireworks. Wednesday was Athletic Day. Thursday was Firemen's Day, with 60 companies. Friday was Fraternal Day, with a "grand parade of Societies and Lodges in uniform from the Cities and Towns of Western New York." Saturday was Rochester Day, with addresses by Rochester luminaries, an industrial parade, and fireworks.

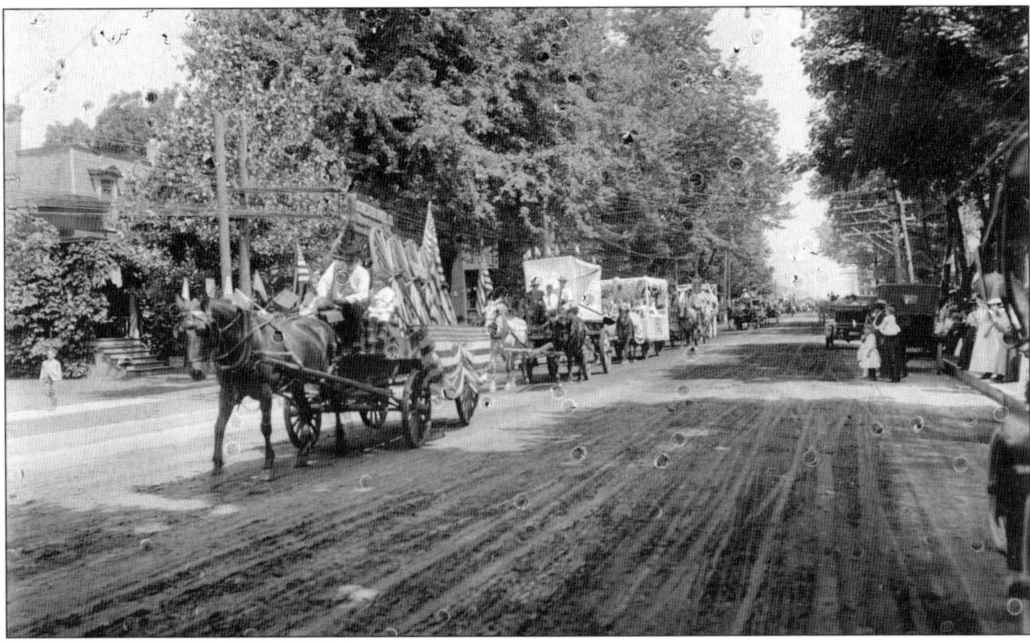

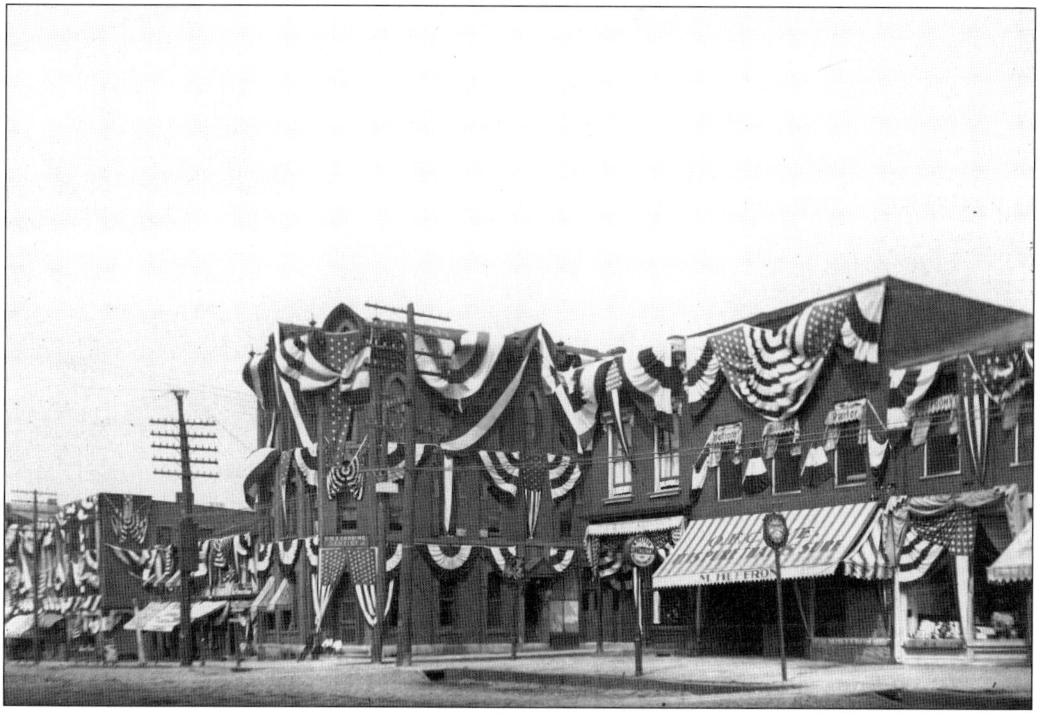

DECORATIONS. Main Street buildings were festooned with bunting and banners during Old Home Week. The Decker Block (page 69) is in the center.

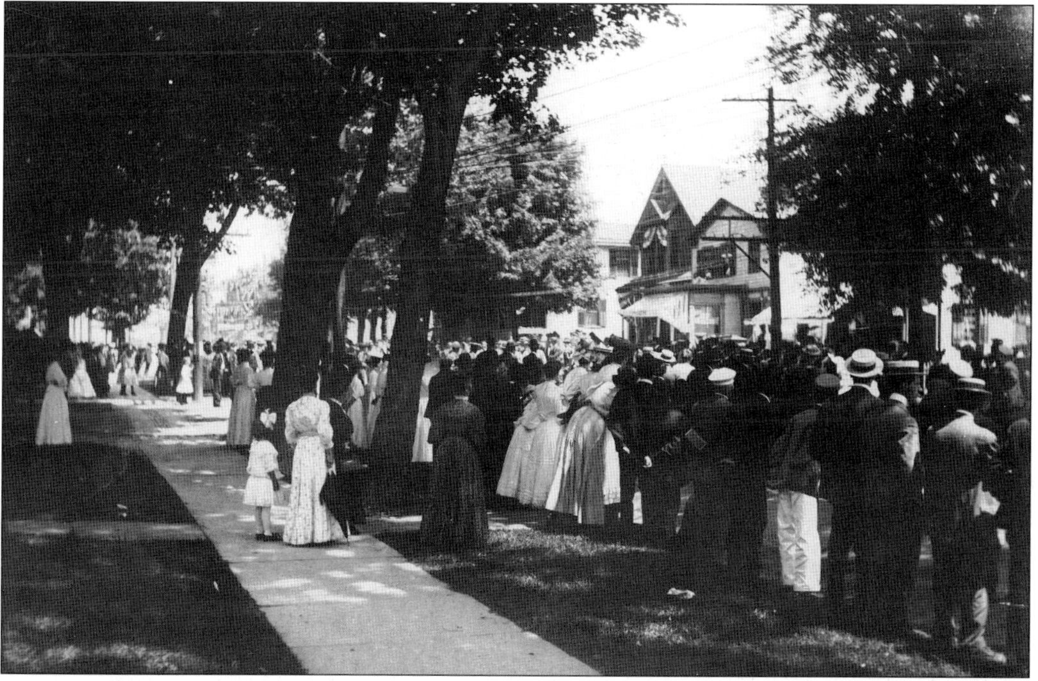

CROWDS. Brockporters and residents of neighboring towns turned out massively for Old Home Week activities. This crowd is awaiting a parade on Main Street. Bunting can be seen on homes in the background.

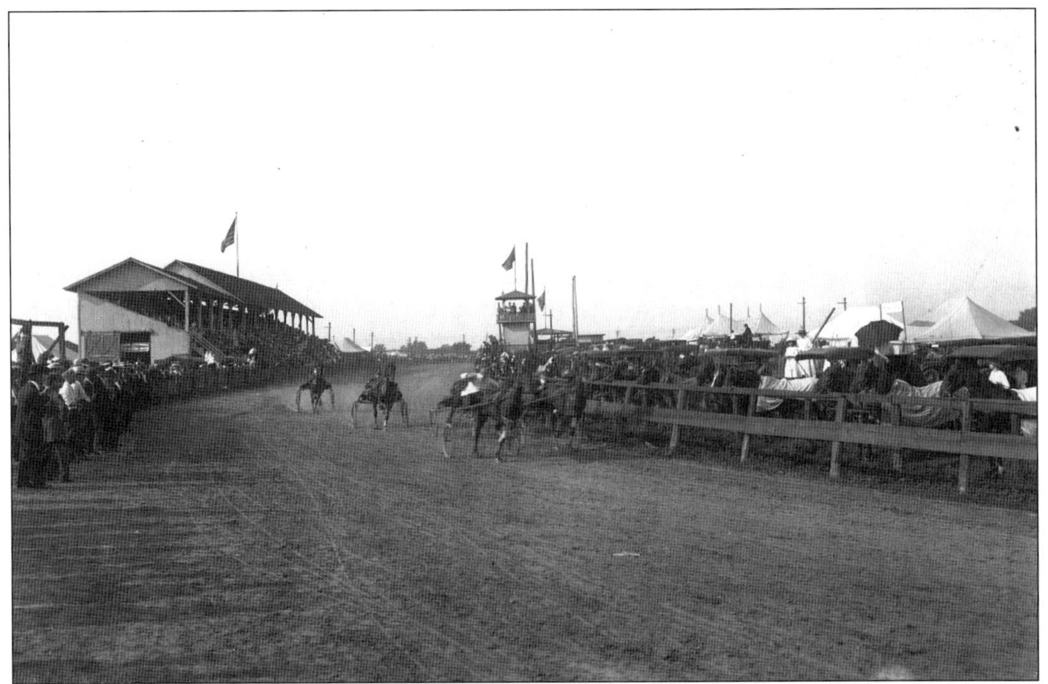

THE COUNTY FAIR. For many years, a major event each autumn was a county agricultural fair. It began in 1859, expired in 1869, came back to life in 1877, and left Brockport in 1932. Typically, the fair lasted four or five days. Two favorite activities were horse racing and auto racing, for which a half-mile track and substantial grandstand were built. These trotters raced on September 6, 1912. The stadium was also the home field for the Brockport Freezers, a semiprofessional baseball team.

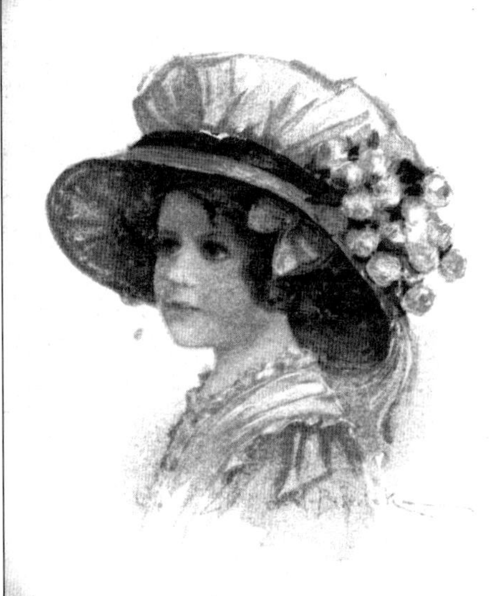

Keep This Blotter!

It is good if presented by a
School Child, for
ONE FREE ADMISSION
to a Tent Show, at Brockport Fair

Thursday, Sept. 2, 1915

Monroe County Fair
BROCKPORT, N. Y.

Sept. 1-2-3-4, 1915

Send for Premium List, W. B. CONKLING, Sec.

A TICKET. This ink blotter is a ticket to a tent show at the 1915 fair. The program for the 1925 fair lists hundreds of categories of competition. The principal classes were horses, cattle, sheep, schoolwork, junior projects, swine, poultry, culinary, fruits, flowers, farm produce, domestic arts, and fine arts.

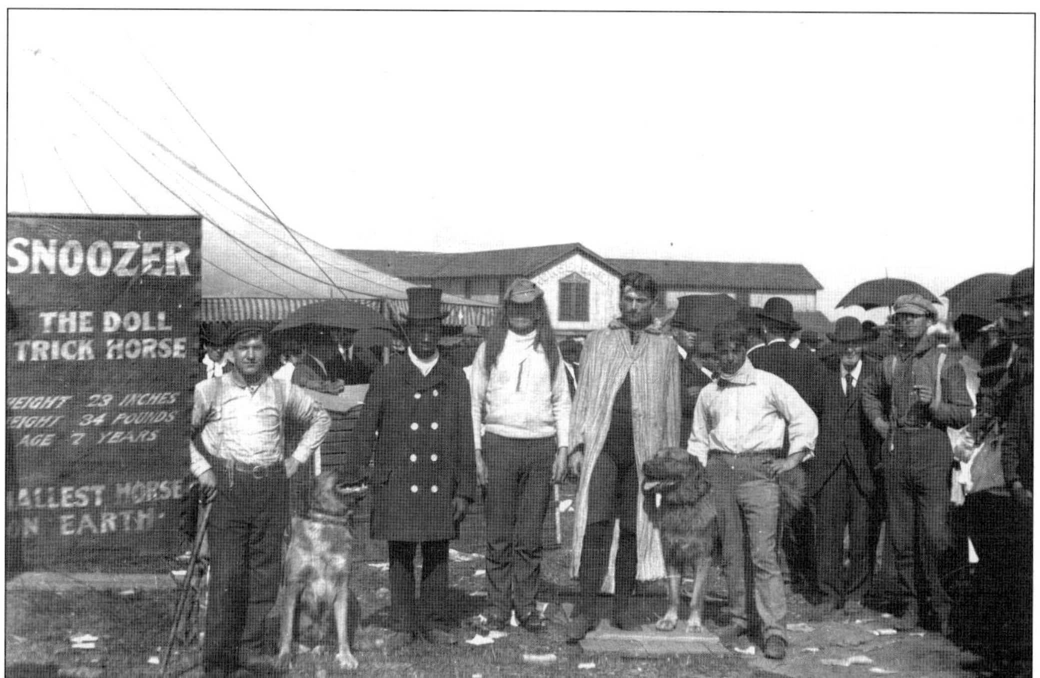

THE TRICK HORSE. The fair included entertainment, such as vaudeville performances, a small circus, band concerts, clowns, freaks and oddities, movies, trained bears, dancing, a "great fireworks exhibit each night," and this trick horse.

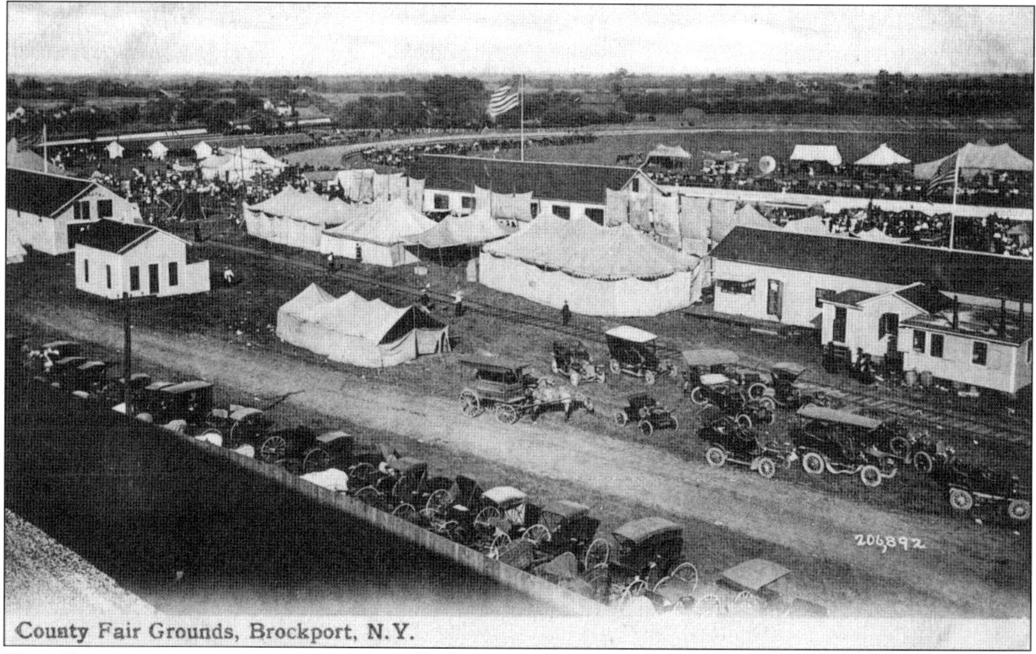

THE FAIRGROUNDS. Permanent buildings at the fairgrounds included a Domestic Hall and a Floral Hall, some livestock sheds, and a dining hall. Large tents were erected especially for the event. The fair was originally located at the end of Fair Street, south of the railroad, but moved later to more spacious grounds at the end of Spring Street, north of the tracks.

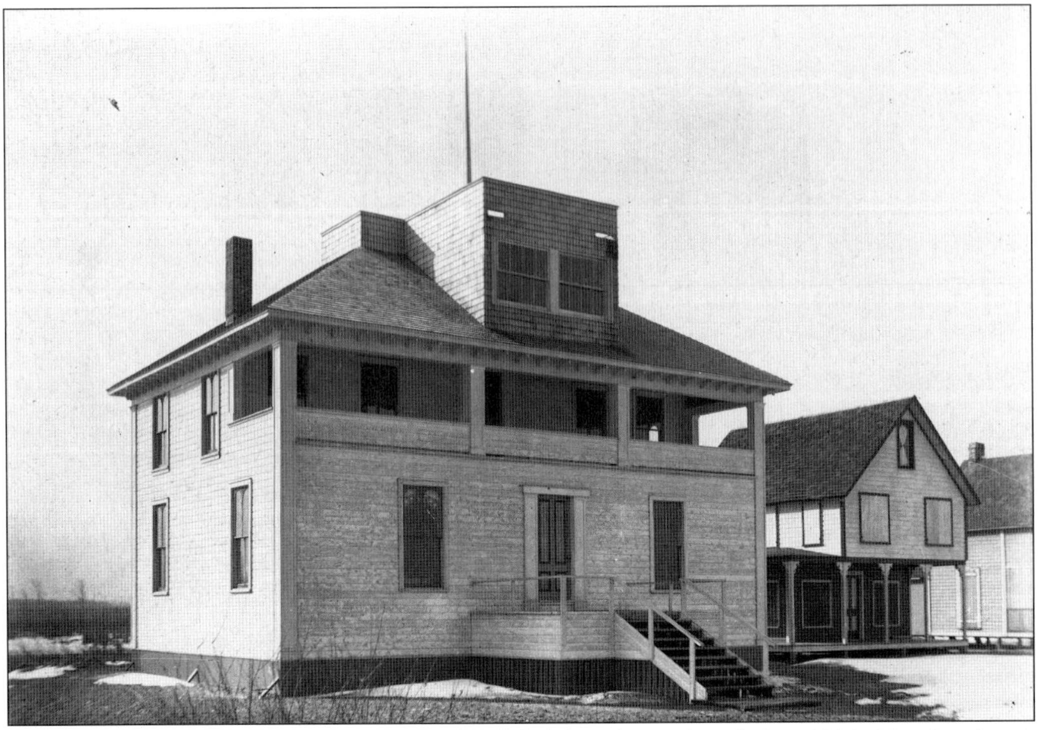

THE BROCKPORT YACHT CLUB. The yacht club (above) was founded in 1904. Membership is restricted to 100 by the capacity of the anchorage. The club has an active social and sailing program, both racing and cruising. The clubhouse was built in 1910 where Sandy Creek enters Lake Ontario, 10 miles north of the village. The buildings in the background are summer cottages. The postcard (below) was mailed July 8, 1907, before the clubhouse was built.

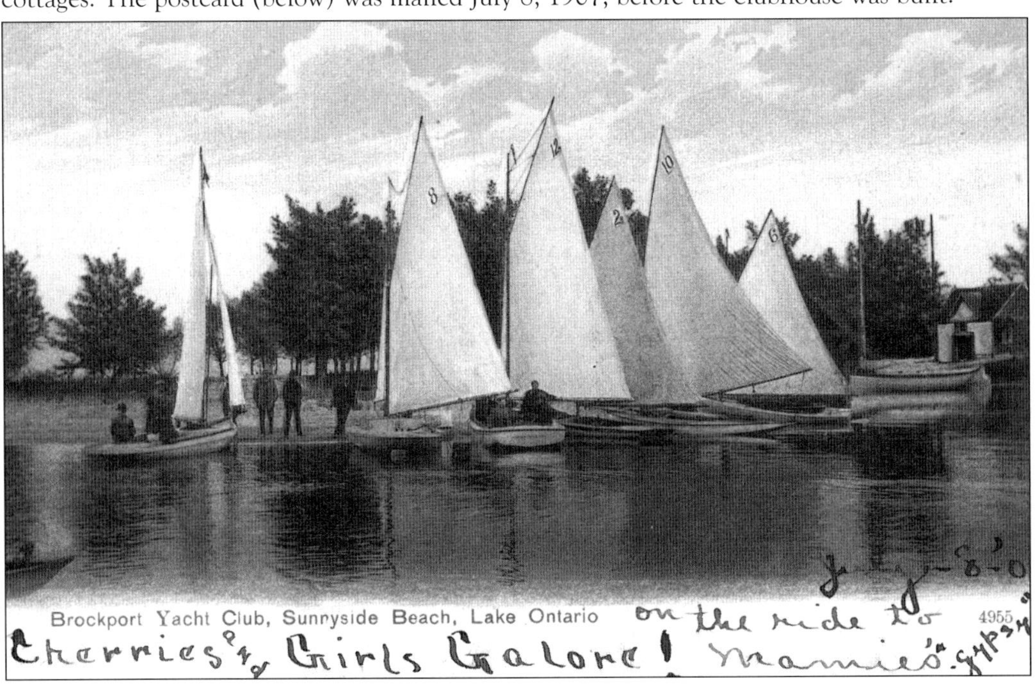

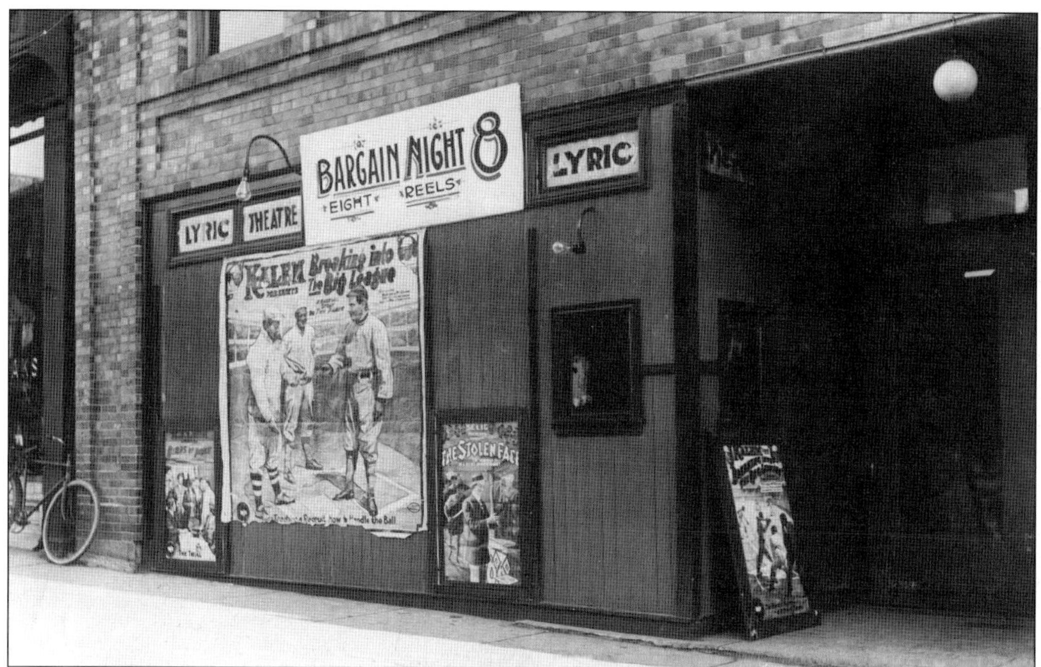

The Movies. The Ward Opera House, on Main Street just south of King Street, was the main venue for theatrical performances in the village. It showed the first movie played in the village, *The Great Train Robbery*, in 1909. The Lyric Theater (above) opened in 1907 on the ground floor of the Winslow Block, at Main and State Streets, and was probably showing movies by 1910. In 1916, it moved to the second floor of the building and became the Strand. In 1946, the Strand was expanded to occupy the entire structure and the façade was remodeled in the modernist style (below). Thus, a motion picture theater has occupied that site continuously for some 90 years, making it one of the oldest in the country.

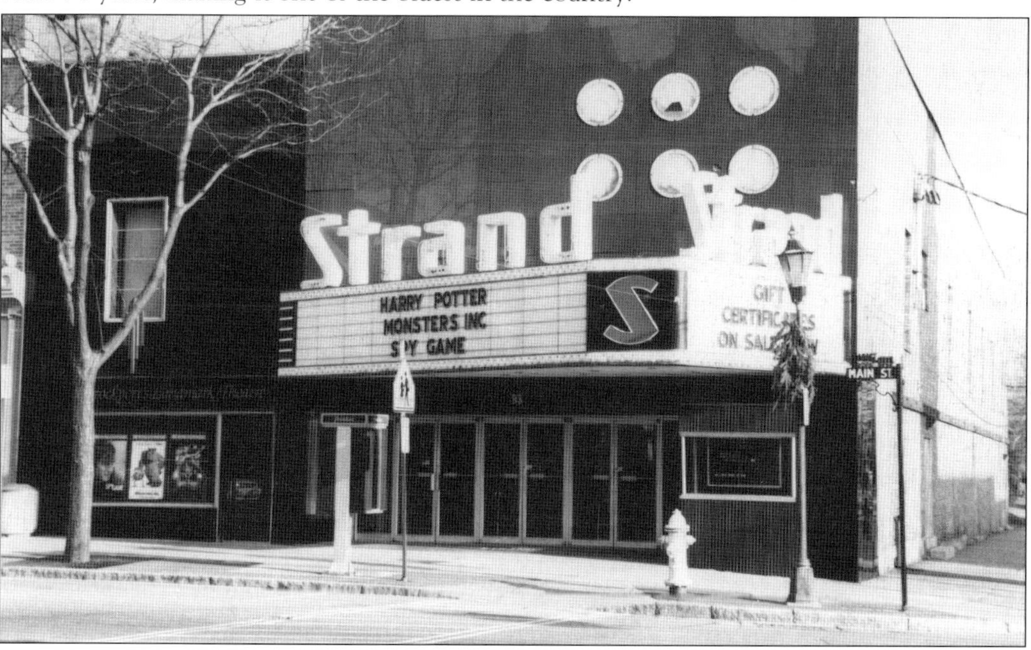

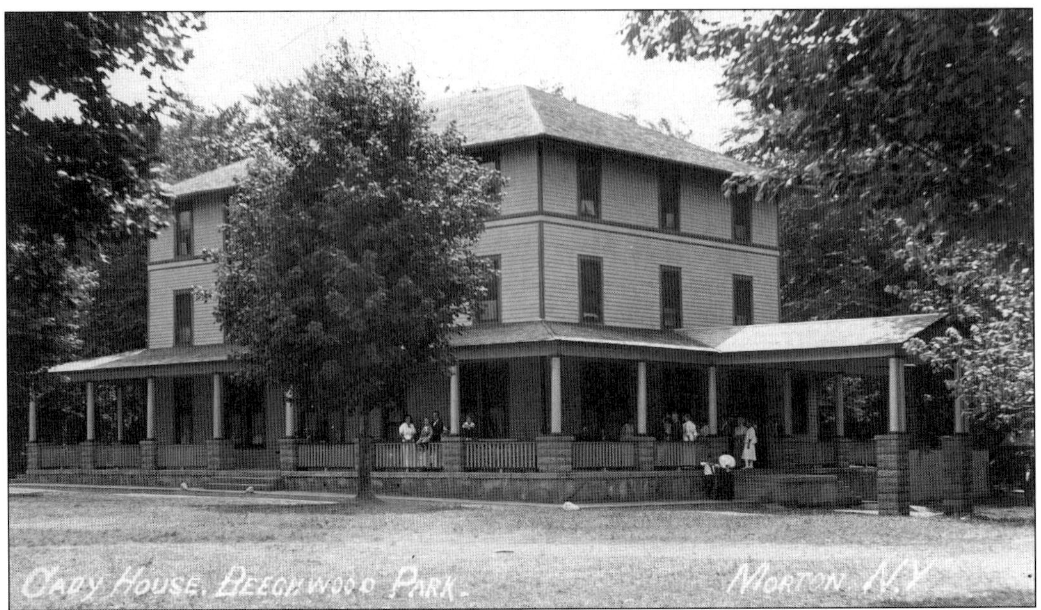

THE CADY HOUSE. Troutburg, straddling County Line Road at Lake Ontario, was a favorite recreation and vacation site for Brockporters in the early 20th century. The Cady House was one of Troutburg's resort hotels, built by Holley lumberman Nerville Cole in 1910. The structure still stands, though it has been boarded up for many years. Many Brockporters owned or rented Troutburg cottages, sometimes spending much of the summer there.

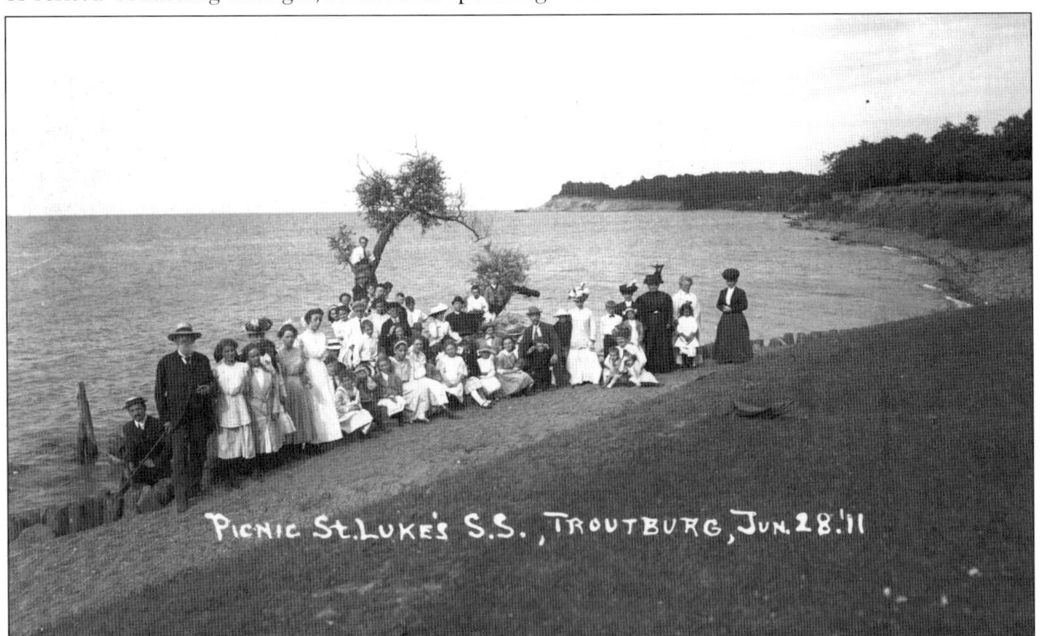

GROUP PICNICS. Troutburg was a popular location for group picnics. Brockport's St. Luke's Episcopal Church held its annual Sunday school picnic there in 1911. In the background is Devil's Nose, a promontory of a hard, durable blend of sand, gravel, and native lime that has not eroded as fast as the adjacent shoreline of softer texture. When Hamlin Beach State Park opened *c.* 1930, larger and nearer Brockport, Troutburg lost much of its attractiveness.

Four

Higher Education

Brockport has been home to a succession of institutions of higher education since the early 1830s. A short-lived Baptist college (1835) was followed by the Brockport Collegiate Institute secondary school (1841), a teacher-training normal school (1867), a teachers college (1942), and a liberal arts college in the State University of New York system (1962). The institution has grown from one building on six acres with a tiny faculty and hardly more students to 66 buildings on a 435-acre campus with 560 faculty members, 8,500 students, 24 academic disciplines, and 17 certification programs.

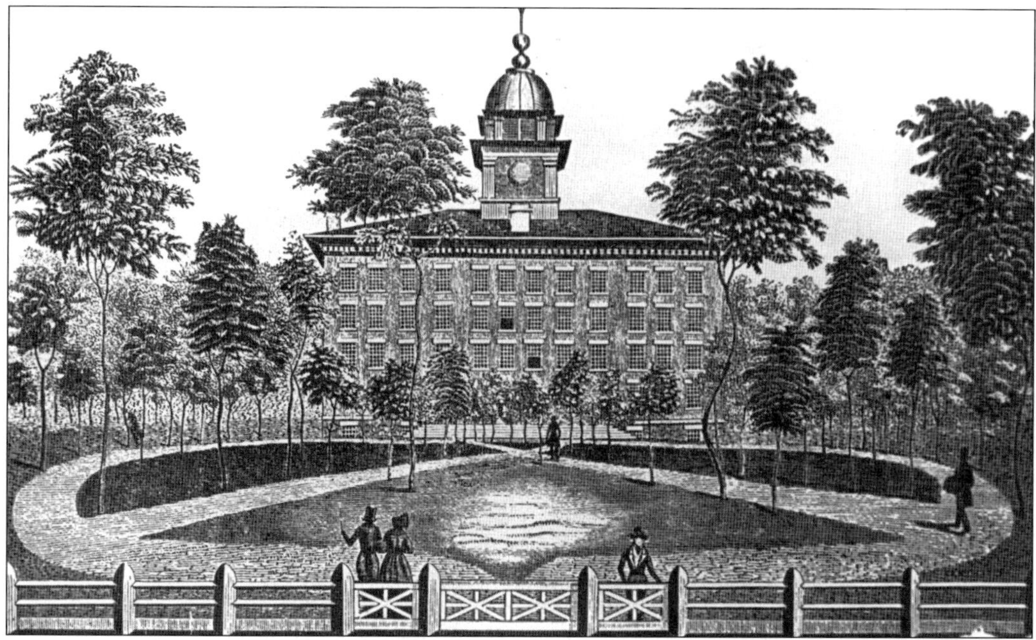

THE BEGINNINGS. In 1830, Hiel Brockway (page 40) offered six acres of village land as a site for a college. The Baptist Missionary Convention of the State of New York accepted the offer and erected the building above where Hartwell now stands. The school opened in 1835 but soon failed financially. In 1841, a group of Brockporters bought the structure and opened the Brockport Collegiate Institute, with 130 students. This academy-type secondary school offered classics, practical and technical courses, and teacher training.

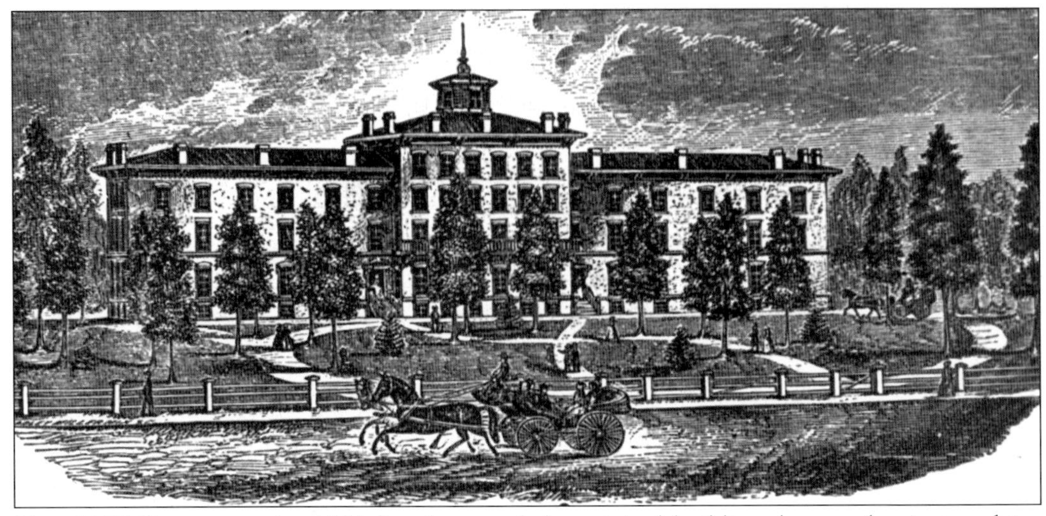

THE 1855 BUILDING. An 1854 fire destroyed the original building, but a subscription drive raised funds to rebuild. School resumed in November 1855. The departments included primary for the first eight grades, academic for the lower two years of high school, collegiate for the upper two years of high school, and teachers, which provided 20 students free teacher training in return for a pledge to teach in district schools.

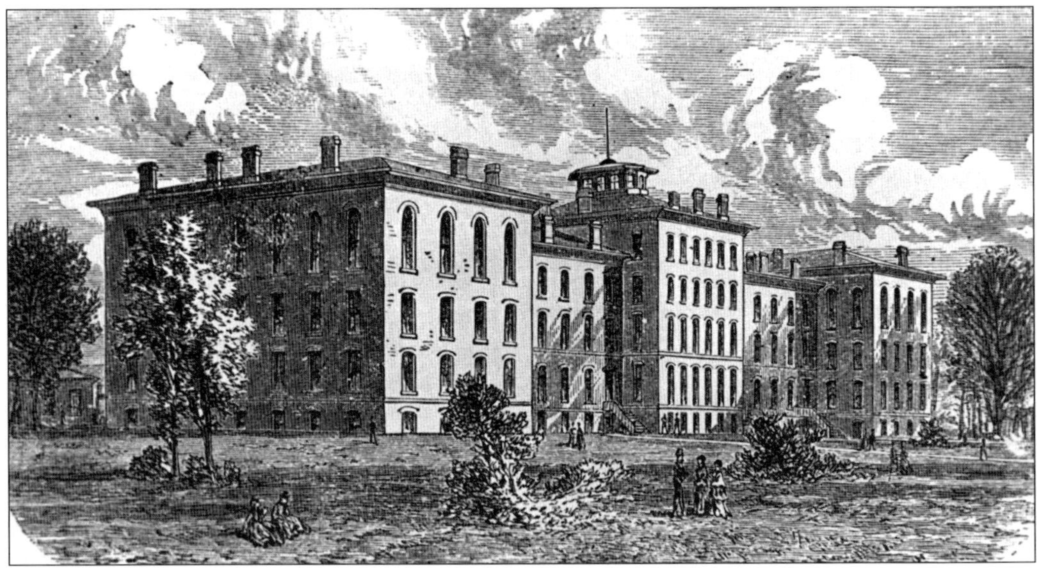

THE NORMAL SCHOOL. In 1866, the state legislature established normal schools at Brockport, Binghamton, Potsdam, and Fredonia and saved the financially floundering institute. The village of Brockport floated a $75,000 bond issue to finance building additions. The normal schools were part of a 19th-century revolution in American education, providing teacher training in instructional methods and subject-matter knowledge. The new name, Brockport State Normal and Training School (commonly referred to as the normal school), reflected this change.

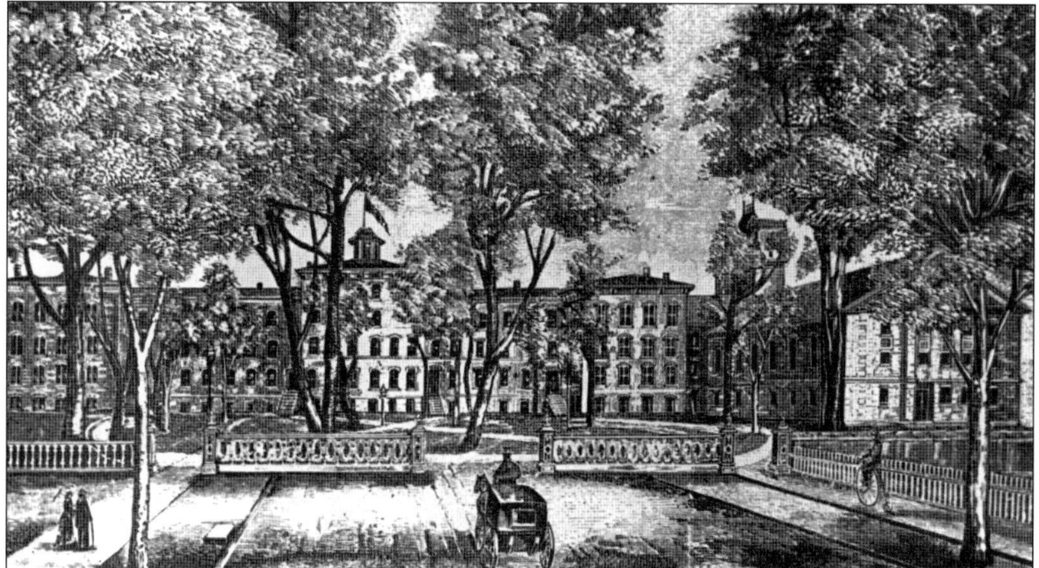

The Training School. The 1899 North Building provided a chapel and Training School quarters. A key element of the teacher training philosophy was a practice, or demonstration, school attached to the normal school. Normal school students, under the supervision of faculty critics, taught local children.

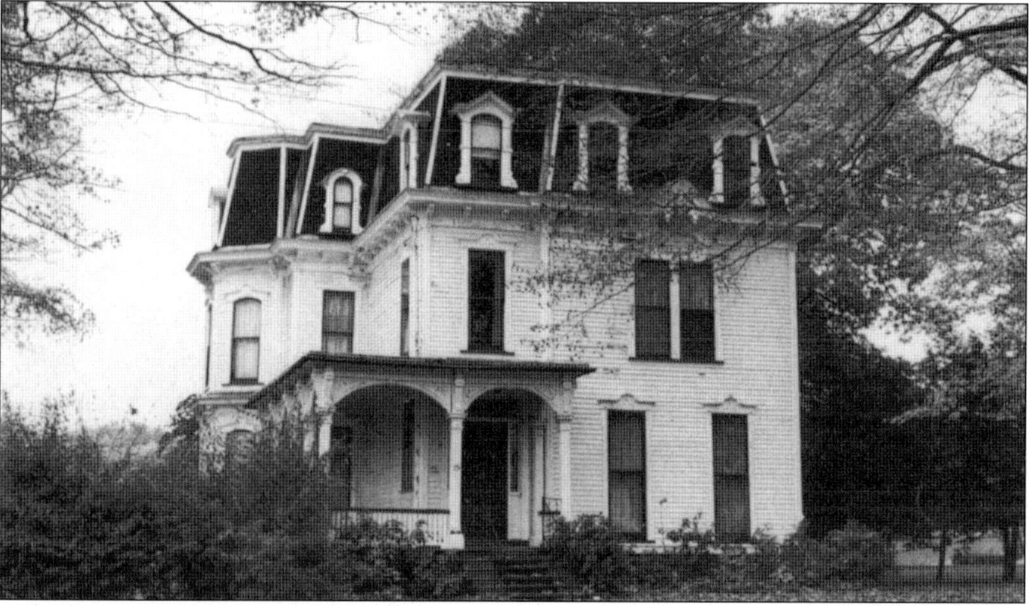

The Harrison House. Edward Harrison (1831–1916) (pages 66 and 98) built this home before 1872. Eloise Wilkin, famous illustrator and Harrison's granddaughter, played here as a child and used it as a model for her illustrations in *The Visit*, by Joan Esley. In 1898, Harrison's daughter, Margaret, sold it to the state of New York. Normal school principals from David Smith, in 1898, to Donald Tower, in 1964, used it as a residence. Its location near the school's main entrance was convenient for watching over the building and students. The State University of New York at Brockport Alumni Association saved it from demolition in the 1980s and restored its Victorian splendor. It is now used for many alumni activities.

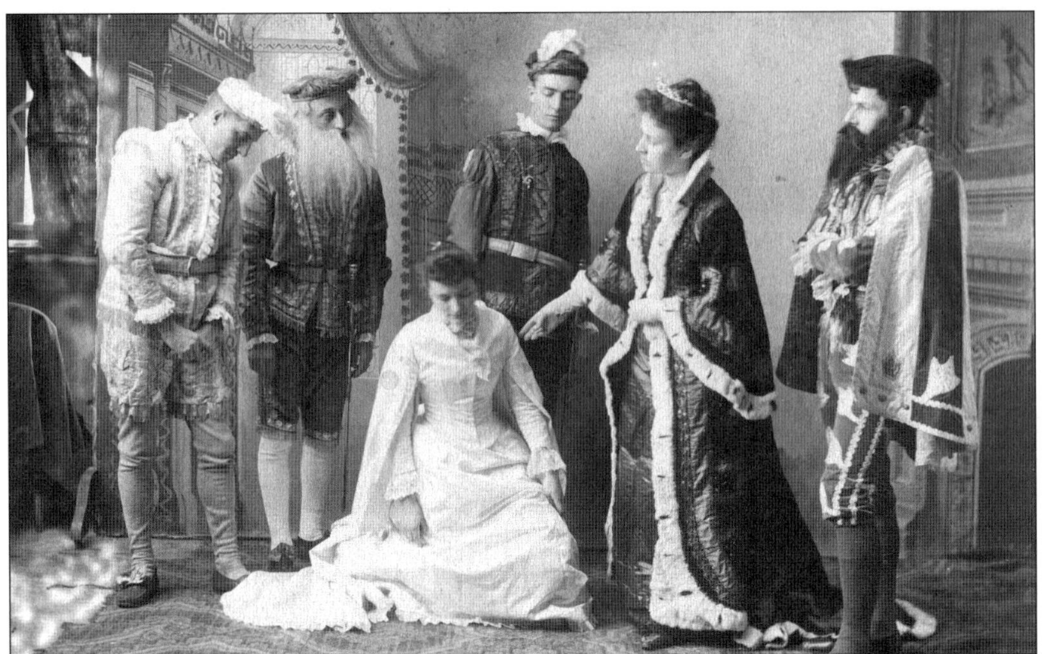

STUDENT SOCIETIES. These forerunners of modern fraternities and sororities contributed to the overall atmosphere of the campus. They provided social and intellectual fora for students. Each society had a room in the school building for formal meetings and social gatherings. The societies offered debates, readings of essays and poems, musical recitals, dances, teas, and other activities. This scene is from a play portraying Queen Elizabeth's wrath at the Earl of Leicester's marriage.

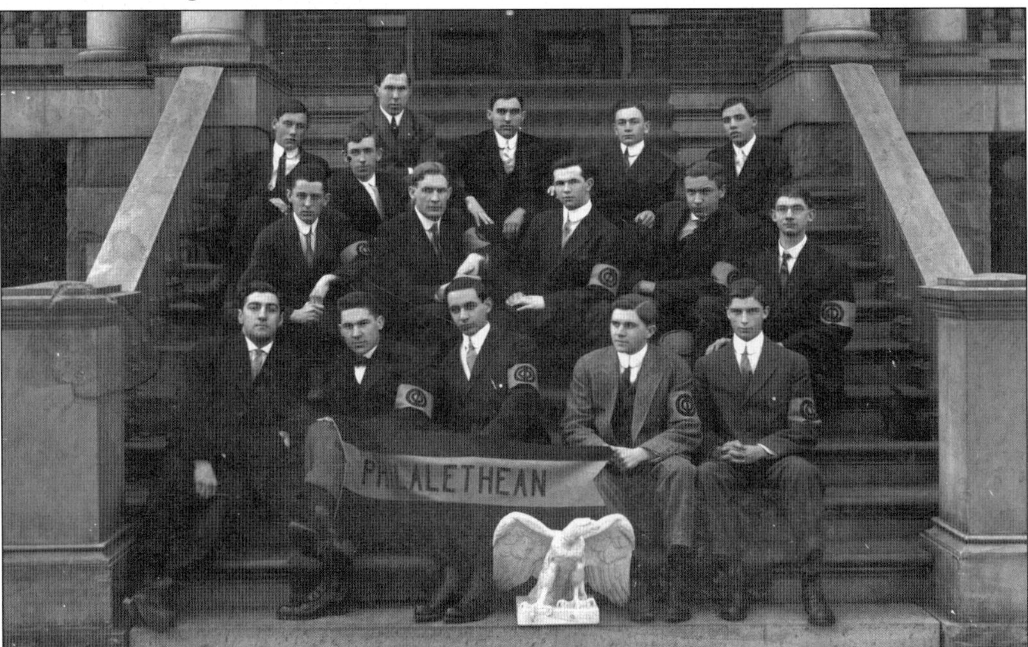

THE PHILALETHEAN. This group formed in 1893 as one of the early men's literary societies. It provided literary entertainments, including debates, readings, musical recitals, dances, and teas.

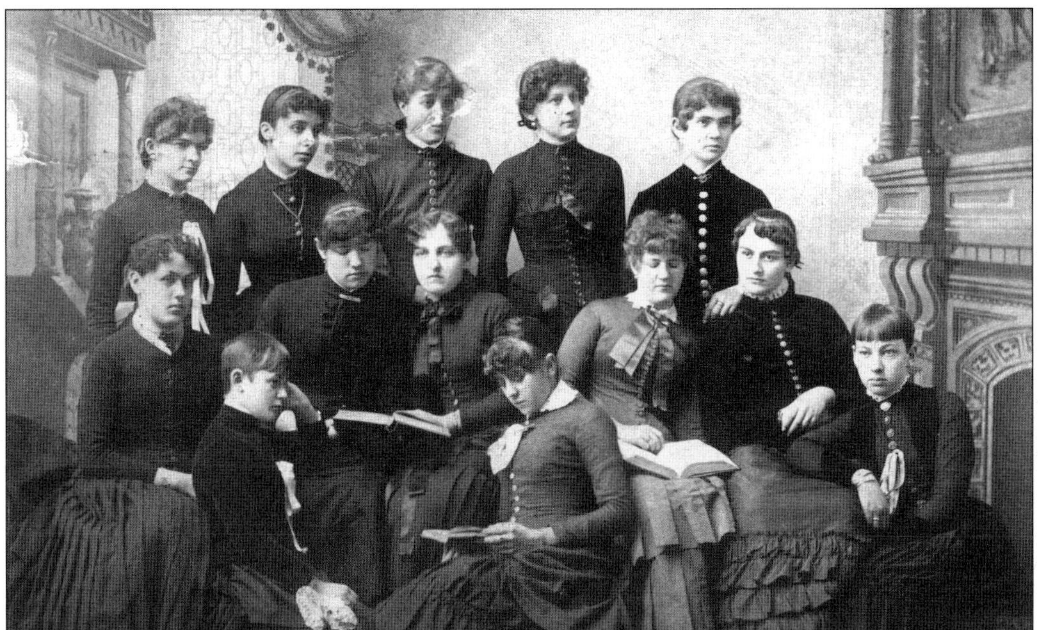

THE ARETHUSA SORORITY. Normal school students founded this society with the support of Principal Charles McLean in 1870. Society members here are in the Arethusa Room at the school. They held literary readings, plays, and dances. Although Arethusa has long been absent from Brockport, it remains active elsewhere and has a website, http://www.arethusa.org.

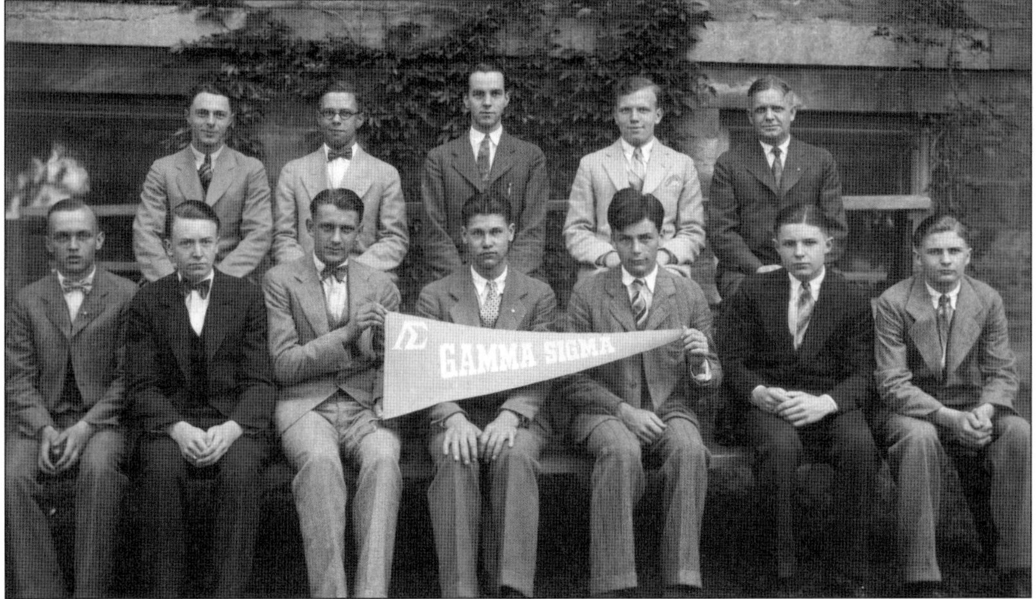

GAMMA SIGMA. The Gamma Sigma Literary Society, later a fraternity, was founded at Brockport, with the support of Principal Charles McLean, in 1869. It sponsored public literary entertainment, often with the Arethusa Society. In 1890, it began to form chapters at other normal schools and secondary schools in the area, beginning at Rochester Free Academy. By 1925, it had 26 chapters in eight states and the District of Columbia. A chapter in Niagara Falls, Ontario, in 1927 made it the first international secondary school fraternity in the world.

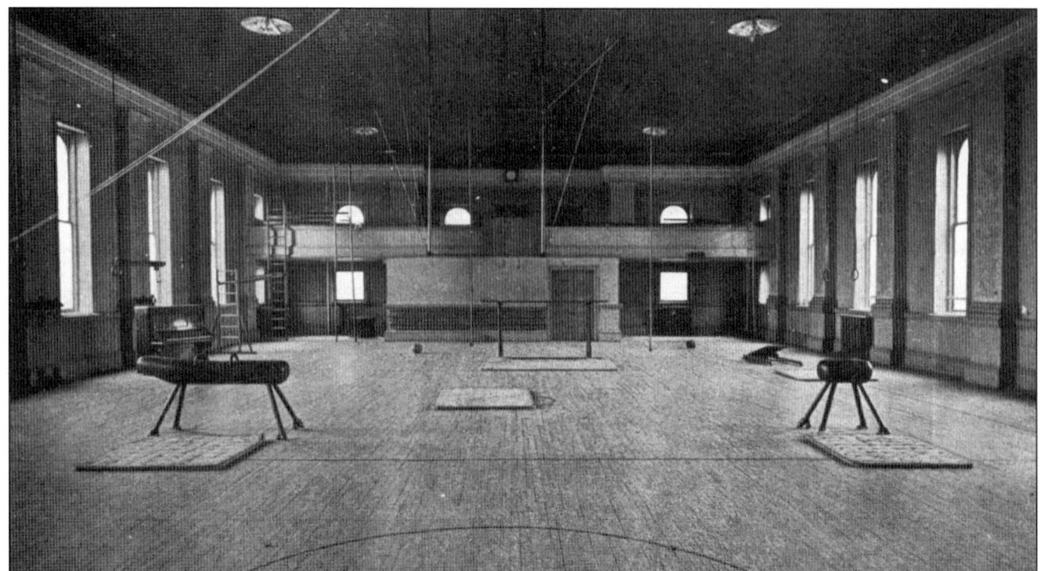

The Gymnasium. The normal school's 1889 chapel in its North Building served as a gymnasium from 1901 until the structure was demolished to make way for Hartwell Hall in 1940. The 1902 yearbook states that "the exceptionally large and well equipped Gymnasium gives ample opportunity for indoor activities."

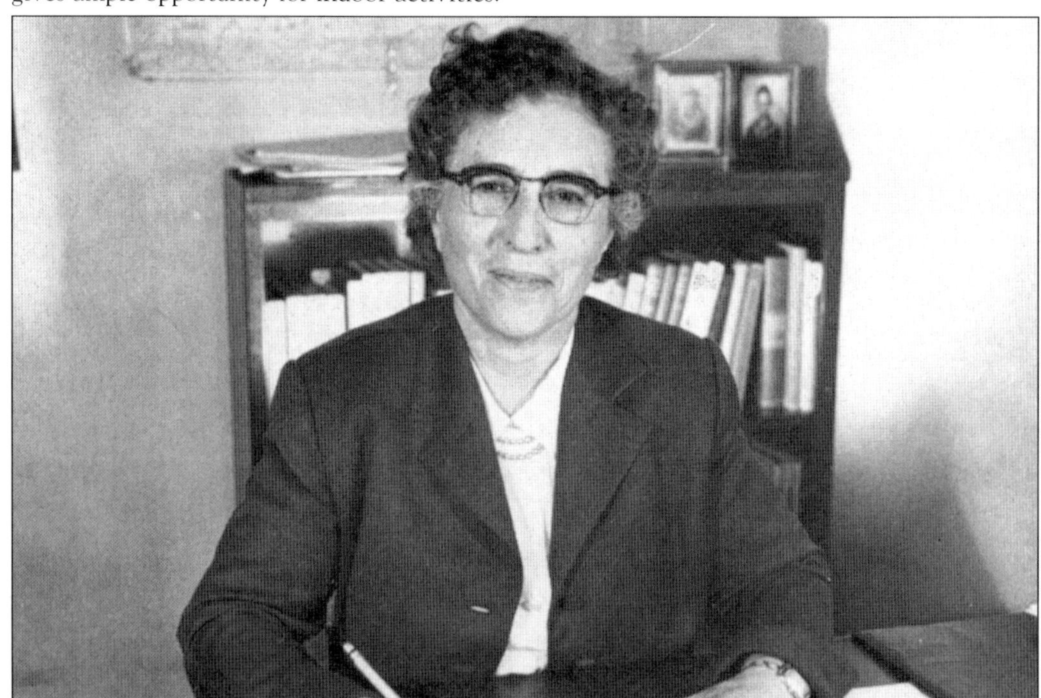

Women's Sports. Leonora M. Schroeder came to Brockport in 1928 and was a leader in women's physical education. She helped found the Women's Athletic Association, which organized women's intramural leagues for basketball, field hockey, swimming, and water ballet. The association also formed an Officials Club for women interested in learning to officiate sports.

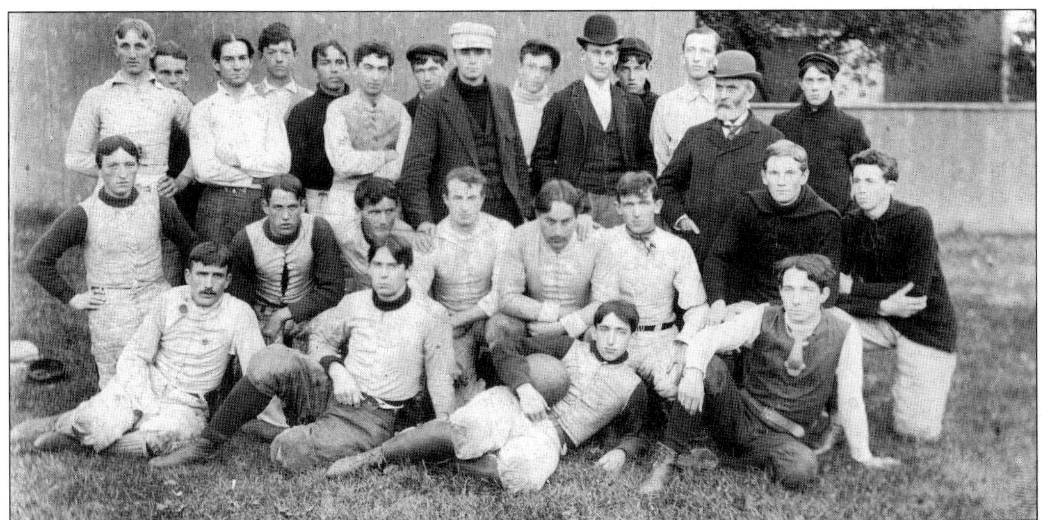

FOOTBALL. Football debuted in 1889. The early contests were intramural, with little in the way of equipment or uniforms, as this 1890 team photograph shows. Intercollegiate football began in 1894 with games between Brockport and the University of Rochester at each institution. By the end of that decade, the football team was playing with considerable regularity against secondary schools in towns such as Pittsford and Albion. That informal program was discontinued in 1916. Regular intercollegiate football began in 1947 with Bob Boozer as coach.

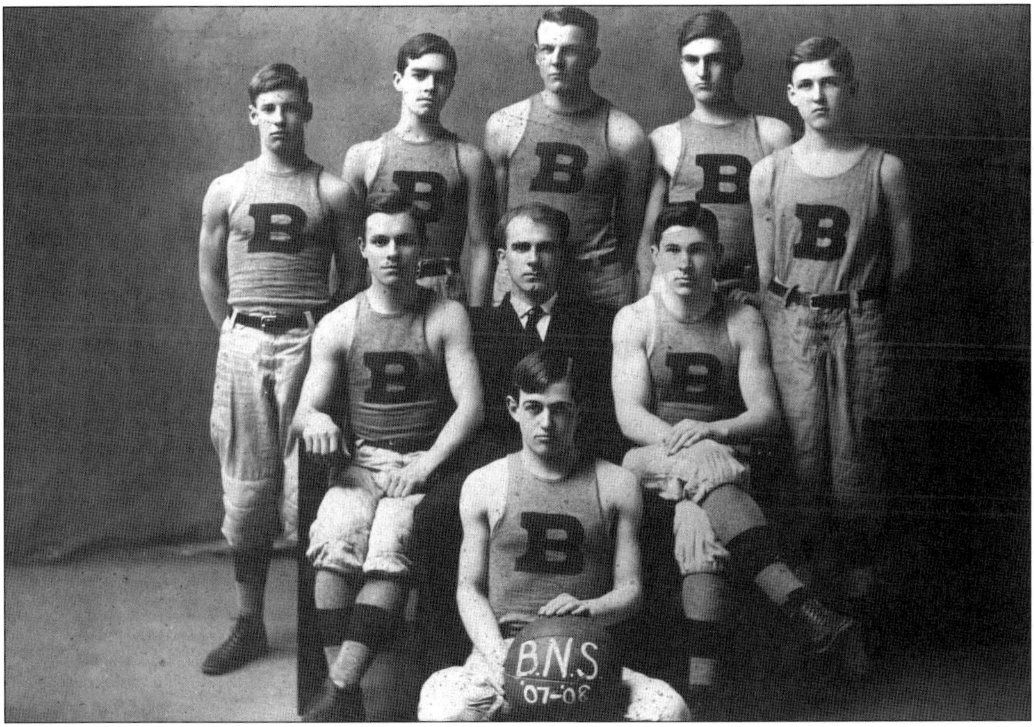

BASKETBALL. The Brockport Normal School Association for the Playing of Basket Ball was formed in 1902. It joined a league of high schools and normal schools. This photograph shows the 1907–1908 team, still in its infancy, as can be seen in the pants it shared with the football team.

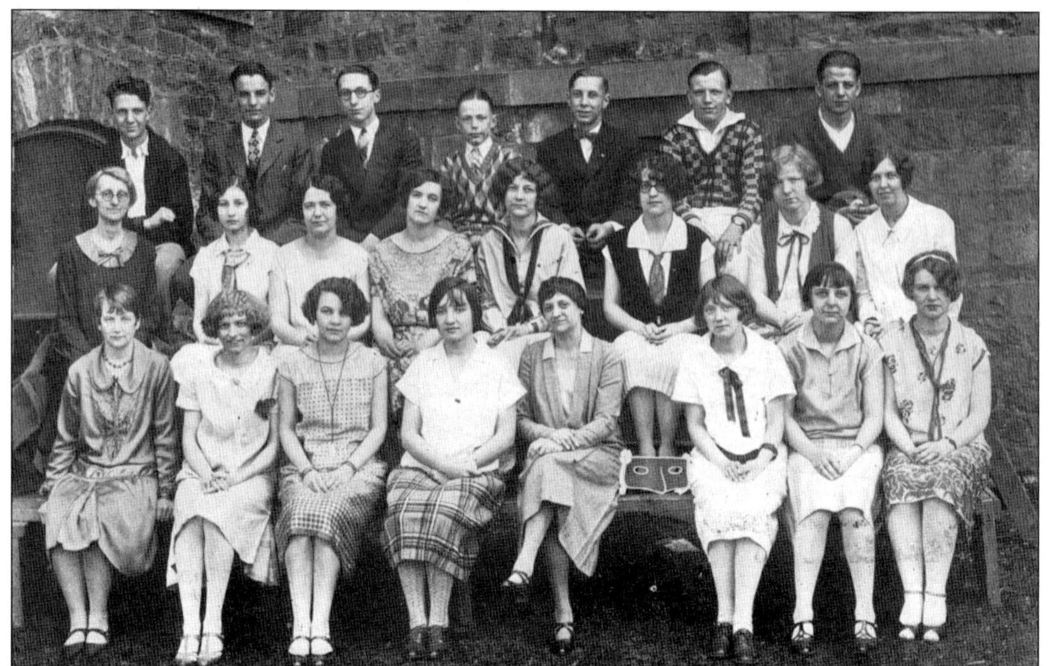

THEATER. Members of the student Magpies dramatic society were required to prove their acting ability. Proceeds from the annual plays benefited the school. The Magpies evolved into the Drama Club of the 1940s and the Harlequins of the 1960s.

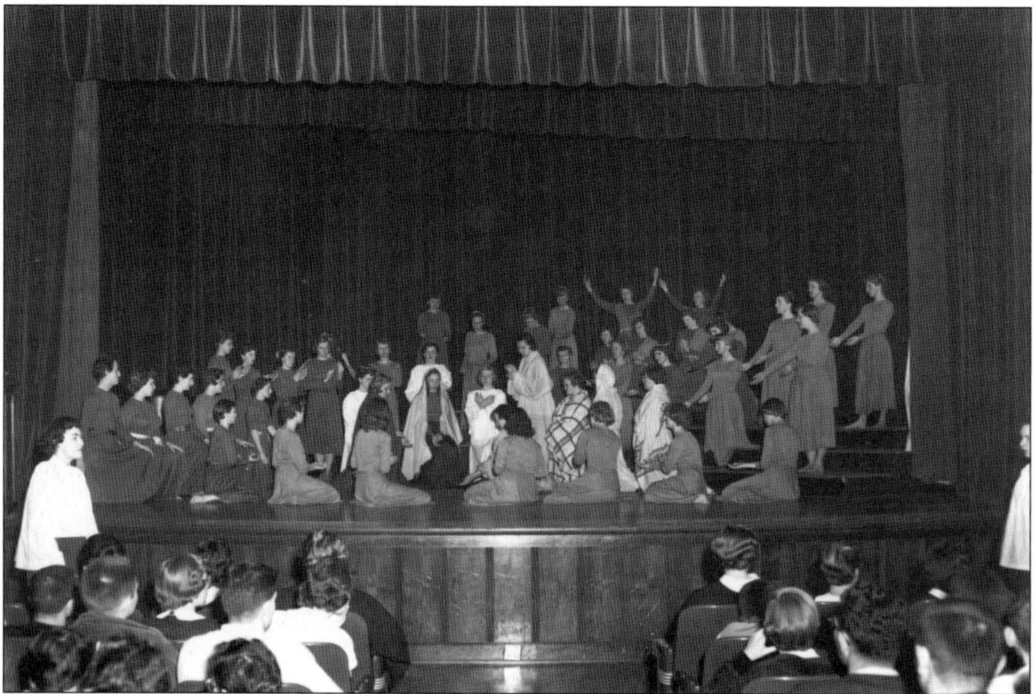

CHRISTMAS. In 1940, Pauline Haynes directed the first Christmas Vespers service, consisting of yuletide carols and Bible readings performed by the Special Chorus and Choir. The Christmas Vespers presented the biblical Christmas story as Prophecy, Birth, and Adoration.

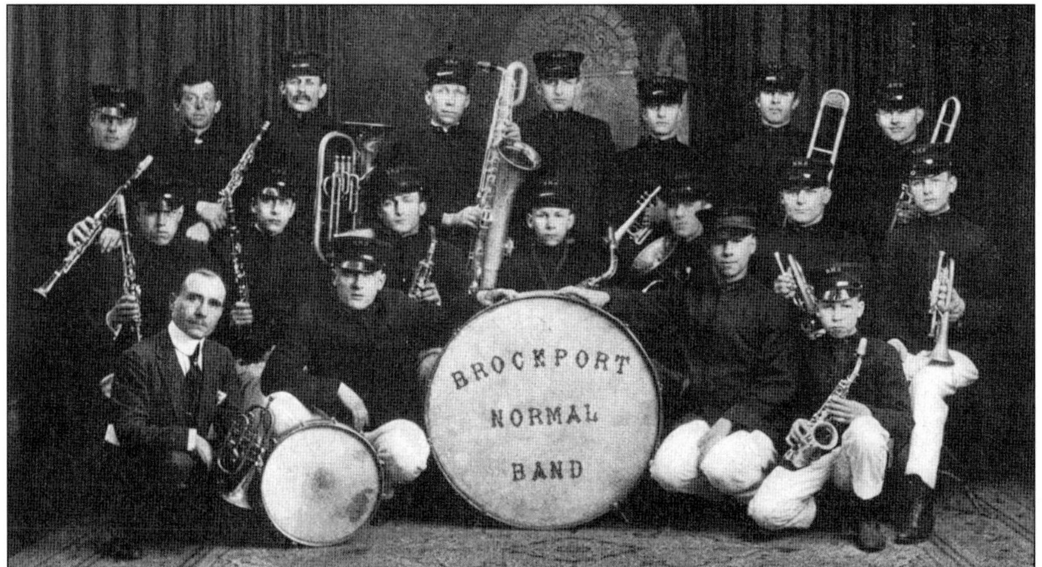

THE BAND. The Brockport Normal Band was formed in 1920. Each member agreed to buy a musical instrument. The members ranged in age from grade-school pupils to normal-school seniors and even some adults. A girls' orchestra also existed then. Instrumental and vocal music continued to be a prominent part of the curriculum and student activities during the remainder of the normal-school years.

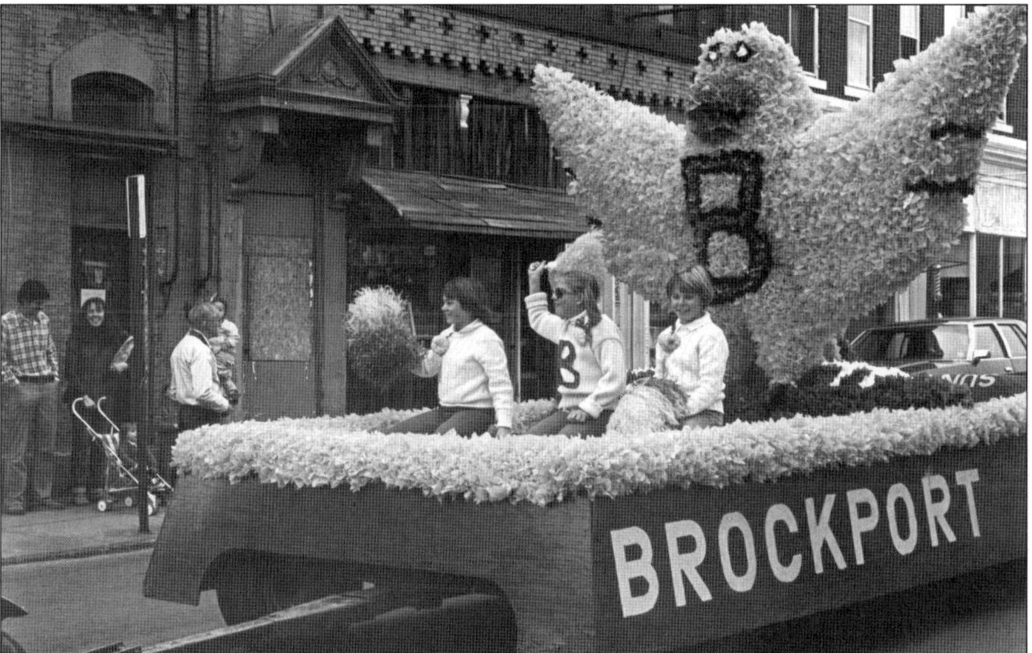

HOMECOMING. Homecoming began in 1931, when a group of former basketball players returned for a get-together and game with the varsity team. It became annual during the 1930s, and class reunions were added after 1943. In 1948, the name Homecoming became official and the program expanded to include a reception, athletic games, buffet supper, dance, parade, and house-decorating contest. The winning float depicts the Brockport Alumni Eagle.

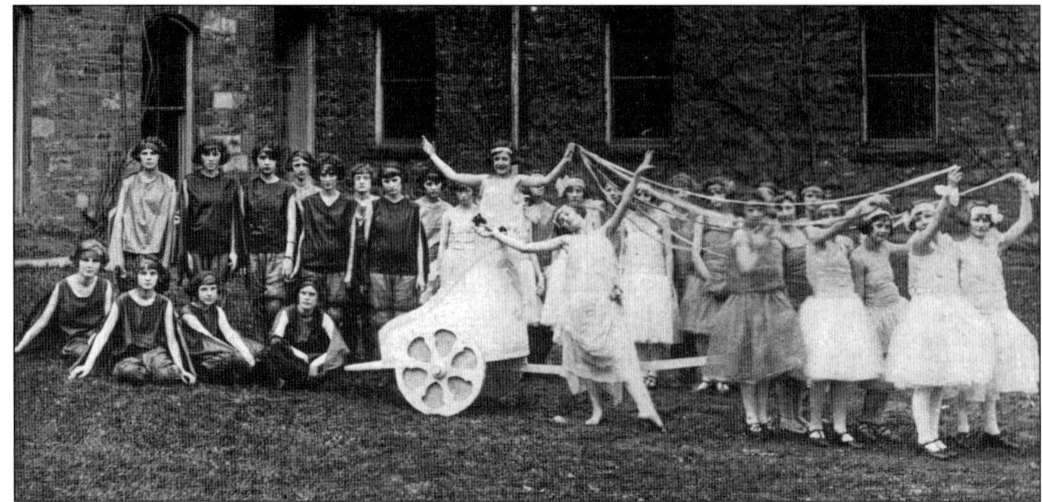

COLOR DAY. These students are ready for the annual Color Day procession at the normal school building. This was an annual event from 1902 to 1937. A typical day included a noon picnic on the lawn, followed by a band concert and a pageant. Students were expected to wear the green and yellow school colors—yellow for dandelions and green for grass.

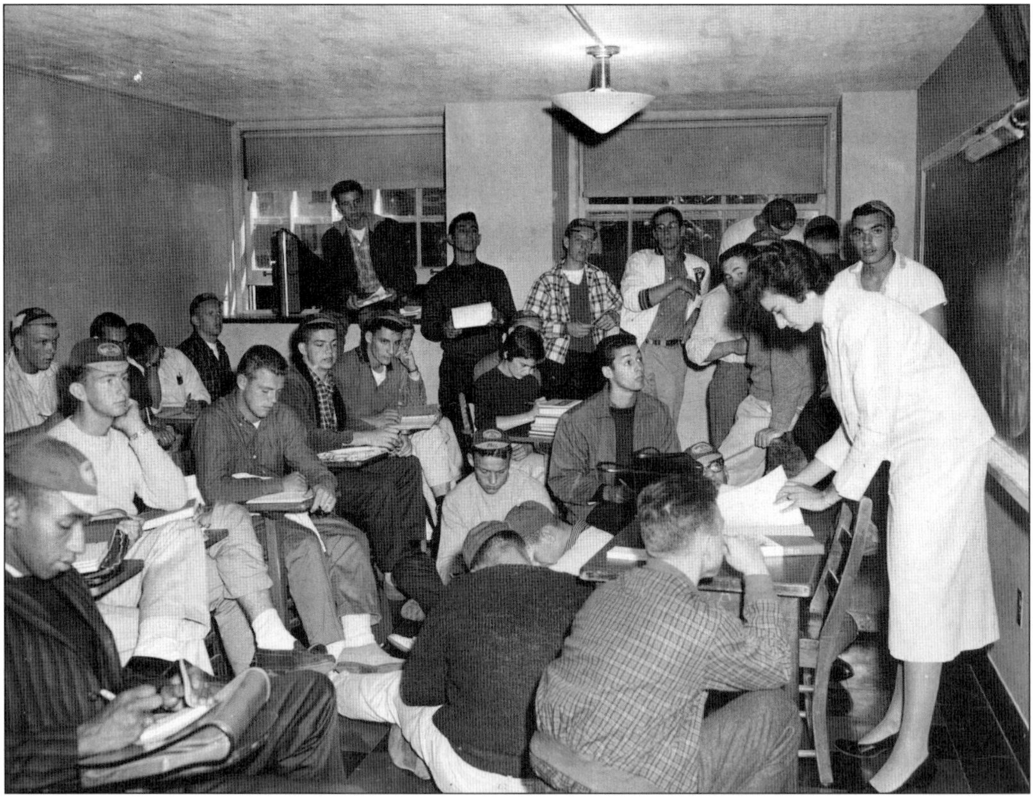

THE RETURNING GIS. A more serious side of student life in the early postwar period was the crowding produced by the influx of veterans on the G.I. Bill. Some classes were so jammed that students had to sit on the floor or windowsills. To alleviate this problem, temporary structures, including a women's dormitory and Quonset huts, were built.

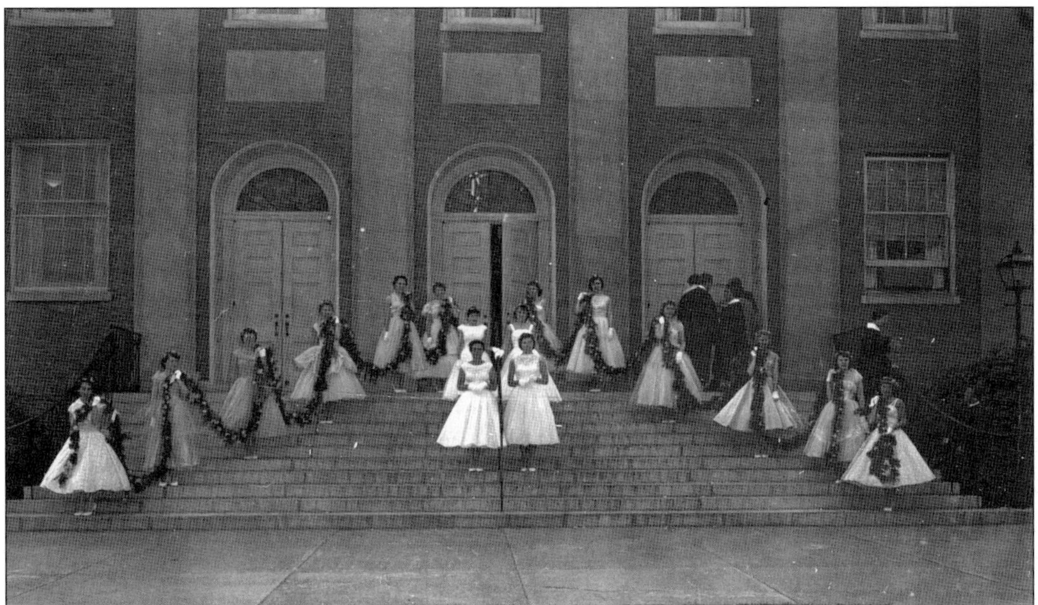

CLASS DAY. A daisy-chain procession was part of Class Day from the late 1960s until 1966. Sophomore girls dressed in pastel gowns and carrying a chain of daisies led the seniors in caps and gowns from the senior luncheon to the Class Day ceremony. Traditional Class Day events included singing the Class Day song, reading the senior will and prophecy, and the moving-up ceremony, in which each class moved into the seats of the class above.

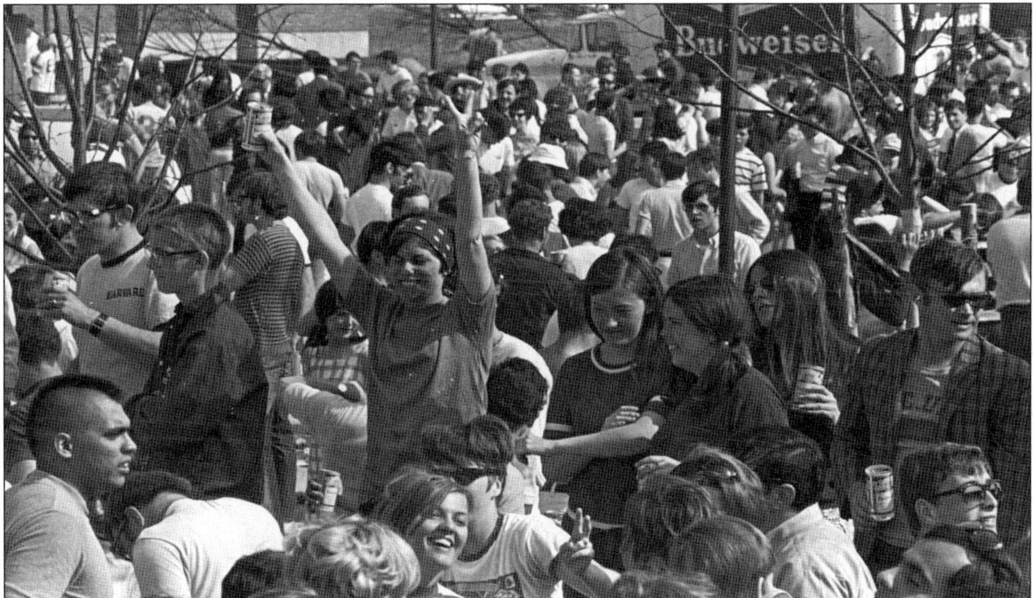

SPRING-IN. The youth revolution of the 1960s changed the character of student celebrations drastically. From *c.* 1969 until 1980, the Brockport Student Government sponsored a rowdy end-of-the-school-year campus bacchanalia with free beer. Crowds of 5,000 to 8,000 attended the 10-hour event. Bands played for hours, and beer trucks dispensed their beverages at dispersed locations to reduce congestion and chaos. Costs and changes in the college alcohol policy ended Spring-In.

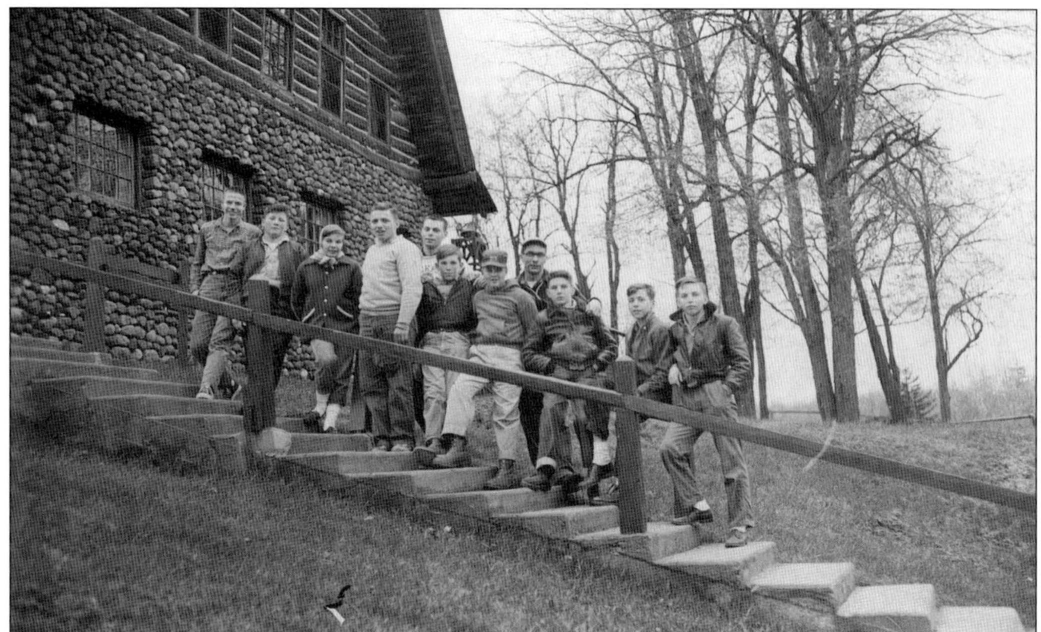

Camp Totem. The 1947 offering of a health and physical major, the first academic specialty, led the college to acquire a site for outdoor education activities. The Gannett foundation and the Susan Lee estate helped it buy a 100-acre private camp, renamed Camp Totem, on the Oswegatchie River in the western Adirondacks in 1952. Campers are seen outside a cabin. The facility housed children, aged 10 to 16, for two- to eight-week sessions. Students taught the campers under the guidance of director Martin Rogers and other faculty. Although a great success, the camp was a long drive from Brockport, and Totem was sold in the early 1960s. The students (below) are juggling at the camp in the 1950s.

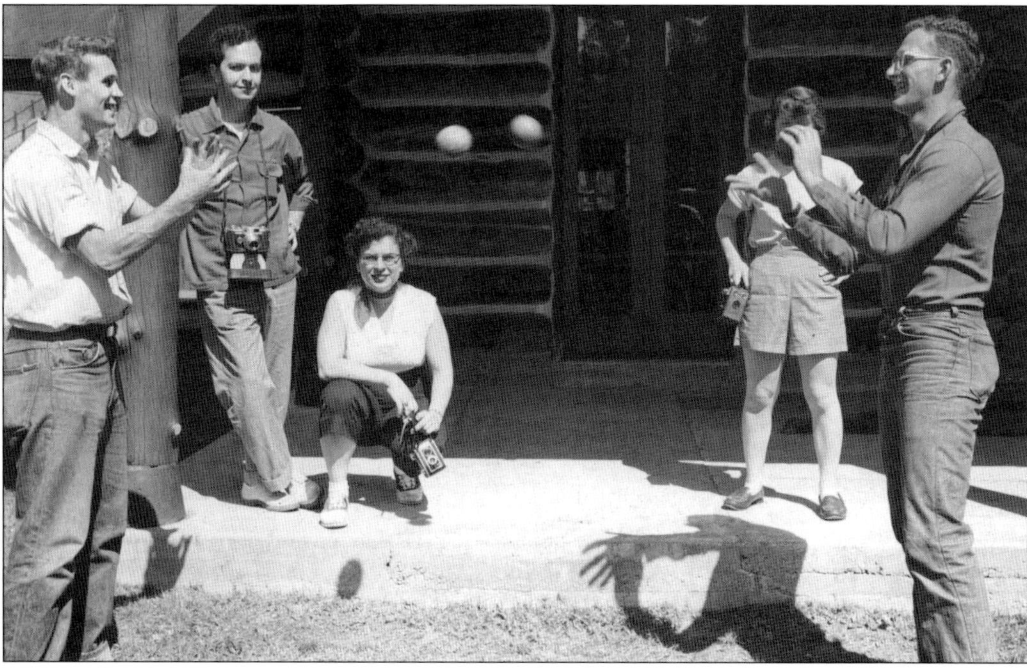

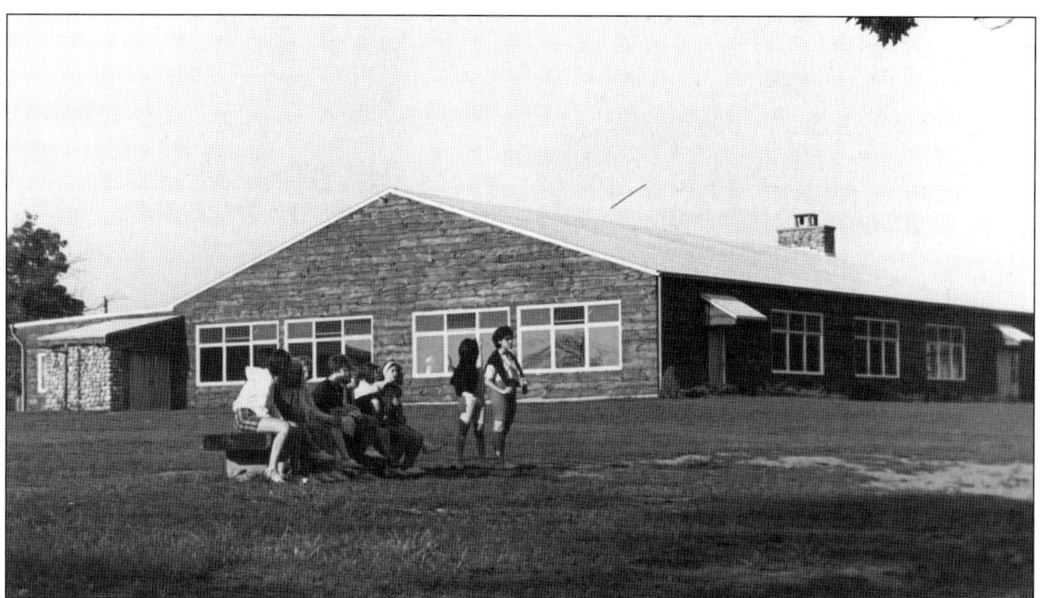

FANCHER CAMPUS. In 1963, the college bought 500 acres of open and wooded land nine miles west of Brockport for outdoor education and recreation and sold Camp Totem. Added to the existing farmhouse and barn were a 65-by-100-foot lodge, a conference center, an outdoor theater, a ski tow, and a swimming pool.

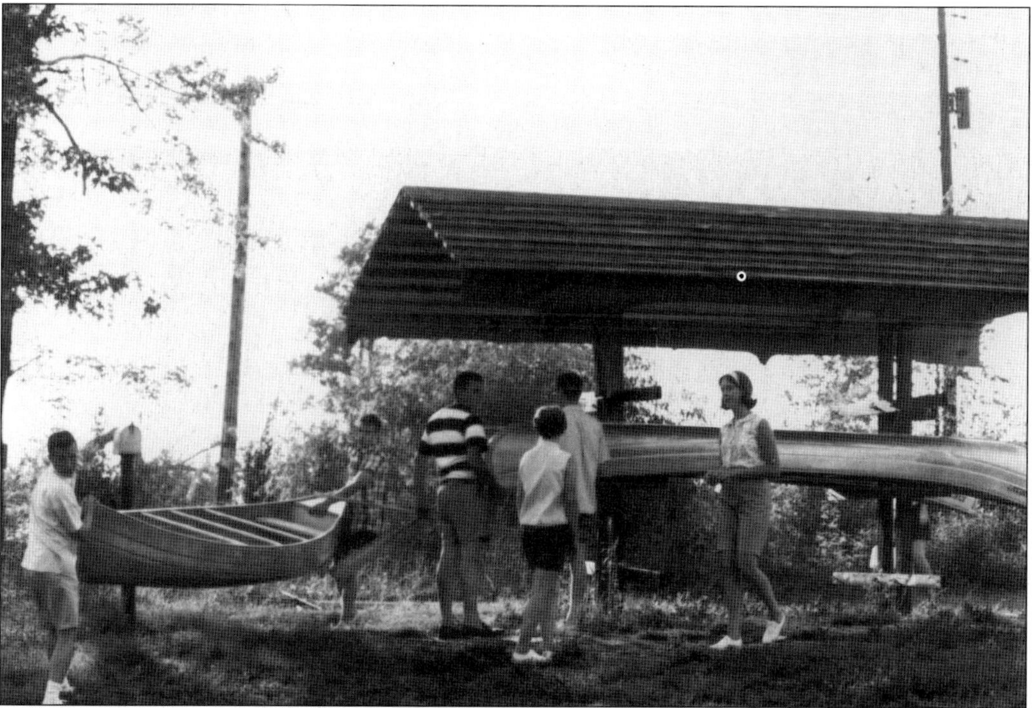

MCCARGO LAKE. The Fancher campus included a 10-acre pond with a beach and floating dock, which enhanced its value as a recreation and education center. For instance, biologists carried out a major grant-funded water research study. However, budgetary constraints and changing curricular needs led to the 1983 sale of the property.

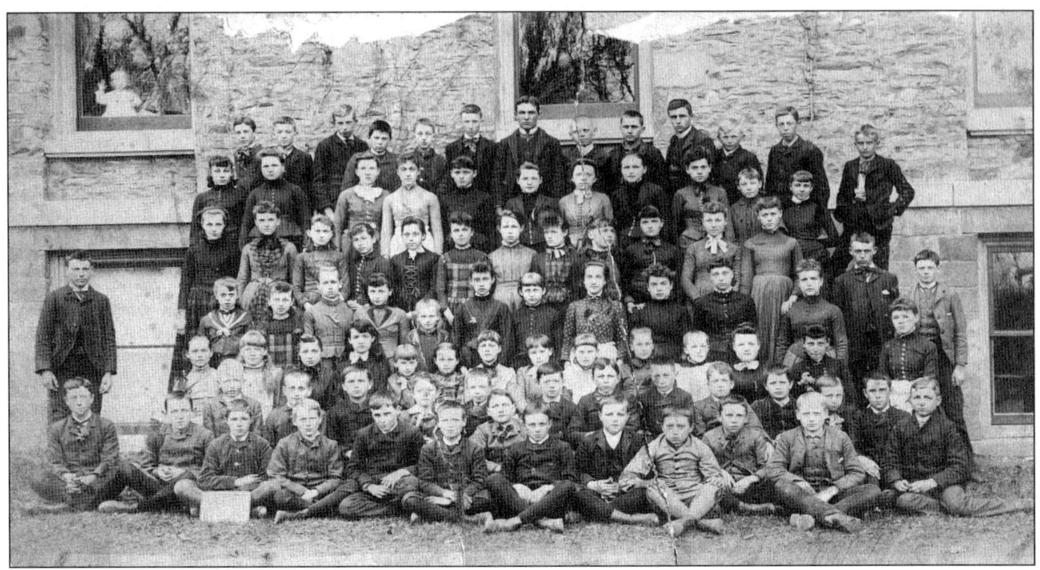

THE PRACTICE SCHOOL. This is the earliest known photograph of students in the teacher-training practice school, *c.* 1890. From 1867 to 1981, Brockport had some form of teaching laboratory arrangement. The school provided education for local children and training for student teachers.

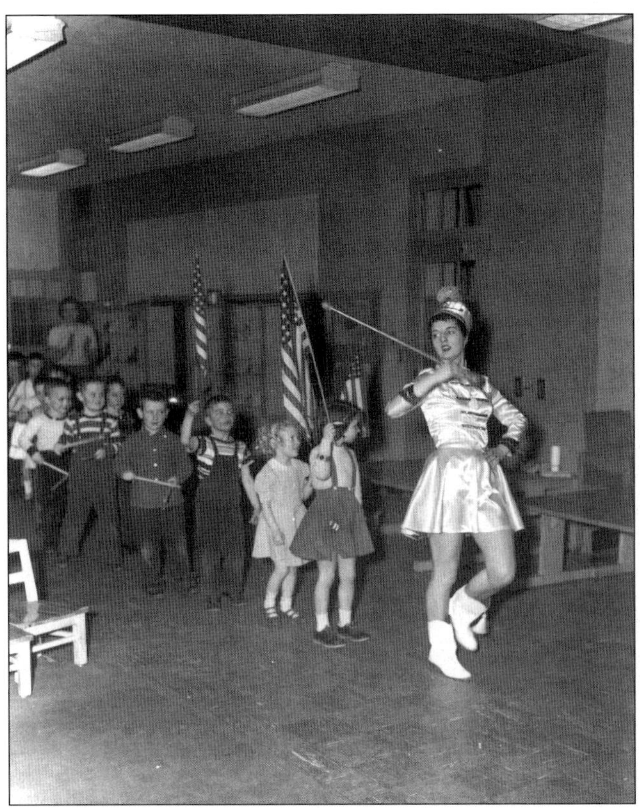

THE CAMPUS SCHOOL. Campus school faculty members were professional teacher-critics, full-time instructors who also supervised the student teachers. A campus school wing was added to the north side of Hartwell Hall in 1952, and a modern laboratory school building housing the Cooper Center for Innovation in Education opened in 1966. However, changes in state policies and in teacher-training practices spelled doom for the program, and it closed in 1981.

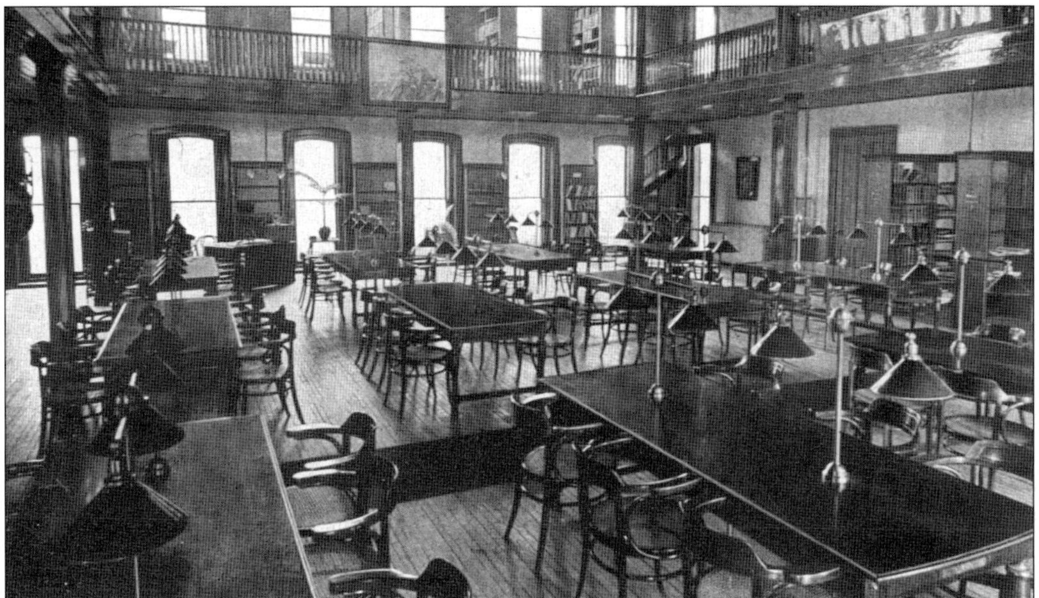

THE LIBRARY. By 1912, the library had grown considerably from its early days when the meager collection was housed in a corridor. It had become an integral part of the school, extending through three floors. The main level included seating for study and stacks for books. The second-floor gallery provided additional stack space. The third level had a map and document room and a classroom for a course in library methods.

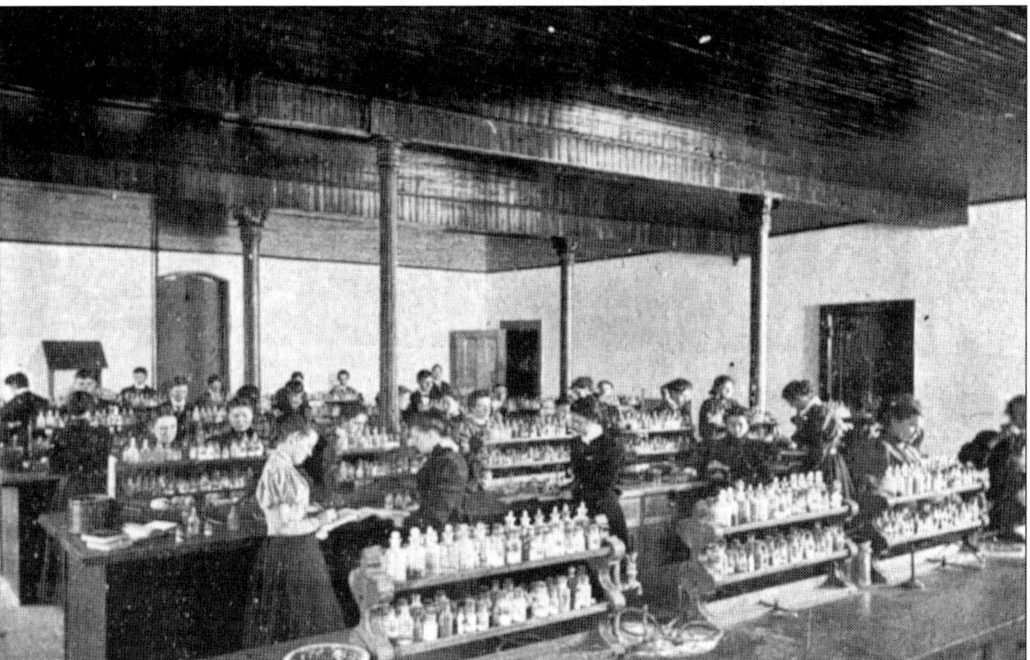

THE CHEMISTRY LABORATORY. The 1899 yearbook describes the chemistry laboratory as "one of the best appointed in the state, having ample table room for 50 students at one time . . . The department has over $2,500 worth of physical apparatus, over 2,500 stereopticon slides and some 3,000 specimens."

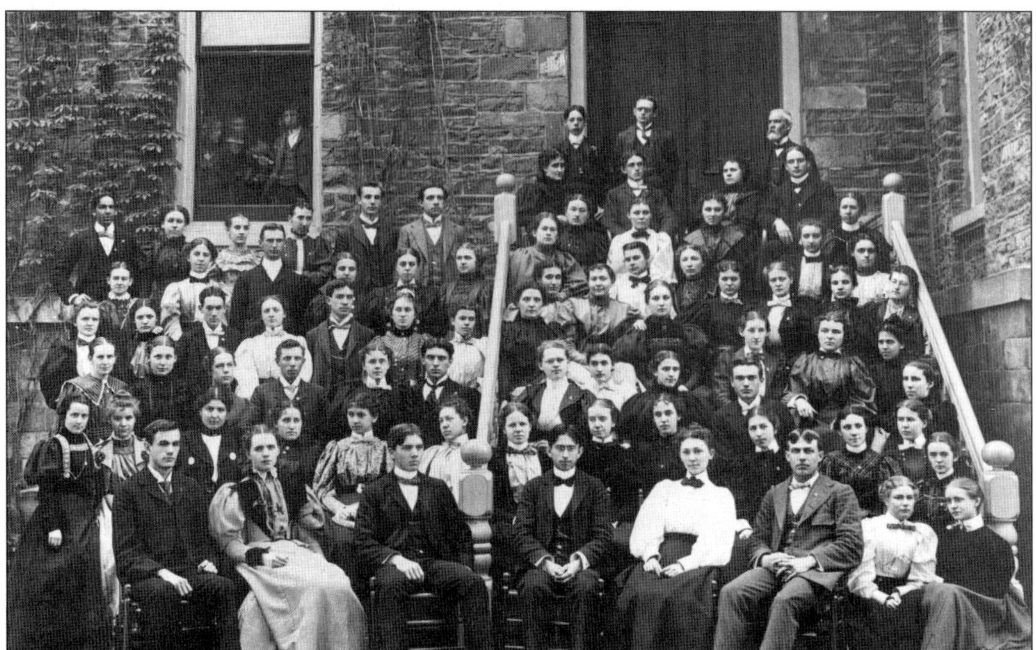

CHARLES D. MCLEAN. In this 1890s photograph, Charles D. McLean (1869–1898) is the bearded man at the upper right. McLean graduated from the Brockport Collegiate Institute in 1850. He became professor of mathematics in 1865 and principal upon the resignation of Malcolm MacVicar. He had the longest tenure in the school's history. He was admired by faculty and students alike and was a dominant figure in the history of the Normal School.

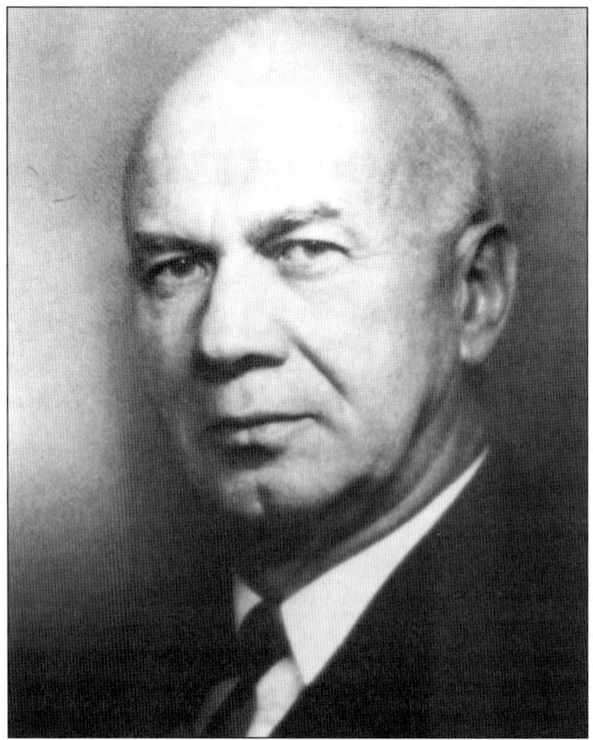

ERNEST HARTWELL. In 1936, when Ernest Hartwell became Brockport's principal, serving until 1944, low enrollment, an inadequate physical plant, and state budgetary problems threatened the school's survival. Working with a group of concerned local citizens and Vincent Dailey (page 101), a politically powerful Brockport native, Hartwell won state and federal funding for a new building, and helped secure 1942 state legislation transforming normal schools, including Brockport, into state teachers colleges.

DONALD TOWER. When Donald Tower (1944–1964) came to the Brockport Collegiate Institute, its enrollment was about 300 and its mission was to train elementary school teachers. The first masters degree program began in 1947 and the curriculum expanded. Enrollment soared and the campus grew correspondingly, displacing adjacent homes. In 1948, it became part of the newly created State University of New York (SUNY) and, in 1962, when SUNY was made a comprehensive system of higher education, Brockport became a state university college. The college's performing arts center is named for Tower because his academic specialization was drama.

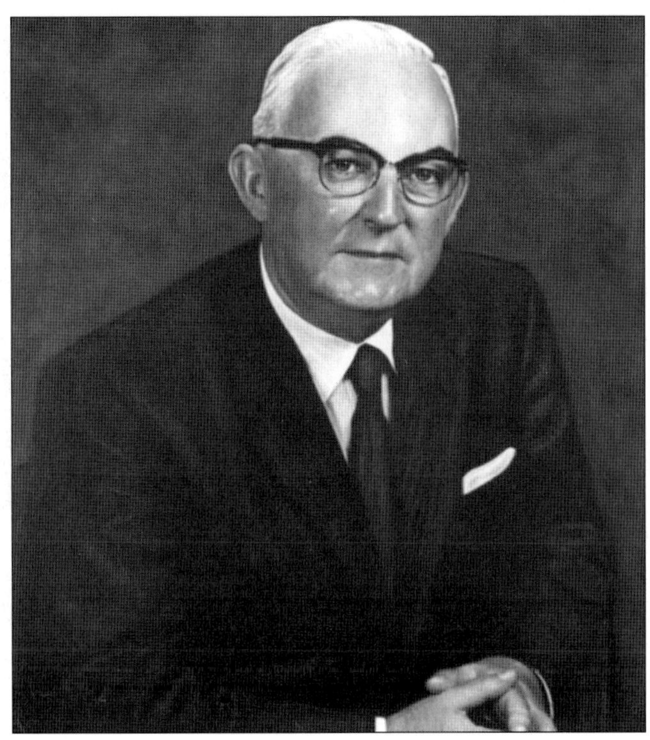

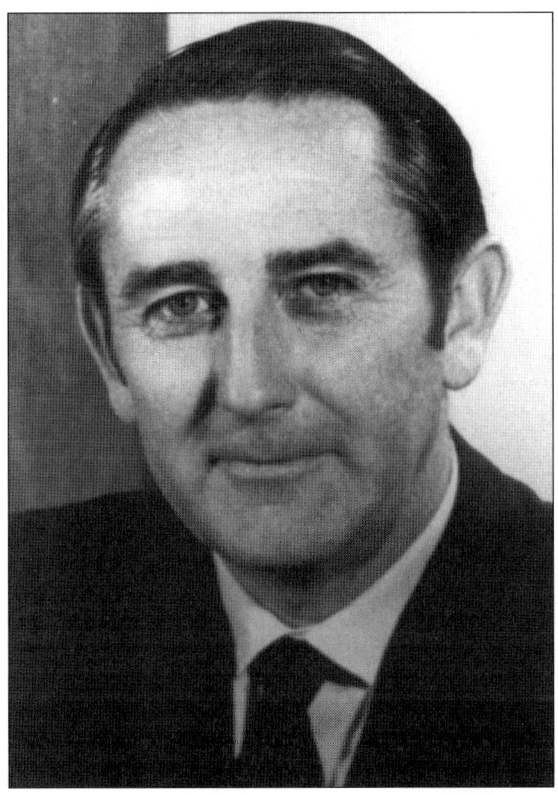

ALBERT W. BROWN. From 1965 to 1981, Albert W. Brown presided over the most dramatic growth and change in the history of the institution. Enrollment grew from about 2,900 students to over 12,000, at its highest. In the middle 1970s, enrollment declined again, stabilizing at about 8,500. Brown also transformed the institution from a teacher-training school to a college of liberal arts and professions; diversified the student body by intensively recruiting minority, adult, and transfer students; and greatly increased off-campus, evening, and overseas courses and programs. John W. Van de Wetering (1981–1997) and Paul Yu (1997–present) have succeeded him.

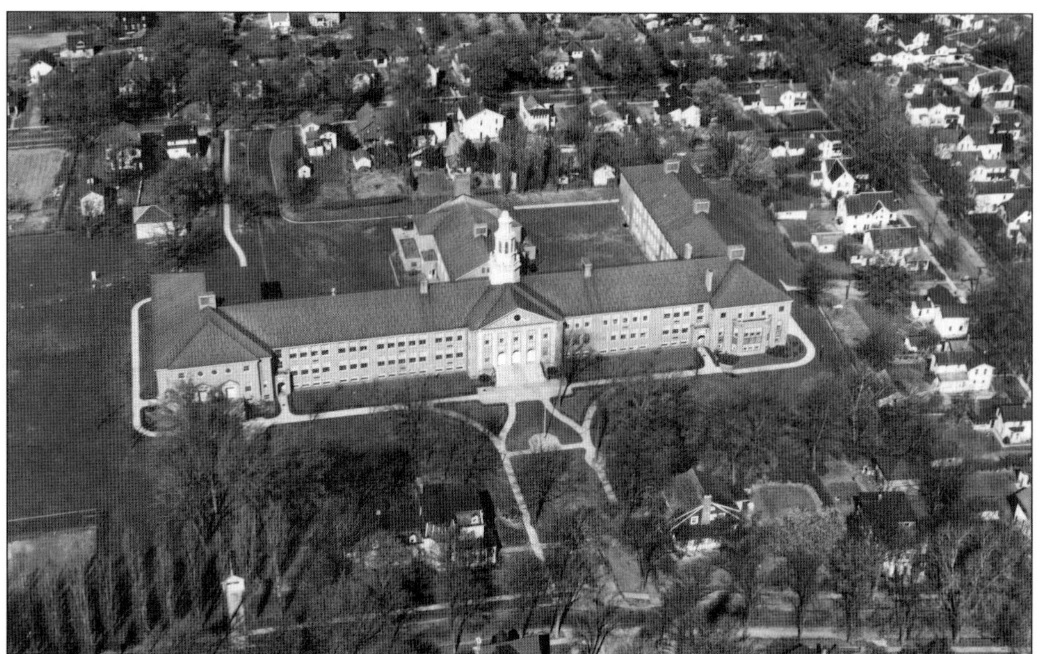

CAMPUS GROWTH. Hartwell Hall (above) was built between 1938 and 1941. In the process, the old building was razed in stages. Folk tradition holds that several ghosts haunt the structure. In the 1940s, this building was the entire school, with classrooms, offices, swimming pool, auditorium, and library. There were a few hundred students and 50 faculty members. After World War II, the physical plant grew enormously, as the 1973 photograph (below) shows, ending with the completion of Drake Memorial Library and the Allen Administration Building in 1973 and the Faculty Office Building in 1974.

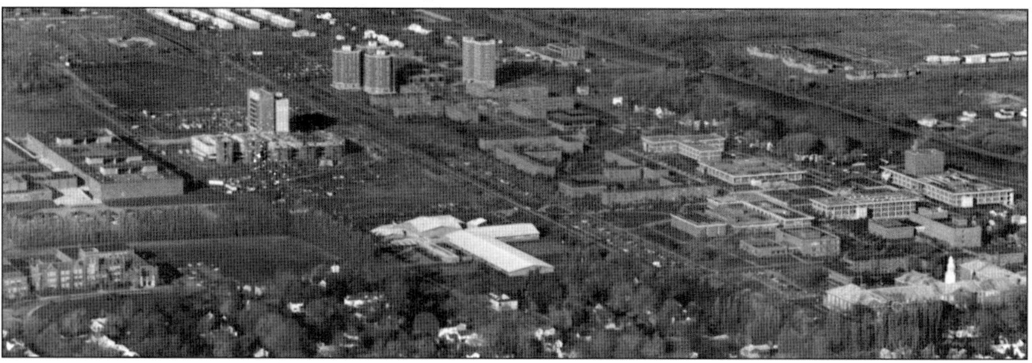

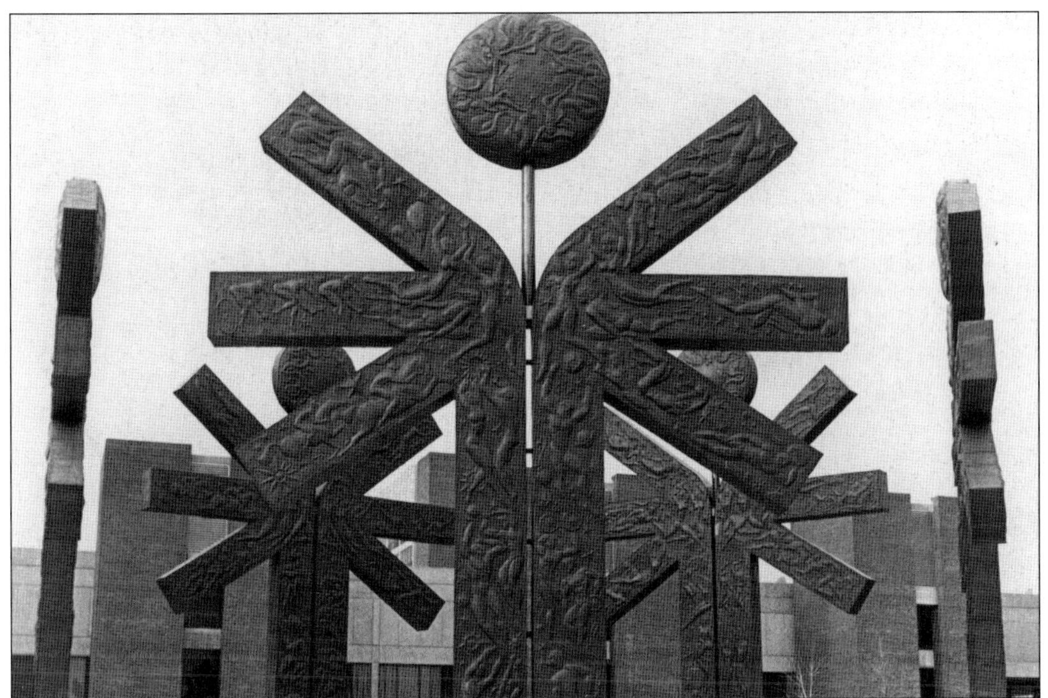

THE SPECIAL OLYMPICS SCULPTURE. In 1979, Zurab Tsereteli created two sculptures for the Brockport campus. *Joy and Happiness to All the Children of the World* was inspired by the International Special Olympics symbol. The stick figures represent the five continents that sent athletes to the 1979 Brockport games. The artist, a native of the Republic of Georgia, was one of the leading artists in the Soviet Union.

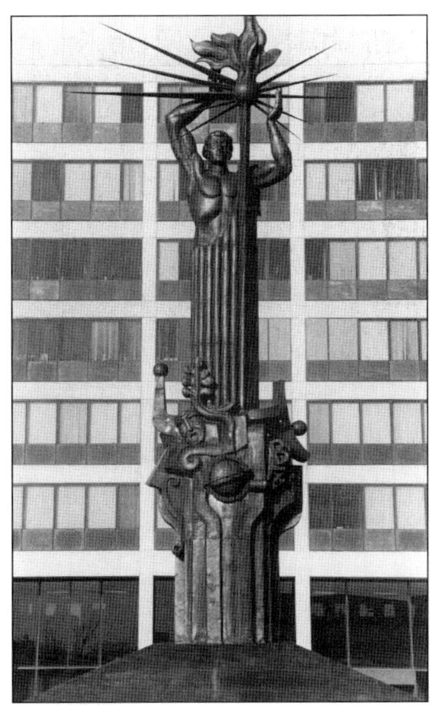

PROMETHEUS. The other Tsereteli sculpture represents Prometheus, the Greek Titan, bringing the spark of knowledge from the gods to human beings. The sculptures were a gift from the Soviet Union of Writers and Artists. Tsereteli waived his usual $250,000 royalty payment because the pieces were for children and students. The bronze works weigh nearly 30 tons and were transported to New York by ship and from there to Brockport on five large trucks. These works are said to be the only large pieces of Socialist Realism art in the Western Hemisphere.

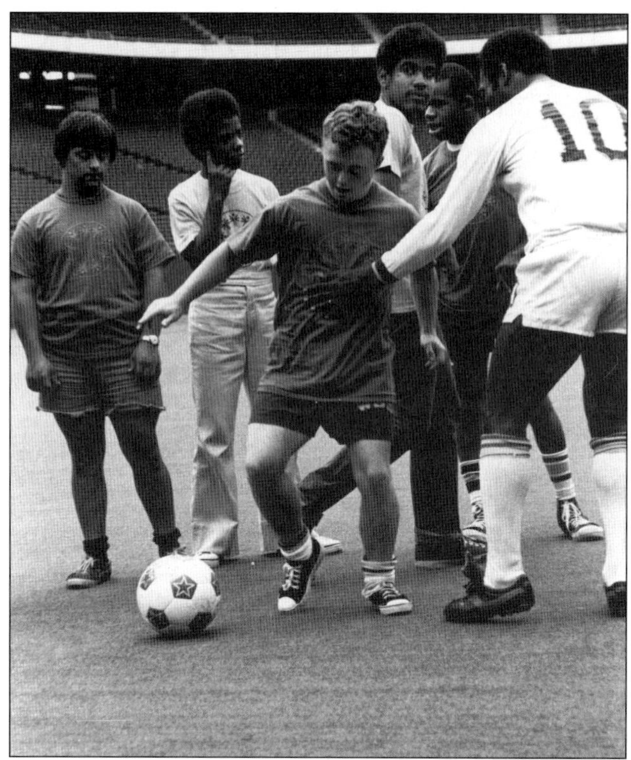

THE SPECIAL OLYMPIANS. The true heroes of the 1979 International Special Olympics in Brockport were its 3,500 physically handicapped athletes, many of whom traveled thousands of miles to attend. Their enthusiasm was overwhelming. Being able to participate was the greatest thrill for many Olympians. Upon completing their events, many athletes rushed to telephone the results to their families at home.

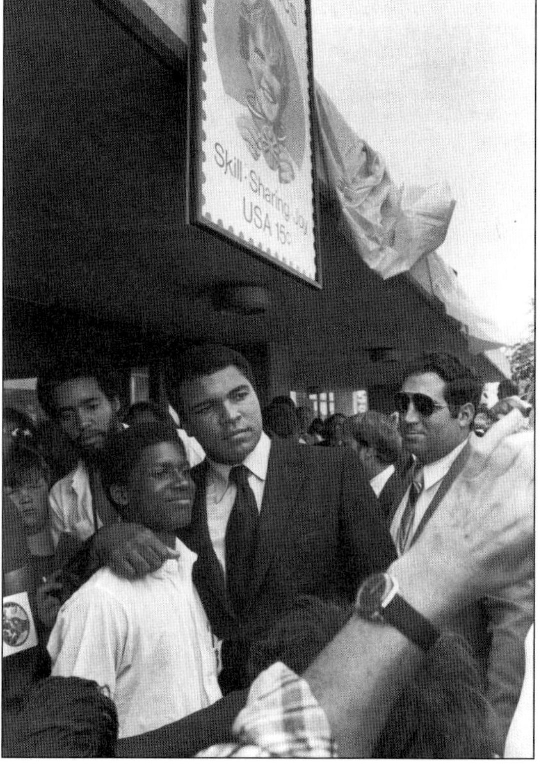

CELEBRITIES. Some 45 to 50 famous professional athletes and other celebrities supported the 1979 event. Among them were Muhammed Ali, Bobby Orr, Phil Esposito, track-and-field star Rafer Johnson, Hank Aaron, Massachusetts Sen. Ted Kennedy, and actress Suzanne Somers. Hundreds of volunteers from Brockport and neighboring communities helped to make the games a success.